Visions

of Excess

Selected Writings,

1927–1939

Georges Bataille

Edited and with an Introduction by Allan Stoekl

Translated by Allan Stoekl,
with Carl R. Lovitt and Donald M. Leslie, Jr.

Theory and History of Literature, Volume 14

University of Minnesota Press, Minneapolis

Published by the University of Minnesota Press
111 Third Avenue South, Suite 290, Minneapolis, MN 55401-2520
http://www.upress.umn.edu
Printed in the United States of America on acid-free paper
Eleventh printing, 2006.
Library of Congress Cataloging in Publication Data

Bataille, Georges, 1897–1962.
  Visions of excess.

  (Theory and history of literature; v. 14)
  Includes bibliographical references and index.
1. Bataille, Georges, 1897–1962—Translations, English.
I. Stoekl, Allan.   II. Title.   III. Series.
PQ2603.A695A27   1985   844'.912   84-20973
ISBN 0-8166-1280-3
ISBN 0-8166-1283-8 (pbk.)

This translation presents selections from
Georges Bataille's *Oeuvres complètes*, 2 volumes,
© J.-J. Pauvert, for "Histoire de l'oeil," and
© Èditions Gallimard, 1970, for the rest of the volumes.

The University of Minnesota
is an equal-opportunity
educator and employer.

Contents

II (1932–1935)

III (1936–1939)

Acknowledgments

I would like first to thank my collaborators on this project, Carl R. Lovitt, who contributed his translation of "The Psychological Structure of Fascism," and Donald M. Leslie, Jr. , who translated "The Old Mole." In addition Carl painstakingly went over most of the translations, checking them against the originals, catching omissions and errors, rewriting awkward sentences, and making a large number of valuable suggestions. Don also read a number of translations and made useful suggestions. This project could not have been completed without their assistance.

I am also grateful to Lindsay Waters and Wlad Godzich of the University of Minnesota Press, for their enthusiasm and encouragement at all stages of the project; to Virginia Hans, for her excellent copyediting; and to my friends Michele Richman, Denis Hollier, Ralph Flores, and Mark Conroy, for their interest, advice, and criticism.

Finally I thank Leah Larsen, without whose acuity, moral support, and love, I would long ago have quit this lugubrious game.

A. S.

Introduction
Allan Stoekl

I

Georges Bataille was born in 1897 and died in 1962; thus he was the contemporary of André Breton (1896–1966) and Louis Aragon (1897–1982), among others. Raised in and around Reims, Bataille experienced a difficult childhood at the hands of a paralyzed and blind, syphilitic father. (At least, so he tells us in the closing section of the novel *Story of the Eye* (I, 76–78)[1]—in the absence of a biography of Bataille, the details of his life that we mention here, details that we should perhaps take with a grain of salt, all come from his own writings.) Bataille and his mother abandoned his father on November 6, 1915, as the Germans approached the area of Reims. Bataille's father, now insane, died shortly thereafter.

Bataille had already revolted as much as he could against his father's rule; he had quit his high school in 1913 (VIII, 459) and had embraced Catholicism— his father was not religious and died refusing the priest (I, 59–61). From this Catholic period (summer 1918) dates Bataille's first published writing, a pamphlet honoring Notre Dame de Reims, the great cathedral nearly destroyed by German shelling (I, 611–16).[2] In this piece, Bataille foresaw a rebirth not only of the cathedral, but of the Christian spirit that made its elevation possible. In 1920, however, Bataille lost his faith, this time for good.

Despite his earlier dropping out of school, Bataille eventually became a good student. He prepared for, and was admitted to, the prestigious Ecole des chartes, where he was trained as a medievalist librarian. After a year in Spain, where he first witnessed bullfights and perhaps saw the enucleation of the eye of the matador Granero on May 7, 1922,[3] Bataille obtained a position at the Bibliothèque Nationale in Paris, which he held until 1942 (when he was forced to leave due to ill health).

Bataille's thesis as a medievalist was an edition of *L'Ordre de Chevalerie*, a medieval romance having to do with the investiture and teaching of knights (I, 99–102). A little later in the decade (1926–28) Bataille published articles on numismatics in *Aréthuse*, a review devoted to art and archeology (I, 108–51).

At the same time, though, Bataille was living a kind of second life (which, as we will see, nevertheless had important connections with his official career as medievalist). In 1924 he had met Michel Leiris, a kindred spirit who soon became associated with the surrealists (VIII, 170–72). Bataille himself was far from being a calm and orderly librarian. In 1926 he wrote a book entitled *W. C.* (later burned by him, although its first chapter, devoted to his heroine Dirty, has been preserved as the opening section of *Blue of Noon*),[4] which had a cover decorated with the sketch of an eye peeping out of the neck-hole of a guillotine and which bore the subtitle *The Eternal Return*. (The first page also carried the lines of a music hall song: "God, how the corpse's blood is sad in the depth of sound.") According to Leiris, one of the book's few readers, it contained an account of Dirty and the narrator having an orgy among fishseller's stalls; the later chapters, again according to Leiris, juxtaposed an "aristocratic luxury" with the lowest vulgarity.[5] It was, in Bataille's estimation, a book "violently opposed to all dignity" (VII, 460) and eventually caused Bataille to undergo a psychoanalytic cure. One of his friends, Dr. Dausse, taken aback by the "virulence and obsessions" of *W. C.* and "The Solar Anus" (1927), arranged for Bataille to be treated by Dr. Adrien Borel (who two years later, in 1929, treated Leiris as well).

As can be seen from the dream fragment with which this collection begins (recorded as part of his cure), Bataille's obsessions were in many ways directly related to Oedipal terrors, perhaps even more Oedipal in that his father was blind. Bataille felt that by August 1927 the cure had done away with "sinister" and apparently violent episodes that threatened him (and perhaps others)—but fortunately it had not done away with the "intellectual violence" (VII, 460) that he would continue to explore for the rest of his life. In fact these obsessions in many ways are the animating force behind Bataille's heterodox "theory," which he began to elaborate after 1927. (We do not intend to imply, however, that Bataille's obsessions as theory are simply reducible to a putative "origin" in neurosis or psychosis, and thus can be simply dismissed. Indeed Bataille's theory itself would tend to make problematic any such naive causal model.)

André Breton, the leader of the surrealists, had an aversion to Bataille. Leiris had told him about *W. C.*, and, on the basis of what he had heard, Breton dismissed Bataille as an "obsessive" (VIII, 173). Bataille had translated some medieval nonsense poems for *La Révolution surréaliste* in 1926, but Breton was not at all interested in extending the collaboration.

Breton at this time was the leading avant-garde intellectual power broker in France, and probably the world. Bataille was a virtually unknown librarian. It certainly would have made sense for Bataille, wanting to express his "intellectual violence," to associate himself with Breton and the surrealists. But the hostility was mutual. Bataille was not interested in renouncing his assault on dignity and beauty, and Breton's concept of the "mental doors opening wide" involved, in Bataille's estimation, precisely an affirmation of an aestheticism and idealism tinged with religion. Bataille by 1927 (in "The Solar Anus") was already developing an approach to what he would call later (in, among other essays, "The Psychological Structure of Fascism") *heterogeneous matter*— matter so repulsive that it resisted not only the idealism of Christians, Hegelians, and surrealists, but even the conceptual edifice-building of traditional materialists. It was indeed an all-out assault on dignity.

Bataille was involved in the founding, in 1929, of a rather luxurious review devoted to art, entitled *Documents*. Collaborating with a group of rebel surrealists (Desnos, Leiris, Limbour), and with a group of more conservative art historians, Bataille contributed a number of articles in which, for the first time, he developed his theory. *Documents* ostensibly presented articles that commented on lavish illustrations of primitive and avant-garde artworks, as well as icons of popular culture (for example, a portrait of the flapper Joan Crawford, her eyes bulging, accompanies Bataille's definition of the 'Eye').[6] But Bataille's essays often violated the general orientation of the review—to the consternation of some of *Documents*' more conservative contributors—commenting as they did on giant photographs of magnified big toes ("The Big Toe") or exposed plant genitalia ("The Language of Flowers"). The latter essay, which ends with a portrait of Sade throwing rose petals into a ditch filled with manure, gave Breton the opportunity he was waiting for to attack Bataille, and, through Bataille, the rebel surrealists who had abandoned and betrayed him.

At the close of the *Second Surrealist Manifesto* (p. 184), citing Marx as his authority[7], Breton in effect condemns Bataille as an "excremental philosopher." Breton specifically dismisses Bataille because he sees a profound contradiction between Bataille's embrace of the heterogeneous—animality, flies, excrement—and his tendency, in spite of all this, to *reason*.

> M. Bataille's misfortune is to reason: admittedly, he reasons like
> someone who "has a fly on his nose", which allies him more closely
> with the dead than with the living, but *he does reason*. He is trying,
> with the help of the tiny mechanism in him which is not completely
> out of order, to share his obsessions: this very fact proves that he can-
> not claim, no matter what he may say, to be opposed to any system,
> like an unthinking brute.

Breton concludes that this disorder—attempting to reason about what is simply unreasonable—is nothing more than pathological: "A state of conscious deficiency, in a form tending to become generalized, the doctors would say" (p. 184). Breton, the former medical technician, even has a term for Bataille's condition: "psychasthenia" (p. 185). In response to the "Language of Flowers," Breton points out that a rose, even if stripped of all its petals, *is still a rose* (p. 186); the most telling remark of Breton is that, in stripping the rose of its petals and throwing them in the manure, Sade only wanted to get rid of the usual trappings of poetic sentiment associated with the rose "in order to try to make the human mind get rid of its chains" (p. 186).

Thus in Breton we see a certain configuration of values that he opposes to Bataille: the refusal of the interpenetration of reason and bestial unreason; the desire to psychoanalyze (hence to categorize and cure Bataille); the ideal image (the rose), and therefore the *mind*.

That Breton had an aversion to filth is fairly apparent;[8] he was taken aback by Dali's inclusion of a shit-smear on the underwear of a little man in the lower right-hand corner of his painting *The Lugubrious Game*. This brown smudge found its champion in Bataille. In a footnote to his essay "The 'Lugubrious Game,' " a clear response to Breton's charges against him, Bataille in fact sees the smudge as a kind of vehicle for liberation: through this stain "a new and real virility is rediscovered by this person [the man in his underwear] in ignominy and horror themselves."

The essay "The 'Lugubrious Game' " must be seen in the context of two fragments, unpublished in Bataille's lifetime, that are, for their scope and theoretical audacity, among his most important writings.[9] These are "The Jesuve" and "The Pineal Eye." Both circle around an "excremental fantasy," a legacy of an anal fixation worked out in Bataille's psychoanalytic cure. This fantasy involves, through the process of evolution, the movement of a tremendous erotic force up from the ape's provocative anus to the erect human's head and brain. The next stage of evolution, manifested by a kind of parodic Nietzschean superman, posits a "pineal eye," a final but deadly erection, which blasts through the top of the human skull and "sees" the overwhelming sun. The point here is not to sublate the anal obsession, but to *embrace* it; the dialectical procedure of the psychoanalytic cure when completed suddenly *falls*, and with it the dialectical movement of human evolution as well. And behind Darwin lurks Hegel: the temporal movement toward erect, properly adjusted, rational man is one with the dialectical movement toward Absolute Spirit. But what happens when this movement is not simply denied—as Breton would have Bataille deny, as contradictory, his own ability to reason—but pushed as far as it can go? The answer is that at the *end* of reason, at the *end* of man, at the *end* of the Cartesian pineal gland (the supposed seat of consciousness) there is only orgasm and a simultaneous fall, a simultaneous death. Death and perversion do not take place in splendid isolation; instead, they are at the endpoint of the human. The energy of obscene, anal sexuality may be temporarily brought to a higher level in the elevated mind, in the ramrod-straight military man, in spirit—but when spirit reaches its full elevation, it *sees* the light of night, it becomes the ejaculation that idealist religious and philosophical systems—Breton's as well as Hegel's—had merely temporarily forgotten and not done away with. At the furthest point of evolution, of absolute knowledge, elevation is the fall; humanity is animality; insight is blindness; health is terminal pathology; God, when he *knows*, is a pig.

Castration is thus not forgotten, sublimated, or sublated, but is ecstatically experienced, as the ax-blade cutting into the ape's anus, as the father's actual castration of the son as a response to the son's total defiance.

But this is more than a simple individual experience of night. Bataille makes it clear in "The Pineal Eye" that his considerations have to do not only with evolution but with larger sociological phenomena. The pineal eye is experienced *communally*; the gibbon is sacrificed, the eye/anus/brain in its ejaculation/defecation/thought becomes an erotic and sacrificial object not just for an isolated individual, but for a cult, a secret society, or perhaps even, by implication, for an entire civilization at the end of history. Hence Bataille's opening remarks on anthropology: what is needed is not simply an anthropology that will reduce myth and collective experience to the status of ideal mental (and academic) categories, but instead an anthropology that will itself provide a living—and orgiastic—myth to overturn, through its experience on a collective level, "modern" sterile bourgeois society.

It must be remembered, however, that evolution (and thus the dialectic) is not simply escaped or done away with. It is impossibly fulfilled, and completed, at the recurrent instant in which it is ruptured and annihilated. Bataille's text itself stands in an impossible neutral space between absolute knowledge and its implacably hostile double, sheer loss. Yet the text is neither one nor the other; it is precisely the conjoining of the two that establishes their identity as automutilation, their violent doubling. In fact one of Bataille's other essays from this period of *Documents* is an affirmation of the madman's duality and automutilation: "Sacrificial Mutilation and the Severed Ear of Vincent Van Gogh."

One could argue that the pattern established in "The Jesuve" and "The Pineal Eye" reappears, in its various guises, throughout the later work of Bataille. But one would have to be careful: Bataille is not simply privileging a new object (excrement, flies, ruptured eyes, the rotten sun, etc.) over the old one (the head, the king, spirit, mind, vision, the sun of reason, etc.). If, as Angus Fletcher has pointed out in *Allegory*,[10] the medieval allegorical imagination posits a fundamental congruence between *hierarchy* in the body and the guaranteed, stable *meaning* of allegory (in the body, the highest element is the head; in society, the king; and in the universe, God), then we must conclude that a theory that simply substituted one hierarchy for another (a hierarchy that favors the *high* replaced by one that favors the *low*) would only inaugurate a new metaphysics and a new stabilized allegorical system of meaning. Filth would replace God.

But Bataille's approach is not that simple. Fully conversant as a medievalist with the theoretical implications of allegory, Bataille precisely recognizes that the *fall* of the elevated and noble threatens the coherent theory of allegory itself. This is not to imply that allegory is simply done away with in Bataille—any more than is the dialectic—but rather, that what Bataille works out is a kind of headless allegory, in which the process of signification and reference associated with allegory continues, but leads to the terminal subversion of the pseudostable references that had made allegory and its hierarchies seem possible. The fall of one system is not stabilized, is not replaced with the elevation of another; the fall in Bataille's allegory is a kind of incessant or repetitious process. Thus filth does not "replace" God; there is no new system of values, no new hierarchy. In the *Documents* articles, Bataille's attention wanders through a disseminated field, a labyrinth, of possibilities; flowers, excrement, toes, Gnosticism, freaks, mouth, sun, severed fingers. Even if it may seem that one term is momentarily privileged (sun/anus), that term itself only signifies the failure of all the other terms to stand clearly in relation to a "higher" signified.[11] Indeed one could argue that for this reason, Bataille's "terminology" itself (and his "theory" as well) is fundamentally unstable, not only in these early writings, but in everything he wrote. The very term *heterogeneous*, positively valued in the early writings, later (in the 1940's) comes to indicate what seems to be the exact opposite.[12] The same change takes place in the word *sovereignty*, indeed even in the figure of Nietzsche, who is taken to task (for being a reactionary) in "The 'Old Mole' and the Prefix *Sur* in the Words *Surhomme* [Superman] and *Surrealist*," but who is, in the later 1930's, seen as a major precursor and, free of all political taint, the victim of Fascist misrepresentation. Among other things, then, Bataille's project must be seen as a kind of allegory of the fall of allegory itself. This fall of allegory is in fact consonant with the fall of the copula in Bataille, and with the ramifications of that fall. (We might speak of the allegory of the fall of the copula.) As we learn in "The Solar Anus,"

> But the *copula* of terms is no less irritating than the *copulation* of bodies. And when I scream I AM THE SUN an integral erection results, because the verb *to be* is the vehicle of amorous frenzy.

> Everyone is aware that life is parodic and that it lacks an interpretation.
> Thus lead is the parody of gold.
> Air is the parody of water.

The copula/copulation dyad is unstable; it is both a function of language and of bodies; because God is dead, a definitive interpretation guaranteed by a stable copula—and mandating its parody, productive copulation—is sacrificed. The unstable copula leads to obscene, parodic, burlesque, and ever-inverted significations; unstable copulation leads to perverse and morbid sexuality. And because of the parodic status of each side of the copula/copulation dyad (in relation to the other), we cannot say that one "causes" the other (that is, we cannot say that the destabilization of signification generates or subsumes the destabilization of sexuality, or vice versa): along with stable signification, a straightforward ("scientific") model of causation is parodied, for example, when "The Solar Anus" presents the copulation of lovers "causing" the earth to turn, their movement a burlesque of the horizontal motion of the locomotive's piston's "causing" the rotation of its wheels.

This is not to say, then, that Bataille wafts off into a purely linguistic or grammatological conundrum. On the contrary, starting with "The 'Old Mole' " (which probably dates from 1929 or 1930), Bataille sees his critique of the elevated—the ideal, the *sur*real—as inseparable from a political critique of fascism. "The 'Old Mole' " (written for the avant-garde review *Bifur* and unpublished in Bataille's lifetime) is an attempt to see irreducibly "base" matter in the context of Marxist revolution. Base materialism, unlike pragmatic or functionalist theories of materialism, does not pass beyond matter in the construction of a "scientific" conceptual edifice. (A materialism that generates abstract "laws" is in complicity with idealism: see the *Documents* article "Materialism.") Instead, base materialism posits a matter that cannot be reduced to systems of scientific or political mastery. Marx's "old mole" burrows under and *sub*verts the idealism that founds and legitimates systems as diverse as authoritarian imperialism (fascism), utopian socialism, the Nietzschean *super*man, and "spiritual" *sur*realism. The imperial eagle that signifies these entities flies over (*sur*), but its easy mastery will be definitively disrupted when the repugnant revolutionaries tear it out of the sky. In Bataille's view, the bourgeois individuals—like Nietzsche or Breton—who foster a desire to revolt by soaring "above" are destined for a fall, and in a way *want* to fall: thus the "Icarian complex," an "unconscious" and pathological desire to fall. Icarian revolt (as opposed to base subversion) is the only pathology Bataille will condemn; it is the pathological refusal to embrace stinking decomposition—an embrace that, from the point of view of any dialectic of the cure, must itself be pathological.

II

But what of the Marxist dialectic in all this? Although Hegel is condemned in "The 'Old Mole,' " a dialectical movement was clearly already implicit in the "Pineal Eye" writings. How can definitively disruptive low matter be joined to a progressive Marxist dialectic (without which there is only utopian idealism), at the same time avoiding a fall into an "abstract and mechanical" Hegelian movement?

This is a major problem. The dialectic, as we know from Alexandre Kojève's reading of Hegel, sets as its major task the recuperation of negativity.[13] Thus the importance of the master-slave dialectic for the Marxist Kojève: the slave gains essential mastery over the master through his constructive use of the dead matter the master would fly above. Bataille, who followed Kojève's lectures throughout the 1930s, soon accepted the inescapability of Hegel and Marxist-Hegelian knowledge (for Kojève's Hegel was thoroughly Marxist). But—and this is the problem—if negativity is always *reappropriated* in the progressive dialectic, how radically perverse and "base" will it be? Does not Bataille's "base matter" itself prove eminently useful, leading outside of itself to finally stable constructs (such as the "end of history"), in which negativity will have no place and in which it will definitively evaporate?

From late 1931 to early 1934 Bataille was involved in an anti-Stalinist Marxist review, *La Critique Sociale*, edited by Boris Souvarine. In the articles he wrote for this review, Bataille attempted to join more systematically his theory of baseness—and now, expenditure—to the class struggle and the Marxist dialectic.

The first effort was an article written with Raymond Queneau, "The Critique of the Foundations of the Hegelian Dialectic" (1932). The goal here is to free dialectical negation from the mechanical abstraction given it (so the article argues) by Engels.

In the crucial "Notion of Expenditure" (1933) Bataille lays his cards on the table. We see here the kind of nonabstract negativity that Bataille would find in the dialectic, animating the class struggle and leading to the final Revolution. This negativity does not have to do with the constructive labor of the slave, but instead finds its "origins" in the destructive orgiastic drive—in *potlatch*—that is, according to Bataille, man's most fundamental "need." Drawing on the anthropological writings of Marcel Mauss, Bataille sees the need to expend not only as one that characterizes society, but as one that enables the rich, who can destroy more than anyone else, to establish themselves *above* the poor, whom they have also destroyed. Although Bataille's approach here bears a superficial resemblance to that of Thorstein Veblen, Bataille goes in exactly the opposite direction. "Conspicuous consumption" for Bataille is not a pernicious remnant of feudalism that must be replaced by total utility; instead, it is the perversion of man's "need to destroy." The noble, and even more hypocritically, the bourgeois, use this "destruction" not to destroy completely, but simply to reaffirm their position in the hierarchy.

Revolution, then, is a liberation of the true nature of expenditure, heretofore only glimpsed in social phenomena such as gambling, ritual destruction, the Christian glorification of Christ's death, and perverse sexuality, and then misconstrued. Through Revolution, for the first time, the "lower" classes take control of the *means of expenditure*. And what they expend is precisely the ruling class, in a bloody and orgiastic social *potlatch*. In this parody of Nietzsche, it is not the rulers who exude force, but those "situated below" who do.

The Marxist dialectic here becomes a parodic dialectic, one of the history of modes of expenditure, of "nonlogical difference"; at the end of history, the proletariat controls not only the means of production—negativity put to work—but the means of destruction as well. Potlatch can no longer be used for reactionary ends: now all human beings are free to lose themselves in it. Production in Bataille's view is clearly subordinate and posterior to destruction: people create in order to expend, and if they retain things they have produced, it is only to allow themselves to continue living, and thus destroying.

Bataille continues this line of argument in his "Psychological Structure of Fascism" (1933). Here again conservation is seen as a kind of aftereffect of loss—or, in the terms of this article, *homogeneity* is an aftereffect of *heterogeneity*. The article sees two forms of heterogeneity in opposition to the simple closed circle of homogeneous consumption and production. One, akin to the "Icarian revolt" in "The 'Old Mole,' " is *imperative*, associable with that which is noble, pure, superior, individual, and so on. This is the master, removed from the daily processes of life. The other is impure, involving untouchable things and people. The imperative, or sovereign, form of heterogeneity goes to aid the homogeneous forces: it guarantees the stability of a society, which can give itself meaning only through the sadistic exclusion of impure heterogeneity. The king or the fascist leader (as imperative heterogeneity) is in a way excluded from the homogeneous activities of society, but he dominates that society and embodies it. The poor, the workers, the ignoble untouchables are also separated from homogeneous society, but they are doomed by it to destruction.

We might briefly indicate at this point one problem with the line of argument in this fascinating and rich article. Bataille elsewhere (in "The Notion of Expenditure") indicates with what ease impure heterogeneity, in the form of the bleeding body of Christ, comes to be imperative heterogeneity: Christ after he has died ascends to heaven and guarantees a finally regressive social structure. Could we not argue that the distinction between the two types of heterogeneity is quite fragile, and that as soon as a given form of impure heterogeneity comes to be seen as a positive value, it will itself inevitably become imperative? In the very act of writing about various forms of trash, in valuing them by devoting articles to them, does not Bataille simply erect them as new privileged values, as privileged as the trashy lumpen proletariat and thugs who have become fascist rulers? And if so, as imperative heterogeneity, are they really so different from fascism and its fetishes? This problem is even more acute in that Bataille notes, at the end of "The Psychological Structure of Fascism," the success fascism has had in stimulating the "renewed affective forces" of powerful crowds. But how easy will it be to separate reactionary ideology and the charisma of the leader from the orgiastic agitation of the mob, if one, as a Marxist, wants to use and promote this agitation?

Clearly the threat of the reestablishment of a new hierarchy is not as easily escaped as we might have thought when we discussed "The Pineal Eye" and the articles from *Documents*. It might seem that once God is dead the risk of fascism is inescapable, because there is nothing to guarantee that a privileged impure heterogeneity will not become imperative.

In fact Bataille faced this problem on a practical as well as a theoretical plane. Bataille founded a political group of intellectuals called Contre-Attaque with (of all people) André Breton in late 1935. 1935–36 was the greatest period of political effervescence in France since the Paris Commune of 1871; it culminated in May-June 1936 with massive strikes in all sectors of the economy and the assumption of power by the Popular Front, an alliance of Socialists and Communists headed by the Socialist Léon Blum.

The reader will note in the speech ("Popular Front in the Street") given by Bataille at a Contre-Attaque meeting in November 1935 the emphasis placed on force, agitation, and violence, to the exclusion of boring political and doctrinal debates. By the time this speech was published in May 1936, Breton's surrealist contingent was already disclaiming any association with Contre-Attaque, labeling it "sur-fasciste" (I, 640–41). Bataille himself in later years did not deny that in this group, among Bataille's friends and even in himself, there was a certain "paradoxical fascist tendency" (VII, 461).

Effervescence, the subversive violence of the masses, the baseness of their refusal to enter into boring discussions—all these things, then, without a clear and correct (even if boring) theory behind them, could easily be reversed into fascism, as Bataille quickly became aware.

Another difficulty in Bataille's arguments, implicit all along, also comes to the fore at this point. To what extent has the dialectic *not* been subverted in any way by Bataille, to what extent, in paying lip service to the limitlessness of this destructive tendency that constitutes man, does Bataille simply establish a new "need" that must in turn be recognized (at the end of history) and satisfied in order to guarantee the stability of society? Boring, useful labor—which certainly constitutes stable society—would in this case only be replaced by the safety valve of sacrificial violence or the scapegoat. These forms of institutionalized violence would be *useful* in that they would guarantee the ultimate permanence of society and of a given social order. This view is frequently found; we see it, in various guises, in Emile Durkheim, in Roger Caillois, and, in the postwar period, in René Girard.[14] Bataille seems to take this position already in "The Notion of Expenditure," when he writes of the "need for limitless loss"—even though he indicates that, in trying to satisfy this "need," people necessarily run the risk of risking themselves totally, like the gambler who cannot stop, or the chief, engaged in *potlatch*, who frenziedly destroys everything, including himself.

But can any one "need" be different in kind from another, even though one is a need for construction and satisfaction, and the other is a need for destruction and loss? And if they are not fundamentally different, how radical is this "need to expend"? How different is it from, say, a need for leisure time, or exercise? If man "produces only in order to expend," is expenditure different in kind from any other human value, such as religion or the family?

III

Bataille's activities after the collapse of Contre-Attaque and up to the start of World War II were divided between two closely linked projects that were nevertheless independent: Acéphale and the Collège de Sociologie. We will discuss Acéphale first.

The public face of Acéphale was the review of the same name, which appeared as a small-format brochure only four times between June 1936 and June 1939. Among the contributors—and members of the Acéphale group—were Bataille (who clearly set the topic for each issue and did a large portion of the writing), Georges Ambrosino, Pierre Klossowski, Jean Wahl, and Jules Monnerot. Bataille was fortunate in having as illustrator André Masson, whose sketches portraying the acephalic man in flight and on the ground set the proper cosmological-orgiastic tone. (Bataille had earlier written "Sacrifices" as a preface to a collection of Masson's drawings.)

While the review was public (indeed, a proposal for an advertisement ran: "If you are not crushed you must subscribe to *Acéphale*"), the Acéphale group itself was considered to be a "secret society," its rituals closed to the public. Clearly Bataille had fundamentally changed his conception of the nature of the political activity to be carried out. Nietzsche now is invoked rather than Marx: *Acéphale* number 2 contains (among other things) responses to right-wing political readings of Nietzsche, showing how the Nazis were misquoting him and misrepresenting his positions ("Nietzsche and the Fascists"). The secret society is a group of adepts, operating in the margins of (and acting against) official society. Bataille for a long time had been interested in marginal groups: Gnostics, madmen, knights, sects of heterodox Christian mystics. The Acéphale group was also outside the mainstream of political life: subversive yet not intended to lead an organized mass movement, the activities of the group would help stimulate a rebirth of the kind of social values Bataille had espoused in the *Critique Sociale* essays: expenditure, risk, loss, sexuality, death. The Acéphale group offered nothing in the way of the standard economic and material promises—that was left to the mainstream groups, though Acéphale was certainly not against progressive reforms in the social and economic spheres. But its main goals were the rebirth of myth and the touching off in society of an explosion of the primitive communal drives leading to sacrifice. Myth, as Bataille states in "The Sorcerer's Apprentice," is the way open to man after the failure of art, science (and scientific notions of causation), and politics to reach these lower—

and more "essential"—human drives, and after their failure as well to lead to a paradoxically rent but "true" existence. Of the mythic figures Bataille proposes (Dionysos, the Crucified, Nietzsche himself), the acephalic man is the most important. As a secret sect, the Acéphale group participated in rites such as a meeting in a "sacred" place near a tree struck by lightning—a point of intersection between lower, chthonian forces and falling higher forces (see the "Instructions for the Meeting in the Forest," II, 277–78). There was even talk of an actual human sacrifice being performed, but it was never carried out.[15]

Clearly much of this orientation is familiar; the low, chthonian forces are related to the big toe, the ape's anus, and the "old mole"; the acephalic man is a not so distant cousin of the duck-headed *archontes* of "Base Materialism and Gnosticism." But we also see a response to the risk of fascism encountered in the Contre-Attaque positions. The secret group will never come to power nor will it be involved with an official party: in its marginality it is closer to the situationists or the *autonomes* of the 1960s or 1970s than it is to any traditional organized party or mass movement. And the Acéphale is precisely *without* a head—whereas many Fascists of the period, such as Drieu la Rochelle (as in his pamphlet *Avec Doriot*),[16] were calling for a return to communal values, the integrated life, etc., but *with* a head, in this case named Doriot, but in others La Rocque, Mussolini, Hitler—or Stalin.

Despite the fact that Bataille at this time was calling himself "ferociously religious," it must be understood that this was a religion celebrating a total lack of religion. The acephalic man through Nietzsche represented the death of God as well as the death of the classical conception of man: "Man will escape from his head as the condemned man escapes from his prison." The "deleterious" time of the eternal return is embraced (as in "The Obelisk" [1938]) and, at its most extreme, the experience of the death of God becomes an unspeakable and unwriteable—yet written—account of the individual's contact, through meditation, with joy, dread, war, and death ("The Practice of Joy before Death" [1939]). This radical negativity finally does not have any usefulness to society (such as acting as a safety valve to let off harmful pressure), but is instead identifiable with mystical experiences that involve a disbelief in the very existence of God.

The Collège de Sociologie was as public as the Acéphale group was private. Its activities centered around biweekly lectures given either by the founding members—Bataille, Roger Caillois, Michel Leiris—or by invited speakers, such as Alexandre Kojève, Anatole Lewitzky, Pierre Klossowski, and others.[17] The effort here was to redefine a "science of the sacred," replacing a narrow functionalist sociology with one that would recognize the importance of the various forms of "expenditure" not only for "primitive" societies, but for modern societies as well. Thus the Collège was meant to study the tendencies of man that the Acéphale group hoped somehow to spark. Both Caillois and Leiris were trained in sociology and anthropology, thus assuring a level of rigor (purposely) excluded from the activities of Acéphale.

The Collège in the years 1937–39 was quite influential, serving as a meeting ground for avant-garde (para- or neo-surrealist) intellectuals and social scientists, each group profiting from the presence of the other. Claude Lévi-Strauss, Jean-Paul Sartre, and Walter Benjamin all attended at one time or another; Benjamin was scheduled to give a lecture in the 1939–40 series,[18] but the war broke out in September, putting an end to the *Collège* and with it an epoch of French literary, artistic, and philosophical activity.

In order to examine the social manifestations of the sacred, it was first necessary to present the way in which communities are "composed"; this in part is Bataille's object in "The Labyrinth" (1936). For Bataille all entities are collections of other entities; there is no simply isolable *ipse* that would represent unitary being. What cells are to a human being, a human being is to that larger organism, the community. Being is not simple identity, but rather rupture or disequilibrium, the sudden change of levels: being is violent *difference*, precariousness and heterogeneity in relation to a given stable group ("the virulent madness of its autonomy in the total night of the world" ["The Labyrinth"]). Being is not totality, but the loss of an element that is impossibly (but necessarily) independent. We can imagine this phenomenon occurring on different levels; on the level of a human body, it might be the momentary autonomy and heterogeneity of the spurt of blood of the sacrificial victim; on the level of a community, it might be the infinite improbability of a *me* in revolt or death (see also, on this problem, "Sacrifices"), or the momentary autonomy of the conjoined being of two lovers; on the scale of the community as well, it might be the revolt of marginal or impoverished groups; on the level of nations, it might be the struggle for independence of a remote and miserable region that dares to fight the capital, where wealth, permanence, power, and divinity are centered. In each case we see a rupture opening to let out the "excess" of an unmaintainable and thus delusive unity, whether that unity is consciousness, the body, a community, or even a nation. "The Obelisk" presents a similar model; there it is a fall from a timeless pyramidal elevation of godhood, kingship, and power, a fall that is nevertheless inherent in the constitution of that elevation.

Finally, Bataille's text itself, in its language, may represent the rupture of unity through a rewriting of "major" philosophies—especially those of Heidegger ("being") and Kierkegaard ("dread")—by a resolutely marginal, fragmentary, and impossible project.[19]

To be sure, there were conflicts in the Collège; the lecture we present here on it, the last given by Bataille at the Collège, shows clearly enough the kinds of objections raised by Leiris and Caillois,[20] who felt Bataille was straying too far in his speculations from the orthodoxy (and "critical distance") of Durkheim and Mauss, and was lingering too much over "morose preconceptions." It seems unlikely that, had Leiris and Caillois been present at the meeting of July 4, 1939, they would have been satisfied by Bataille's remarks. In any case, he continued his research in what for him were the most basic questions of anthropology and sociology, and this work led in the postwar period to the extremely important *La Part Maudite* (1949; *The Cursed Share*, untranslated) (VII, 17-179), as well as to *L'Erotisme* (1957; translated as *Death and Sensuality*).[21]

If the theoretical orientation of Acéphale moved toward a radical "individual" experience of non-sense, it would seem that the Collège was oriented in the opposite direction, toward a consideration of the human being and human expenditure as a function of collective (or social) needs or desires. Here we run up against the problem that we broached at the end of the last section: how radical is this expenditure if it merely fulfills another need of society and through this fulfillment guarantees society's perpetual subsistence? Bataille states this problem at the end of the "College of Sociology" lecture of July 4, 1939: " . . . it is difficult to know to what extent the community is but the favorable occasion for a festival and a sacrifice, or to what extent the festival and the sacrifice bear witness to the love given to the community."

Bataille here confronts as a kind of "impasse" the "last question of man." Is the community a means to the end of free expenditure, or is this expenditure a means to the end of a stable community? It would seem that any theory concerned with the various forms that a community can take and with the mutations of communities throughout history (problems tackled by Bataille both in the Collège lectures and in *La Part maudite*) must value the community itself (and the definitive form(s) it will take at the "end of history") over a radical negativity that is in itself unknowable and ungraspable.

But the *Acéphale* writings apparently go in the opposite direction: the last issue of *Acéphale*, number 5, appearing in June 1939 (and entitled "Madness, War, and Death"), puts forward a largely individual experience, which seems to go beyond the constraints of any notion of community, sect, or life itself ("The Practice of Joy before Death").

It would seem that either direction would lead to an impasse. The valuing of community or society over the radicality of experience itself would, in the end, result in a vision of an ultimate homogeneous social structure that *uses* sacrifice or festivals; such a community could not be seen as different in kind from a bourgeois and finally even a Marxist society erected on the principles of classical utility (that is, on the denial of expenditure without return). This at least would be the necessary point of view of the "acephalic" position. On the other hand, the sheer negativity of the individual or the elite Acéphale group, seen for a moment from the point of view of the larger community, can only be a nihilistic emptiness that, headless or not, elevates itself as an absolute and therefore leads at best to simple individual death or wandering, and at worst to extremely sinister political configurations (regimes of the right are only too happy, as is well known, to make use of previously unharnessed violence).

At this point we do not want to suggest that there is necessarily a solution to this problem; indeed it is probably not solvable. But this very insolvability may be the most radical moment in Bataille's text, a moment of automutilation or "nonlogical difference" in which two necessary and incompatible positions impossibly meet. Bataille's radicality, then, may stem not so much from the content of his "positions" themselves as from their violent interaction. This may in fact be one of the things implied in Bataille's statement "I MYSELF AM WAR" (in "The Practice of Joy before Death"). It should be remembered that at no time in the later 1930s—or after, for that matter—did Bataille deny or refuse Kojève's Marxist Hegel (see, in this context, the "Letter to X, Teacher of a Course on Hegel" [1937; V, 369-71]). Yet the joining of a constructive dialectic of any sort, or its telos, to a definitively "unemployable" negativity could only result in a profoundly fissured writing.[22] One can in fact follow this fissure in Bataille's writings of the war years and the postwar period: the aphoristic *Somme Athéologique* (1943-45; *The Summa Atheologica*, untranslated), which values individual contingency, loss, and fragmentation, is doubled and defied by another group of texts, including *La Part maudite* and *L'Erotisme*, which put forward a finally coherent theory of history and society (a society that has expenditure as its most fundamental phenomenon).

We must not conclude from this, however, that Bataille's text, in its automutilation, is simply a sterile (antisocial and apolitical) negativity into which one willingly enters and which leads nowhere but ever further into itself. If Bataille's text is double, it leads necessarily and impossibly in two directions at once: to choose one direction—in this case one that leads away from society and social analysis—at the expense of the other is to reduce a bicephalic text to a monocephalic one, to choose the secret rites of the Acéphale (performed this time with only a text as the victim and the labyrinth) and to refuse the public and even political activity of the Collège. This is a choice that Bataille himself refused to make. And in the current "end of history" the labor of the "recognition" of unrecognizable negativity has just begun.

Notes

1. All references to Bataille in French, unless otherwise noted, are to the *Oeuvres Complètes* in nine volumes (so far) (Paris: Gallimard, 1970—). The volume number precedes the page number. *Histoire de l'oeil* (1928) has been published in a translation by J. Neugroschel as *Story of the Eye* (New York: Urizen Books, 1977). The description of Bataille's father is on pp. 106-10 of the English translation.

2. See Denis Hollier's *La Prise de la Concorde: Essais sur Georges Bataille* (Paris: Gallimard, 1974) for an examination of the importance of architecture's rise and fall in Bataille.

3. As recounted in *Histoire de l'oeil* (I, 52-56) and *Story of the Eye*, pp. 72-74.

4. See *Le Bleu du ciel*, in volume III of the *Oeuvres Complètes*. The English translation, by H. Mathews, is *Blue of Noon* (New York: Urizen Books, 1978).

5. Michel Leiris, "De Bataille l'Impossible à l'impossible *Documents*" in *Brisées* (Paris: Mercure de France, 1966), p. 258. This article originally appeared in *Critique* 195-96 (1963), *Hommage à Georges Bataille*.

6. *Documents* 1. no. 4 (1929): 216.

7. André Breton, *Manifestoes of Surrealism*, trans. R. Seaver and H. R. Lane (Ann Arbor: University of Michigan Press, 1969).

8. See Hollier's *La Prise de la Concorde*, p. 202. I am indebted to Hollier's analysis of the Bataille-Breton conflict, especially in regard to the question of "pathology."

9. For more on the "Pineal Eye" in Bataille, and its implications for philosophy, see Rodolphe Gasché's *System und Metaphorik in der Philosophie von Georges Bataille* (Bern: Peter Lang, 1978). The "Pineal Eye" writings may be the "unpublished essay on the inferiority complex," of which "The 'Lugubrious Game' " is a part. See "The 'Lugubrious Game,' " note 1.

10. Fletcher introduces the term *kosmos* to indicate a visual-allegorical representation:

Just how kosmos is the essential type of an allegorical image will appear as soon as the term is defined. It signifies 1) a universe, and 2) a symbol that implies a rank in a hierarchy. As the latter it will be attached to, or associated with, or even substituted for, any object which the writer wants to place in hierarchical position. The classic example of kosmos is the jewelry worn by a lady to show her social status, or any other such sartorial emblems of position.

As in English, the Greek term *kosmos* has a double meaning, since it denotes both a *large-scale order* (macrocosmos) and the small-scale *sign of that order* (microcosmos).

See Angus Fletcher, *Allegory* (Ithaca: Cornell University Press, 1964), pp. 109-110.

11. Bataille's anal sun can be seen shining (or defecating) in two of Jacques Derrida's most important essays: "La Mythologie blanche," in *Marges de la philosophie* (Paris: Minuit, 1972), pp. 247-324 ("The White Mythology," in *Margins of Philosophy*, trans. A. Bass [Chicago: University of Chicago Press, 1982], pp. 207-71); and "La Pharmacie de Platon," in *La Dissémination* (Paris: Seuil, 1972), pp. 69-197 ("Plato's Pharmacy," in *Dissemination*, trans. B. Johnson [Chicago: University of Chicago Press, 1981], pp. 61-171).

12. See Joseph Libertson, "Bataille and Communication: From Heterogeneity to Continuity," in *MLN* 89 (May 1974): 669-98, for an examination of the changing meaning of the word *heterogeneity* in Bataille's writing.

13. Alexandre Kojève, *Introduction à la lecture de Hegel*, ed. R. Queneau (Paris: Gallimard, 1947). See especially Appendix II, "L'Idée de la mort dans la philosophie de Hegel," pp. 527-73. Translated as *Introduction to the Reading of Hegel*, assembled by R. Queneau, trans. J. H. Nichols, Jr., ed. A. Bloom (New York: Basic Books, 1969). Unfortunately, this reediting of the Queneau edition omits the important essay "L'Idée de la mort dans la philosophie de Hegel."

14. See Emile Durkheim, *Les Formes élémentaires de la vie religieuse* (Paris: Alcan, 1912) (*The Elementary Forms of the Religious Life*, trans. J. W. Swain [London: Allen and Unwin, 1926]); Roger Caillois, *L'Homme et le sacré* (Paris: Gallimard, 1939) (*Man and the Sacred*, trans. M. Barash [Glencoe, Ill.: The Free Press of Glencoe, 1960]); René Girard, *La Violence et le sacré* (Paris: Grasset, 1972) (*Violence and the Sacred*, trans. P. Gregory [Baltimore: The Johns Hopkins University Press, 1977]).

For a detailed analysis of the influence of Mauss and Durkheim on Bataille, see Michele Richman's *Reading Georges Bataille: Beyond the Gift* (Baltimore: The Johns Hopkins University Press, 1982).

15. See "The *Collège de Sociologie*: Paradox of an Active Sociology," by Roger Caillois. In

Sub-Stance 11-12 (1975): 61–64. This short article is a concise statement of Caillois's objections to Bataille and Bataille's projects.

16. Drieu La Rochelle, *Avec Doriot* (Paris: Gallimard, 1937). See especially the article "Noël pour le peuple," pp. 111–15.

17. Denis Hollier has edited all the lectures given by Bataille and the other Collège contributors in *Le Collège de Sociologie* (Paris: Gallimard, Collection "Idées," 1979).

18. The reader will note many parallels between the projects of Bataille and Benjamin. Benjamin too attempted to find an alternative to both idealism and traditional materialism (which starts out with material facts but then goes "beyond" them to construct an abstract, conceptual edifice). Benjamin's way out was to propose his theory of "constellations," which involved a materialism that recognizes empirical facts, but which refuses to situate them in a higher "order." See especially the "Epistemo-Critical Prologue" of Benjamin's *Origin of German Tragic Drama*, trans. J. Osborne (London: NLB, 1977), pp. 27-56. On "Constellations," see Susan Buck-Morss, *The Origin of Negative Dialectics* (New York: The Free Press, 1977), pp. 90–95.

Bataille states in "The Psychological Structure of Fascism" that "Heterogeneous reality is that of a force or shock," and Benjamin as well was concerned with shock and (like Bataille) with situating shock in relation to the dialectic or the progression of history. But, especially in the later Benjamin, this shock (when *in* history) comes to be associated with the "Messiah" or with "Messianic time," whereas for Bataille the experience of heterogeneous shock is associated precisely with the *death* of God. See Benjamin's "Theses on the Philosophy of History," in *Illuminations*, trans. H. Zohn, ed. H. Arendt (New York: Shocken Books, 1969), pp. 253–64. (On Benjamin at the Collège, see Hollier's *Collège de Sociologie*, p. 586).

19. Bataille expressed his marginal relation to Heidegger in this way: "Even more than the text of Volume One of *Being and Time* (. . .) Heidegger's inability to finish it by writing Volume Two underlined my similarity to him" (V, 217). Bataille is similar to the great philosopher not only in his ideas, but above all in his silences, his incoherencies, his inability to express his (non) "ideas."

20. See the letter of Leiris to Bataille, written on July 3, 1939 (II, 454–55).

21. *L'Erotisme* (Paris: Minuit, 1957) has not yet been collected in Bataille's *Oeuvres Complètes*. *L'Erotisme* has been translated as *Death and Sensuality*, ed. R. Kastenbaum (1962; reprint, New York: Arno, 1977).

22. Bataille's position vis-à-vis Marxism is, to say the least, a complex one. While it seems that, at least up until 1936, Bataille was trying to join his notion of expenditure to the negativity envisaged by Marxism, it is clear that already in 1935, in his novel *Le Bleu du ciel (Blue of Noon)*, Bataille recognizes a rending conflict between a devotion to expenditure and a devotion to the revolutionary productivity and utility valorized by Marxism. In his later writings (of the 1940s and 50s) Bataille is no longer overtly Marxist, but the problem of inner conflict or sundering, outlined in *Le Bleu du ciel*, remains constant. See, in this context, the chapters "Politics, Mutilation, Writing: Bataille's *Le Bleu du ciel*" and "Betrayal in the Later Bataille" in my book *Politics, Writing, Mutilation: The Cases of Bataille, Blanchot, Roussel, Leiris, and Ponge*, forthcoming from the University of Minnesota Press.

Bataille's "Letter to X" (Kojève) of 1937, pertinent in this context, while not in the present collection, will be included in the translation of Denis Hollier's anthology, *Le Collège de Sociologie*, forthcoming from the University of Minnesota Press.

I
(1927–1930)

Figure 1. Bataille (left) with his father and brother, ca. 1898. (Photo courtesy of Société Nouvelle des Editions Pauvert.)

[Dream]

In the street in front of the house we lived in in Reims. I leave on a bicycle. Paved street and streetcar rails. very annoying on a bicycle. paved street one doesn't know whether to go left or right. multiplication of streetcar rails. I brush against a streetcar but there is no accident. I would like to reach the place where after a turn there is a smooth road but from now on it is no doubt too late and the wonderful smooth road on which you go up and then down with the speed you gain [is] now paved. In fact when I turn the road is no longer as it was before they redid it but in order to redo it they have transformed it into an immense trench in which pronounced ⌐‾⌐ stand out. I see these strong supports but more and more I see them in precarious forms first they are formed by the frames of barrels with disjointed planks in circles that will have to be filled with earth then more and more disjointed barrels to erect. One proceeds as it follows extremely virile and brutal cellar workers and even [horrible *blacks*] arrive to set up the long and thin tottering barrel. Suddenly an atrocious darkness descends; I go around in the form of an American gentleman. To erect the barrel it is necessary to pull on thick cords black with soot on which animals such as enormous atrocious rats are hung by the tail but which threaten to bite, but they must be killed. The cellar workers are with great pleasure in contact with this scum which they joyfully hang up but the American visitor in his suit risks being stained and bitten and he is not a little disgusted and frightened. however he stands his ground with difficulty the slimy and bloody fish or dead but menacing rats at the level of his face.

The association was thus established.

Horrible rats and all the terrors of childhood. The cellar one goes down into with a candle.

Terror of spiders.

And then suddenly I remember having gone down into the cellar with my father, a candle in my hand. Dream of the bear with a candlestick.

Terrors of childhood spiders etc. linked to the memory of having my pants pulled down on my father's knees.

Kind of ambivalence between the most horrible and the most magnificent.

I see him spread his obscene hands over me with a bitter and blind smile. This memory seems to be the most terrible of all. One day returning from vacation I find him again showing me the same affection.

Waking up I associate the horror of rats with the memory of my father correcting me with a blow in the form of a bloody toad into which a vulture (my father) sinks his beak. My buttocks are bare and my stomach is bloody. Very blinding memory like the sun seen through the lids of closed eyes, in red. My father himself, I imagine that, since he is blind, he also sees the sun in blinding red. Parallel to this memory my father sitting.

This has the effect of reminding me that my father being young would have wanted to do something atrocious to me with pleasure.

I'm something like three years old my legs naked on my father's knees and my penis bloody like the sun.

This for playing with a hoop.

My father slaps me and I see the sun.

The Solar Anus

It is clear that the world is purely parodic, in other words, that each thing seen is the parody of another, or is the same thing in a deceptive form.

Ever since sentences started to *circulate* in brains devoted to reflection, an effort at total identification has been made, because with the aid of a *copula* each sentence ties one thing to another; all things would be visibly connected if one could discover at a single glance and in its totality the tracings of an Ariadne's thread leading thought into its own labyrinth.

But the *copula* of terms is no less irritating than the *copulation* of bodies. And when I scream I AM THE SUN an integral erection results, because the verb *to be* is the vehicle of amorous frenzy.

Everyone is aware that life is parodic and that it lacks an interpretation.
Thus lead is the parody of gold.
Air is the parody of water.
The brain is the parody of the equator.
Coitus is the parody of crime.

Gold, water, the equator, or crime can each be put forward as the principle of things.

And if the origin of things is not like the ground of the planet that seems to be the base, but like the circular movement that the planet describes around a mobile center, then a car, a clock, or a sewing machine could equally be accepted as the generative principle.

The two primary motions are rotation and sexual movement, whose combination is expressed by the locomotive's wheels and pistons.

These two motions are reciprocally transformed, the one into the other.

Thus one notes that the earth, by turning, makes animals and men have coitus, and (because the result is as much the cause as that which provokes it) that animals and men make the earth turn by having coitus.

It is the mechanical combination or transformation of these movements that the alchemists sought as the philosopher's stone.

It is through the use of this magically valued combination that one can determine the present position of men in the midst of the elements.

An abandoned shoe, a rotten tooth, a snub nose, the cook spitting in the soup of his masters are to love what a battle flag is to nationality.

An umbrella, a sexagenarian, a seminarian, the smell of rotten eggs, the hollow eyes of judges are the roots that nourish love.

A dog devouring the stomach of a goose, a drunken vomiting woman, a sobbing accountant, a jar of mustard represent the confusion that serves as the vehicle of love.

A man who finds himself among others is irritated because he does not know why he is not one of the others.

In bed next to a girl he loves, he forgets that he does not know why he is himself instead of the body he touches.

Without knowing it, he suffers from the mental darkness that keeps him from screaming that he himself is the girl who forgets his presence while shuddering in his arms.

Love, or infantile rage, or a provincial dowager's vanity, or clerical pornography, or the diamond of a soprano bewilder individuals forgotten in dusty apartments.

They can very well try to find each other; they will never find anything but parodic images, and they will fall asleep as empty as mirrors.

The absent and inert girl hanging dreamless from my arms is no more foreign to me than the door or window through which I can look or pass.

I rediscover indifference (allowing her to leave me) when I fall asleep, through an inability to love what happens.

It is impossible for her to know whom she will rediscover when I hold her, because she obstinately attains a complete forgetting.

The planetary systems that turn in space like rapid disks, and whose centers also move, describing an infinitely larger circle, only move away continuously from their own position in order to return to it, completing their rotation.

Movement is the figure of love, incapable of stopping at a particular being, and rapidly passing from one to another.

But the forgetting that determines it in this way is only a subterfuge of memory.

A man gets up as brusquely as a specter on a coffin and falls in the same way.

He gets up a few hours later and then he falls again, and the same thing happens every day; this great coitus with the celestial atmosphere is regulated by the terrestrial rotation around the sun.

Thus even though terrestrial life moves to the rhythm of this rotation, the image of this movement is not the turning earth, but the male shaft penetrating the female and almost entirely emerging, in order to reenter.

Love and life appear to be separate only because everything on earth is broken apart by vibrations of various amplitudes and durations.

However, there are no vibrations that are not conjugated with a continuous circular movement; in the same way, a locomotive rolling on the surface of the earth is the image of a continuous metamorphosis.

Beings only die to be born, in the manner of phalluses that leave bodies in order to enter them.

Plants rise in the direction of the sun and then collapse in the direction of the ground.

Trees bristle the ground with a vast quantity of flowered shafts raised up to the sun.

The trees that forcefully soar end up burned by lightning, chopped down, or uprooted. Returned to the ground, they come back up in another form.

But their polymorphous coitus is a function of uniform terrestrial rotation.

The simplest image of organic life united with rotation is the tide.

From the movement of the sea, uniform coitus of the earth with the moon, comes the polymorphous and organic coitus of the earth with the sun.

But the first form of solar love is a cloud raised up over the liquid element.

The erotic cloud sometimes becomes a storm and falls back to earth in the form of rain, while lightning staves in the layers of the atmosphere.

The rain is soon raised up again in the form of an immobile plant.

Animal life comes entirely from the movement of the seas and, inside bodies, life continues to come from salt water.

The sea, then, has played the role of the female organ that liquifies under the excitation of the penis.

The sea continuously jerks off.

Solid elements, contained and brewed in water animated by erotic movement, shoot out in the form of flying fish.

The erection and the sun scandalize, in the same way as the cadaver and the darkness of cellars.

Vegetation is uniformly directed towards the sun; human beings, on the other hand, even though phalloid like trees, in opposition to the other animals, necessarily avert their eyes.

Human eyes tolerate neither sun, coitus, cadavers, nor obscurity, but with different reactions.

When my face is flushed with blood, it becomes red and obscene.

It betrays at the same time, through morbid reflexes, a bloody erection and a demanding thirst for indecency and criminal debauchery.

For that reason I am not afraid to affirm that my face is a scandal and that my passions are expressed only by the JESUVE.

The terrestrial globe is covered with volcanoes, which serve as its anus.

Although this globe eats nothing, it often violently ejects the contents of its entrails.

Those contents shoot out with a racket and fall back, streaming down the sides of the Jesuve, spreading death and terror everywhere.

In fact, the erotic movements of the ground are not fertile like those of the water, but they are far more rapid.

The earth sometimes jerks off in a frenzy, and everything collapses on its surface.

The Jesuve is thus the image of an erotic movement that burglarizes the ideas contained in the mind, giving them the force of a scandalous eruption.

This eruptive force accumulates in those who are necessarily situated below.

Communist workers appear to the bourgeois to be as ugly and dirty as hairy sexual organs, or lower parts; sooner or later there will be a scandalous eruption in the course of which the asexual noble heads of the bourgeois will be chopped off.

Disasters, revolutions, and volcanoes do not make love with the stars.

The erotic revolutionary and volcanic deflagrations antagonize the heavens.

As in the case of violent love, they take place beyond the constraints of fecundity.

In opposition to celestial fertility there are terrestrial disasters, the image of terrestrial love without condition, erection without escape and without rule, scandal, and terror.

Love, then, screams in my own throat; I am the *Jesuve*, the filthy parody of the torrid and blinding sun.

I want to have my throat slashed while violating the girl to whom I will have been able to say: you are the night.

The Sun exclusively loves the Night and directs its luminous violence, its ignoble shaft, toward the earth, but it finds itself incapable of reaching the gaze or the night, even though the nocturnal terrestrial expanses head continuously toward the indecency of the solar ray.

The *solar annulus* is the intact anus of her body at eighteen years to which nothing sufficiently blinding can be compared except the sun, even though the *anus* is the *night*.

The Language of Flowers

It is vain to consider, in the appearance of things, only the intelligible signs that allow the various elements to be distinguished from each other. What strikes human eyes determines not only the knowledge of the relations between various objects, but also a given decisive and inexplicable state of mind. Thus the sight of a flower reveals, it is true, the presence of this well-defined part of a plant, but it is impossible to stop at this superficial observation; in fact, the sight of this flower provokes in the mind much more significant reactions, because the flower expresses an obscure vegetal resolution. What the configuration and color of the corolla reveal, what the dirty traces of pollen or the freshness of the pistil betray doubtless cannot be adequately expressed by language; it is, however, useless to ignore (as is generally done) this inexpressible *real presence* and to reject as puerile absurdities certain attempts at symbolic interpretation.

That most of the juxtapositions of the *language of flowers* would have a fortuitous and superficial character could be foreseen even before consulting the traditional list. If the dandelion conveys *expansion*, the narcissus *egoism*, and the wormwood flower *bitterness*, one can all too easily see why. At stake here is clearly not the divination of the secret meaning of flowers, and one can easily make out the well-known property or the adequate legend. One would look in vain, moreover, for parallels that strikingly convey a hidden understanding of the things here in question. It matters little, in fact, that the columbine is the emblem of sadness, the snapdragon the emblem of desire, the waterlilly the emblem of indifference . . . It seems opportune to recognize that such approximations can be renewed at will, and it suffices to assign a primordial importance to much simpler interpretations, such as those that link the rose or the spurge to love. Not that, doubtless, these two flowers alone can designate human love—even if there is a more exact correspondence (as when one has the spurge say: "It is you who have awakened my love," so troubling when conveyed by such a shady flower), it is to flowers in general, and not to any specific flower, that one is tempted to attribute the strange privilege of revealing the presence of love.

But this interpretation seems unsurprising: in fact love can be posited from the outset as the natural function of the flower. Thus the symbolic quality would be due, even here, to a distinct property and not to an appearance that mysteriously strikes the human sensibility. Therefore it would only have a purely subjective value. Men have linked the brilliance of flowers to their amorous emotions because, on either side, it is a question of phenomena that precede fertilization. The role given to symbols in psychoanalytic interpretations, moreover, would corroborate an explanation of this type. In fact it is almost always an accidental parallel that accounts for the origin of substitutions in dreams. Among other things, the value given to pointed or hollowed-out objects is fairly well known.

In this way one quickly dismisses the opinion that external forms, whether seductive or horrible, reveal certain crucial resolutions in all phenomena, which human resolutions would only amplify. Thus there would be good reason to renounce immediately the possibility of replacing the *word* with the *appearance* as an element of philosophical analysis. It would be easy to show that only the *word* allows one to consider the characteristics of things that determine a relative situation, in other words the properties that permit an external action. Nevertheless, the *appearance* would introduce the decisive values of things . . .

It appears at first that the symbolic meaning of flowers is not necessarily derived from their function. It is evident, in fact, that if one expresses love with the aid of a flower, it is the corolla, rather than the useful organs, that becomes the sign of desire.

But here a specious objection could be raised against interpretation through the objective value of *appearance*. In fact the substitution of juxtaposed elements for essential elements is consistent with all that we spontaneously know about the emotions that motivate us, since the object of human love is never an organ, but the person who has the organ. Thus the attribution of the corolla to love can easily be explained: if the sign of love is displaced from the pistil and stamens to the surrounding petals, it is because the human mind is accustomed to making such a displacement with regard to people. But even though there is an undeniable parallelism in the two substitutions, it would be necessary to attribute to some puerile Providence a singular desire to satisfy people's manias: how in fact can one explain how these garish elements, automatically substituted for the essential organs of the flower, develop in such a brilliant way?

It would obviously be simpler to recognize the aphrodisiac properties of flowers, such as odor and appearance, which have aroused men's and women's amorous feelings over the centuries. Something is explosively propagated in nature, in the springtime, in the same way that bursts of laughter are propagated, step by step, each one provoking and intensifying the next. Many things can be altered in human societies, but nothing will prevail against the natural truth that a beautiful woman or a red rose signifies love.

An equally inexplicable and equally immutable reaction gives the girl and the rose a very different value: that of ideal beauty. There are, in fact, a multitude of beautiful flowers, since the beauty of flowers is even less rare than the beauty of girls, and characteristic of this organ of the plant. It is surely impossible to use an abstract formula to account for the elements that can give the flower this quality. It is interesting to observe, however, that if one says that flowers are beautiful, it is because they seem to *conform to what must be*, in other words they represent, as flowers, the human *ideal*.

At least at first glance, and in general: in fact, most flowers are badly developed and are barely distinguishable from foliage; some of them are even unpleasant, if not hideous. Moreover, even the most beautiful flowers are spoiled in their centers by hairy sexual organs. Thus the interior of a rose does not at all correspond to its exterior beauty; if one tears off all of the corolla's petals, all that remains is a rather sordid tuft. Other flowers, it is true, present very well-developed and undeniably elegant stamens, but appealing again to common sense, it becomes clear on close examination that this elegance is rather satanic: thus certain kinds of fat orchids, plants so shady that one is tempted to attribute to them the most troubling human perversions. But even more than by the filth of its organs, the flower is betrayed by the fragility of its corolla: thus, far from answering the demands of human ideas, it is the sign of their failure. In fact, after a very short period of glory the marvelous corolla rots indecently in the sun, thus becoming, for the plant, a garish withering. Risen from the stench of the manure pile—even though it seemed for a moment to have escaped it in a flight of angelic and lyrical purity—the flower seems to relapse abruptly into its original squalor: the most ideal is rapidly reduced to a wisp of aerial manure. For flowers do not age honestly like leaves, which lose nothing of their beauty, even after they have died; flowers wither like old and overly made-up dowagers, and they die ridiculously on stems that seemed to carry them to the clouds.

It is impossible to exaggerate the tragicomic oppositions indicated in the course of this death-drama, endlessly played out between earth and sky, and it is evident that one can only paraphrase this laughable duel by introducing, not as a sentence, but more precisely as an ink stain, this nauseating banality: *love smells like death*. It seems, in fact, that desire has nothing to do with ideal beauty, or, more precisely, that it only arises in order to stain and wither the beauty that for many sad and well-ordered personalities is only a limit, a *categorical imperative*. The most admirable flower for that reason would not be represented, following the verbiage of the old poets, as the faded expression of an angelic ideal, but, on the contrary, as a filthy and glaring sacrilege.

There is good reason to insist upon the exception represented, in this respect, by the flower on the plant. In fact, if one continues to apply the method of interpretation introduced here, on the whole the external part of the plant is endowed with an unambiguous meaning. The appearance of leafy stems generally gives the impression of strength and dignity. Without a doubt the insane contortions of tendrils and the unusual lacerations of foliage bear witness to the fact that all is not uniformly correct in the impeccable erection of plants. But nothing contributes more strongly to the peace in one's heart and to the lifting of one's spirits, as well as to one's loftier notions of justice and rectitude, than the spectacle of fields and forests, along with the tiniest parts of the plant, which sometimes manifest a veritable architectural order, contributing to the general impression of correctness. No crack, it seems—one could stupidly say no *quack*—conspicuously troubles the decisive harmony of vegetal nature. Flowers themselves, lost in this immense movement from earth to sky, are reduced to an episodic role, to a diversion, moreover, that is apparently misunderstood: they can only contribute, by breaking the monotony, to the inevitable seductiveness produced by the general thrust from low to high. And in order to destroy this favorable impression, nothing less is necessary than the impossible and fantastic vision of roots swarming under the surface of the soil, nauseating and naked like vermin.

Roots, in fact, represent the perfect counterpart to the visible parts of a plant. While the visible parts are nobly elevated, the ignoble and sticky roots wallow in the ground, loving rottenness just as leaves love light. There is reason to note, moreover, that the incontestable moral value of the term *base* conforms to this systematic interpretation of the meaning of roots: what is *evil* is necessarily represented, among movements, by a movement from high to low. That fact is impossible to explain if one does not assign moral meaning to natural phenomena, from which this value is taken, precisely because of the striking character of the *appearance*, the sign of the decisive movements of nature.

Besides, it would seem impossible to eliminate an opposition as flagrant as the one that differentiates stem from root. One legend in particular demonstrates the morbid interest, which has always been more or less pronounced, in the parts that shove themselves into the earth. The obscenity of the mandrake root is undoubtedly fortuitous, like the majority of specific symbolic interpretations, but it is no coincidence that this type of emphasis, to which the mandrake root owes a legendary satanism, is based on an obviously ignoble form. The symbolic values of the carrot and the turnip are also fairly well known.

It was more difficult to show that the same opposition appeared in an isolated part of the plant, the flower, where it takes on an exceptionally dramatic meaning.

There can be no doubt: the substitution of natural forms for the abstractions currently used by philosophers will seem not only strange but absurd. It is probably fairly unimportant that philosophers themselves have often had to have recourse, though with repugnance, to terms that derive their value from the production of these forms in nature, as when they speak of *baseness*. No blindness interferes with defending the perogatives of abstraction. This substitution, moreover, threatens to carry one too far: it would result, in the first place, in a feeling of freedom, the free availability of oneself in every sense, which is absolutely unbearable for the most part, and the troubling contempt for all that is still—thanks to miserable evasions—*elevated*, noble, sacred . . . Don't all these beautiful things run the risk of being reduced to a strange *mise en scène*, destined to make sacrilege more impure? And the disconcerting gesture of the Marquis de Sade, locked up with madmen, who had the most beautiful roses brought to him only to pluck off their petals and toss them into a ditch filled with liquid manure—in these circumstances, doesn't it have an overwhelming impact?

Materialism

Most materialists, even though they may have wanted to do away with all spiritual entities, ended up positing an order of things whose hierarchical relations mark it as specifically idealist. They situated dead matter at the summit of a conventional hierarchy of diverse facts, without perceiving that in this way they gave in to an obsession with the *ideal* form of matter, with a form that was closer than any other to what matter *should be*. Dead matter, the pure idea, and God in fact answer a question in the same way (in other words perfectly, and as flatly as the docile student in a classroom)—a question that can only be posed by philosophers, the question of the essence of things, precisely of the *idea* by which things become intelligible. Classical materialists did not really even substitute causation for the *must be* (the *quare* for the *quamobrem*, or, in other words, determinism for destiny, the past for the future). Their need for external authority in fact placed the *must be* of all appearance in the functional role they unconsciously assigned the idea of science. If the principle of things they defined is precisely the stable element that permitted science to constitute an apparently unshakeable position, a veritable divine eternity, this choice cannot be attributed to chance. The conformity of dead matter to the idea of science is, among most materialists, substituted for the religious relations earlier established between the divinity and his creatures, the one being the *idea* of the others.

Materialism will be seen as a senile idealism to the extent that it is not immediately based on psychological or social facts, instead of on artificially isolated physical phenomena. Thus it is from Freud, among others—rather than from long-dead physicists, whose ideas today have no meaning—that a representation of matter must be taken. It is of little importance that the fear of psychological complications (a fear that only bears witness to intellectual weakness) causes timid souls to see in this attitude an aversion or a return to spiritual values. When the word *materialism* is used, it is time to designate the direct interpretation, *excluding all idealism*, of raw phenomena, and not a system founded on the fragmentary elements of an ideological analysis, elaborated under the sign of religious relations.

Eye

Cannibal delicacy. It is known that civilized man is characterized by an often inexplicable acuity of horror. The fear of insects is no doubt one of the most singular and most developed of these horrors as is, one is surprised to note, the fear of the eye. It seems impossible, in fact, to judge the eye using any word other than *seductive*, since nothing is more attractive in the bodies of animals and men. But extreme seductiveness is probably at the boundary of horror.

In this respect, the eye could be related to the cutting edge, whose appearance provokes both bitter and contradictory reactions; this is what the makers of the *Andalusian Dog*[1] must have hideously and obscurely experienced when, among the first images of the film, they determined the bloody loves of these two beings. That a razor would cut open the dazzling eye of a young and charming woman—this is precisely what a young man would have admired to the point of madness, a young man watched by a small cat, a young man who by chance holding in his hand a coffee spoon, suddenly wanted to take an eye in that spoon.

Obviously a singular desire on the part of a white, from whom the eyes of the cows, sheep, and pigs that he eats have always been hidden. For the eye—as Stevenson exquisitely puts it, a *cannibal delicacy*—is, on our part, the object of such anxiety that we will never bite into it. The eye is even ranked high in horror, since it is, among other things, the *eye of conscience*. Victor Hugo's poem is sufficiently well known; the obsessive and lugubrious eye, the living eye, the eye that was hideously dreamed by Grandville in a nightmare he had shortly before his death;[2] the criminal "dreams that he has just struck down a man in a dark wood . . . Human blood has been spilled and, to use an expression that

[Derniers dessins de J.-J. Grandville. — Premier rêve. — Crime et expiation.]

Figure 2. Last illustrations of J. J. Grandville: ''First Dream: Crime and Expiation'' (1847). Phot. Bibl. nat. Paris.

presents a ferocious image to the mind, *he made an oak sweat*.[3] In fact, it is not a man, but a tree trunk . . . bloody . . . that thrashes and struggles . . . under the murderous weapon. The hands of the victim are raised, pleading, but in vain. Blood continues to flow." At that point an enormous eye appears in the black sky, pursuing the criminal through space and to the bottom of the sea, where it devours him after taking the form of a fish. Innumerable eyes nevertheless multiply under the waves.

On this subject, Grandville writes: "Are these the eyes of the crowd attracted by the imminent spectacle of torture?" But why would these absurd eyes be attracted, like a cloud of flies, by something so repugnant? Why as well, on the masthead of a perfectly sadistic illustrated weekly, published in Paris from 1907 to 1924, does an eye regularly appear against a red background, above a bloody spectacle? Why isn't the *Eye of the Police*—similar to the eye of human justice in the nightmare of Grandville—finally only the expression of a blind thirst for blood? Similar also to the eye of Crampon, condemned to death and approached by the chaplain an instant before the blade's fall: he dismissed the chaplain, but enucleated himself and gave him the happy gift of his torn-out eye, *for this eye was made of glass*.

Notes

1. This extraordinary film is the work of two young Catalans: the painter Salvador Dali, one of whose characteristic paintings we reproduce below (p. 25), and the director Luis Bunuel. See the excellent photographs published by the *Cahiers d'art* (July 1929, p. 230), by *Bifur* (August 1929, p. 105) and by *Variétés* (July 1929, p. 209). This film can be distinguished from banal avant-garde productions, with which one might be tempted to confuse it, in that the screenplay predominates. Several very explicit facts appear in successive order, without logical connection it is true, but penetrating so far into horror that the spectators are caught up as directly as they are in adventure films. Caught up and even precisely caught by the throat, and without artifice; do these spectators know, in fact, where they—the authors of this film, or people like them—will stop? If Bunuel himself, after the filming of the slit-open eye, remained sick for a week (he, moreover, had to film the scene of the asses' cadavers in a pestilential atmosphere), how then can one not see to what extent horror becomes fascinating, and how it alone is brutal enough to break everything that stifles?

2. Victor Hugo, a reader of *Le Magazin pittoresque*, borrowed from the admirable written dream *Crime and Expiation*, and from the unprecedented drawing of Grandville, both published in 1847 (pp. 211-14), the story of the pursuit of a criminal by an obstinate eye; it is scarcely useful to observe, however, that only an obscure and sinister obsession, and not a cold memory, can explain this resemblance. We owe to Pierre d'Espezel's erudition and kindness our awareness of this curious document, probably the most beautiful of Grandville's extravagant compositions.

[The poem by Victor Hugo to which Bataille refers is "La Conscience" (in the collection *La Légende des siècles* [Paris: Gallimard, Bibliothèque de la Pléiade, 1950], pp. 26-27). The poem in fact presents the eye of God following Cain, even into a (self-imposed) tomb. Tr.]

3. ["Faire suer un chêne" (literally, "to make an oak sweat") is a slang expression that could be translated as "to exploit a guy" or "to rip off a guy." Tr.]

The Big Toe

The big toe is the most *human* part of the human body, in the sense that no other element of this body is as differentiated from the corresponding element of the anthropoid ape (chimpanzee, gorilla, orangutan, or gibbon). This is due to the fact that the ape is tree dwelling, whereas man moves on the earth without clinging to branches, having himself become a tree, in other words raising himself straight up in the air like a tree, and all the more beautiful for the correctness of his erection. In addition, the function of the human foot consists in giving a firm foundation to the erection of which man is so proud (the big toe, ceasing to grasp branches, is applied to the ground on the same plane as the other toes).

But whatever the role played in the erection by his foot, man, who has a light head, in other words a head raised to the heavens and heavenly things, sees it as spit, on the pretext that he has this foot in the mud.

Although within the body blood flows in equal quantities from high to low and from low to high, there is a bias in favor of that which elevates itself, and human life is erroneously seen as an elevation. The division of the universe into subterranean hell and perfectly pure heaven is an indelible conception, mud and darkness being the *principles* of evil as light and celestial space are the *principles* of good: with their feet in mud but their heads more or less in light, men obstinately imagine a tide that will permanently elevate them, never to return, into pure space. Human life entails, in fact, the rage of seeing oneself as a back and forth movement from refuse to the ideal, and from the ideal to refuse—a rage that is easily directed against an organ as *base* as the foot.

The human foot is commonly subjected to grotesque tortures that deform it and make it rickety. In an imbecilic way it is doomed to corns, calluses, and bunions, and if one takes into account turns of phrase that are only now disappearing, to the most nauseating filthiness: the peasant expression ''her hands are as dirty as feet,'' while no longer true of the entire human collectivity, was so in the seventeenth century.

Man's secret horror of his foot is one of the explanations for the tendency to conceal its length and form as much as possible. Heels of greater or lesser height, depending on the sex, distract from the foot's low and flat character.

Besides, this uneasiness is often confused with a sexual uneasiness; this is especially striking among the Chinese, who, after having atrophied the feet of women, situate them at the most excessive point of deviance. The husband himself must not see the nude feet of his wife, and it is incorrect and immoral in general to look at the feet of women. Catholic confessors, adapting themselves to this aberration, ask their Chinese penitents ''if they have not looked at women's feet.''

The same aberration is found among the Turks (Volga Turks, Turks of Central Asia), who consider it immoral to show their nude feet and who even go to bed in stockings.

Nothing similar can be cited from classical antiquity (apart from the use of very high soles in tragedies). The most prudish Roman matrons constantly allowed their nude toes to be seen. On the other hand, modesty concerning the feet developed excessively in the modern era and only started to disappear in the nineteenth century. M. Salomon Reinach has studied this development in detail in the article entitled ''Pieds pudiques'' [''Modest Feet''],[1] insisting on the role of Spain, where women's feet have been the object of the most dreaded anxiety and thus were the cause of crimes. The simple fact of allowing the shod foot to be seen, jutting out from under a skirt, was regarded as indecent. Under no circumstances was it possible to touch the foot of a woman, this liberty being, with one exception, more grave than any other. Of course, the foot of the queen was the object of the most terrifying prohibition. Thus, according to Mme D'Aulnoy, the Count of Villamediana, in love with Queen Elizabeth, had the idea of starting a fire in order to have the pleasure of carrying her in his arms: ''Almost the entire house, worth 100,000 écus, was burned, but he was consoled by the fact that, taking advantage of so favorable an occasion, he took the sovereign in his arms and carried her into a small staircase. He took some liberties there, and, *something very much noticed in this country, he even touched her foot*. A little page saw it, reported it to the king, and the latter had his revenge by killing the count with a pistol shot.''

It is possible to see in these obsessions, as M. Reinach does, a progressive refinement of modesty that little by little has been able to reach the calf, the ankle, and the foot. This explanation, in part well founded, is however not sufficient if one wants to account for the hilarity commonly produced by simply imagining the *toes*. The play of fantasies and fears, of human necessities and aberrations, is in fact such that fingers have come to signify useful action and firm character, the toes stupor and base idiocy. The vicissitudes of organs, the profusion of stomachs, larynxes, and brains traversing innumerable animal species and individuals, carries the imagination along in an ebb and flow it does not willingly follow, due to a hatred of the still painfully perceptible frenzy of the bloody palpitations of the body. Man willingly imagines himself to be like the god Neptune, stilling his own waves, with majesty; nevertheless, the bellowing waves of the viscera, in more or less incessant inflation and upheaval, brusquely put an end to his dignity. Blind, but tranquil and strangely despising his obscure baseness, a given person, ready to call to mind the grandeurs of human history, as when his glance ascends a monument testifying to the grandeur of his nation, is stopped in mid-flight by an atrocious pain in his big toe because, though the most noble of animals, he nevertheless has corns on his feet; in other words, he has feet, and these feet independently lead an ignoble life.

Corns on the feet differ from headaches and toothaches by their baseness, and they are only laughable because of an ignominy explicable by the mud in which feet are found. Since by its physical attitude the human race distances itself *as much as it can* from terrestrial mud—whereas a spasmodic laugh carries joy to its summit each time its purest flight lands man's own arrogance spread-eagle in the mud—one can imagine that a toe, always more or less damaged and humiliating, is psychologically analogous to the brutal fall of a man—in other words, to death. The hideously cadaverous and at the same time loud and proud appearance of the big toe corresponds to this derision and gives a very shrill expression to the disorder of the human body, that product of the violent discord of the organs.

The form of the big toe is not, however, specifically monstrous: in this it is different from other parts of the body, the inside of a gaping mouth, for example. Only secondary (but common) deformations have been able to give its ignominy an exceptionally burlesque value. Now it is easy, most often, to account for burlesque values by means of extreme seductiveness. But we are led here to distinguish categorically two radically opposed kinds of seductiveness (whose habitual confusion entails the most absurd misunderstandings of language).

If a seductive element is to be attributed to the big toe, it is evidently not one to satisfy such exalted aspirations as, for example, the perfectly indelible taste that, in most cases, leads one to prefer elegant and correct forms. On the contrary, if one chooses, for example, the case of the Count of Villamediana, one can affirm that the pleasure he derived from touching the queen's foot specifically derived from the ugliness and infection represented by the baseness of the foot, in practice by the most deformed feet. Thus, supposing that the queen's foot was perfectly pretty, it still derived its sacrilegious charm from deformed and muddy feet. Since a queen is *a priori* a more *ideal* and ethereal being than any other, it was human to the point of laceration to touch what in fact was not very different from the stinking foot of a thug. Here one submits to a seduction radically opposed to that caused by light and ideal beauty; the two orders of seduction are often confused because a person constantly moves from one to the other, and, given this back and forth movement, whether it finds its end in one direction or the other, seduction is all the more acute when the movement is more brutal.

As for the big toe, classic foot fetishism leading to the licking of toes categorically indicates that it is a phenomenon of base seduction, which accounts for the burlesque value that is always more or less attached to the pleasures condemned by pure and superficial men.

The meaning of this article lies in its insistence on a direct and explicit questioning of *seductiveness*, without taking into account poetic concoctions that are, ultimately, nothing but a diversion (most human beings are naturally feeble and can only abandon themselves to their instincts when in a poetic haze). A return to reality does not imply any new acceptances, but means that one is seduced in a base manner, without transpositions and to the point of screaming, opening his eyes wide: opening them wide, then, before a big toe.

Note

1. In *L'Anthropologie*, 1903, pp. 733–36; reprinted in *Cultes, mythes et religions*, 1905, vol 1, pp. 105–10.

The "Lugubrious Game"

Intellectual despair results in neither weakness nor dreams, but in violence. Thus abandoning certain investigations is out of the question. It is only a matter of knowing how to give vent to one's rage; whether one only wants to wander like madmen around prisons, or whether one wants to overturn them.[1]

To halfheartedness, to loopholes and deliria that reveal a great poetic impotence, one can only oppose a black rage and even an incontestable bestiality; it is impossible to get worked up other than as a pig who rummages in manure and mud uprooting everything with his snout—and whose repugnant voracity is unstoppable.

If the forms brought together by a painter on a canvas had no repercussion, and for example, since we are speaking of voracity—even in the intellectual order—if horrible shadows that collide in the head, if jaws with hideous teeth had not come out of Picasso's skull to terrify those who still have the impudence to think honestly, then painting at the very most would be good for distracting people from their rage, as do bars or American films. But why hesitate to write that when Picasso paints, the dislocation of forms leads to that of thought, in other words that the immediate intellectual movement, which in other cases leads to the idea, aborts. We cannot ignore that flowers are aphrodisiacs, that a single burst of laughter can traverse and stir up a crowd, that an equally obstinate abortion is the shrill and incendiary blast of the *non serviam* that the human brute opposes to the idea. And the idea has over man the same degrading power that a harness has over a horse; I can snort and gasp: I go, no less, right and

Figure 3. "The Lugubrious Game" by Salvador Dali. © S.P.A.D.E.M.,
Paris/V.A.G.A., New York, 1983.

B. Désirs du sujet exprimés par une ascension ailée des objets du désir. Le caractère burlesque et provoquant de cette expression marque la recherche volontaire de la punition.

D. Figuration du sujet contemplant avec complaisance sa propre émasculation et donnant l'amplification poétique.

A. Figuration du sujet au moment de l'émasculation. L'émasculation est exprimée par le déchirement de la partie supérieure du corps.

C. Figuration du sujet souillé échappant à l'émasculation par une attitude ignominieuse et écœurante. La souillure est à la fois cause primitive et remède.

SCHÉMA PSYCHANALYTIQUE DES FIGURATIONS CONTRADICTOIRES DU SUJET DANS "LE JEU LUGUBRE" DE SALVADOR DALI.

left, my head bridled and pulled by the idea that brutalizes all men and causes them to be docile—the idea in the form of, among other things, a piece of paper adorned with the arms of the State. Taking into account trickery, human life always more or less conforms to the image of a soldier obeying commands in his drill. But sudden cataclysms, great popular manifestations of madness, riots, enormous revolutionary slaughters—all these show the extent of the inevitable backlash.

This leads me to state, almost without introduction, that the paintings of Picasso are hideous, that those of Dali are frighteningly ugly.[2] One is a victim of the awkwardness of words, or even of an evil spell resulting from the practices of black magic, when one attempts to believe otherwise. All it takes is to imagine suddenly the charming little girl whose soul would be Dali's abominable mirror, to measure the extent of the evil. The tongue of this little girl is not a tongue but a she-rat. And if she still appears admirably beautiful, it is, as they say, because black blood is beautiful, flowing on the hide of a cow or on the throat of a woman. (If violent movements manage to rescue a being from profound boredom, it is because they can lead—through some obscure error—to a ghastly satiating ugliness. It must be said, moreover, that ugliness can be hateful without any recourse and, as it were, through misfortune, but nothing is more common than the equivocal ugliness that gives, in a provocative way, the illusion of the opposite. As for irrevocable ugliness, it is exactly as detestable as certain beauties: the beauty that conceals nothing, the beauty that is not the mask of ruined immodesty, the beauty that never contradicts itself and remains eternally at attention like a coward.)

Little by little the contradictory signs of servitude and revolt are revealed in all things. The great constructions of the intellect are, finally, prisons: that is why they are obstinately overturned. Dreams and illusory Cimmerii remain within reach of the zealously irresolute, whose unconscious calculations are not so clumsy since they innocently shelter revolt from laws. Besides, how could one not admire the loss of will, the blind manner, the drifting uncertainty rang-

Figure 4. Psychoanalytic Schema of the Contradictory Representations of the Subject in "Lugubrious Game" of Salvador Dali.

A. Representation of the subject at the moment of emasculation. The emasculation is expressed by the laceration of the upper part of the body.

B. The subject's desires expressed by a winged ascension of the objects of desire. The burlesque and provocative character of this expression indicates the voluntary pursuit of punishment.

C. Representation of the soiled subject escaping emasculation through an ignominious and nauseating posture. The stain is both original cause and remedy.

D. Representation of the subject contemplating with complacency his own emasculation and giving a poetic amplification.

ing from willful distraction to attentiveness? It is true that I am speaking here of what already sinks into oblivion when Dali's razors carve into our faces the grimaces of horror that probably risk making us vomit like drunkards this servile nobility, this idiotic idealism that leaves us under the spell of a few comical prison bosses.

Dogs, vaguely sick from having so long licked the fingers of their masters, howl themselves to death in the countryside, in the middle of the night. These frightening howls are answered—as thunder is answered by the racket of rain—by cries so extreme that one cannot even talk of them without excitement.

A few days before July 14, 1789, the Marquis de Sade, for years doomed to rage in his cell in the Bastille, excited the crowd around the prison by scream-ing insanely into the pipe that was used to carry off his filthy water—an insane cry that was doubtless the most far-reaching ever to strain a larynx. This scream is reported historically as follows: "People of Paris," shouted Sade, "they are killing the prisoners!" Practically the scream of an old *rentière* with her throat slashed at night in a suburb. It is known that Governor Launay, justifiably fright-ened by the riot that was starting to explode, had the frenzied prisoner trans-ferred to another prison; this however did not prevent his head, only a few hours later, from terrifying the town on the end of a pike.

But if one wants explicitly to account for the excessive character of this scream, it is necessary to refer to the deposition of Rose Keller, which accuses Sade of inflicting cruelties upon her. This deposition, recently discovered by M. Maurice Heine,[3] is categorical. The young woman recounts that, after being tor-tured with a whip, she tried to move, with her tears and entreaties, a man both so pleasing and so evil; and as she invoked everything in the world that was saintly and touching, Sade, suddenly gone wild and hearing nothing, let out hor-rifying and perfectly nauseating screams . . .

It is well known that a long-standing uneasiness, going back a number of years, has no other meaning than the feeling that something is missing from exis-tence; it is hardly useful to insist upon the fact that it is for want of the power to let out or hear such screams that, on all sides, restless people have plainly lost their heads, condemning human life to boredom and disgust, while pretend-ing at that very instant to conserve and even to defend it, at the first opportunity, heroically, against stains that seem to them ignoble.

This is said without any critical intention, for it is evident that violence, even when one is beside oneself with it, is most often of sufficient brutal hilarity to exceed questions about people. My only desire here—even if by pushing this bestial hilarity to its furthest point I must nauseate Dali—is to squeal like a pig before his canvases.

For reasons which, out of consideration for him, I put off explaining,[4] Dali has refused to allow the reproduction of his paintings in this article, thus doing me an honor that was as unexpected as I may believe it was persistently sought. I am not unaware of the cowardice and the poverty of spirit reflected, by and large, in the attention paid to his recent productions, to minor and major discoveries. Having gotten caught up in the game, I at least have the good fortune to speak of a man who will necessarily take this article as a provocation and not as a traditional bit of flattery, who will hate me, as I am well aware, as a *provocateur*.

Nowhere, no doubt, from one end to the other of the regions inhabited by the bourgeoisie, is there anything going on that is noticeably different from the rest, from the past, from political traditions, from literary traditions; nevertheless, and moreover without attaching any other importance to it, I can say that from now on it is impossible to retreat and hide in the "wonderland" of Poetry without being publicly condemned as a coward.

Notes

1. This is a portion of an unpublished essay on the inferiority complex. The title is borrowed from the painting by Salvador Dali, whose schema is reproduced on p. 26 (this painting belongs to the Viscount de Noailles and appeared in the Dali show at the Galerie Goemans in November 1929). The *Lugubrious Game*, as moreover the text of the schema indicates, is nothing other than the complex in question. This complex was already apparent in relatively early Dali paintings. *Blood is Sweeter than Honey* (published in *Documents* 4) is characteristic; the body with the head, hands, and feet cut off, the head with the face cut, the ass, symbol of grotesque and powerful virility, lying dead and decomposed, the systematic fragmentation of all the elements of the painting . . .

Even more explicit is the episode of the sliced eye in *An Andalusian Dog*, the film of Luis Bunuel and Salvador Dali (see *Documents* 4, p. 218, and the text of the screenplay in *Revue du cinema*, November 1929, and *Révolution surréaliste 12*, December 1929).

Bunuel himself told me that this episode was the invention of Dali, to whom it was directly suggested by the real vision of a narrow and long cloud cutting across the lunar surface (I can add here that the dead and decomposing asses that reappear in *An Andalusian Dog* represent an obsession shared by Buñuel and Dali, and go back for each of them to the identical discovery, during childhood, of a decomposing ass-cadaver in the countryside).

Even the title, *Lugubrious Game*, adopted by Dali can be taken as an indication of the explicit value of this painting, in which the genesis of emasculation and the contradictory reactions it carries with it are translated with an extraordinary wealth of detail and power of expression. Without pretending to exhaust the psychological elements of this painting, I can indicate here their general development. The very act of emasculation is expressed by Figure A, whose body, from the waist up, is completely torn off. The provocation that immediately caused this bloody punishment is expressed in B by dreams of virility of a puerile and burlesque temerity (the masculine elements are represented not only by the bird's head but by the colored umbrella, the feminine elements by men's hats). But the profound and early cause of the punishment is nothing other than the ignoble stain of the man in his underwear (C), a stain moreover without provocation, since a new and real virility is rediscovered by this person in ignominy and horror themselves. Yet the statue on the left (D) still personifies the unusual satisfaction found in sudden emasculation and betrays a hardly virile need for the poetic amplification of the game. The hand concealing the virility of the head is a suppression of a rule in the painting of Dali, in which persons who for the most part have lost their heads find them only on the condition that they grimace with horror. This permits one to inquire seriously about the orientation of those who see here for the first time *the mental windows opening wide*, who place an emasculated poetic complacency where there appears only the screaming necessity of a recourse to ignominy.

2. That is, moreover, the only similarity between two bodies of work, which differ from each other as much as a cloud of flies differs from an elephant.

3. I must thank M. Maurice Heine, to whom nothing about Sade is unknown, who kindly authorized me to mention the facts that he recounted orally to me. These facts are found in the deposition of Rose Keller, which is included among the authentic documents of a trial soon to be published, through M. Heine's efforts, by Stendhal and Co.

4. I must say that it is not at all a question of something people commonly would call "suspect," but *certain* stories of the "artistic and literary milieu" genre could in any case provoke intractable disgust.

Formless

A dictionary begins when it no longer gives the meaning of words, but their tasks. Thus *formless* is not only an adjective having a given meaning, but a term that serves to bring things down in the world, generally requiring that each thing have its form. What it designates has no rights in any sense and gets itself squashed everywhere, like a spider or an earthworm. In fact, for academic men to be happy, the universe would have to take shape. All of philosophy has no other goal: it is a matter of giving a frock coat to what is, a mathematical frock coat. On the other hand, affirming that the universe resembles nothing and is only *formless* amounts to saying that the universe is something like a spider or spit.

The "Old Mole" and the Prefix *Sur* in the Words *Surhomme* [Superman] and *Surrealist*

In history as in nature, decay is the laboratory of life.

Karl Marx

If we were to identify under the heading of *materialism* a crude liberation of human life from the imprisonment and masked pathology of ethics, an appeal to all that is offensive, indestructible, and even despicable, to all that overthrows, perverts, and ridicules spirit, we could at the same time identify *surrealism* as a childhood disease of this base materialism: it is through this latter identification that the current prerequisites for a consistent development may be specified forcefully and in such a manner as to preclude any return to pretentious idealistic aberrations.

Sufficient agreement exists concerning present social conditions, bourgeois moral values, and the intellectual edifice that supports them. For quite some time, all thinking that has not undermined this dilapidated edifice has immediately taken on its demeanor of senile trickery and comical smugness. But it is useless to insist here on the bankruptcy of bourgeois culture, on the necessity of destroying one day even its memory, and beginning now to establish a new basis for mental agitation. To whatever extent the unhappy bourgeois has maintained a human vulgarity, a certain taste for virility, disaffection with his own class quickly turns into stubborn hatred. And we must insist from the outset that a still relatively new form of intellectual activity, not yet castrated and domesticated, is linked by the force of things to the uprising of the lower classes against present-day work.

It remains to be seen how this force acts, how what passes through bourgeois heads alienated from practical considerations and given over most often to shrill frenzy can be associated with the ongoing upheaval of all human structures, with a series of social collapses and catastrophes whose magnitude and character naturally exceed the reach of even radical ambitions.

I

In the first place, it is not surprising that any subversion within the bourgeois intellectual domain begins with forms that correspond very imperfectly to the solution of such difficulties. Instead of relying on presently lower forms whose interplay will in the end destroy bourgeois prisons, subversion seeks immediately to create its own values in order to oppose established values, concerned as it is as much with the stifling effect of the present moral order as with the material conditions of the proletariat. Thus it finds itself, scarcely alive, searching for an authority *above* the one that has provoked the revolt. Abused by a system that threatens to crush or domesticate them, individuals have put themselves, in practical terms, at the mercy of what appears to them, through blinding flashes and disheartening attacks of empty verbiage, to be above all the pitiful contingencies of their human existence, for example *spirit, surreal, absolute,* etc. At first the "surrealist revolution" was independent of the revolt of the lower classes, indeed was defined as nothing but a confused mental state to which was added violent verbiage asserting the necessity of a dictatorship of *spirit*. Subsequently surrealism has recognized the legitimacy of the organizational endeavors and even the principles of Marxist communism, seeing therein the only means to bring about an indispensable revolution in the real world. But the surrealists continued persistently to express their basic predilection for values *above* the "world of facts" with such banal formulas as "revolt of the Spirit," etc. (*The Revolution First and Always*).

It is of course difficult to avoid a feeling of contempt for revolutionaries to whom the revolution is not, before all else, *the decisive phase of the class struggle*. Nevertheless we are not concerned with ephemeral reactions, but with a verification of a general nature: *any member of the bourgeoisie who has become conscious that his most vigorous and vital instincts, if he does not repress them, necessarily make him an enemy of his own class, is condemned, when he loses heart, to forge at once values situated ABOVE all those values, bourgeois or otherwise, conditioned by the order of real things.*

The inevitable character of this exhausting subterfuge is easy moreover to display in broad terms. It is sufficient to recall in the first place that there had not been, before Marx, any revolutionary movement free of idealism (in the most vulgar sense of the word). At even a relatively recent date, the works of Hugo manifested with great literary brilliance this infantile ethical tendency of revolutionary unrest. While enjoying to the full his class privileges, the bourgeois readily develops a transferred inferiority complex. His "guilt feelings" (resulting from a psychological impulse inherent to consciousness that risks calling into question his personal right to trample down the unfortunate) are skillfully shifted to the bourgeoisie in its entirety. Thus displaced, the guilty conscience expresses itself with a disgusting idealistic verbal outpouring that gives free rein to a craving for cheap utopian blindness. With few exceptions, this is the pitiful psychology of bourgeois revolutionaries before the Marxist organization of the class struggle. It leads to a representation of revolution as a redemptive light rising *above* the world, *above* classes, the overflowing of spiritual elevation and Lamartinian bliss.

II

The necessities of political action eliminated these archaic deviations a long time ago. But if one considers, *apart* from large economic upheavals, the psychological perturbations that accompany them (or, more exactly, are a *consequence* of them), one must note the tenacity of developments consistent with the archaic schema of prematerialist revolutions.

But before turning to the description of moral deviations, we will find it useful to refer to the general and essential contradiction of the high and the low, under, for example, its political forms, namely, in the opposition between the eagle and the "old mole."

From the point of view of appearance and brilliance, the eagle is obviously the more virile conception of the two. Not only does it rise in radiant zones of the solar sky, but it resides there with uncontested glamour. The eagle's hooked beak, which cuts all that enters into competition with it and cannot be cut, suggests its sovereign virility. Thus the eagle has formed an alliance with the sun, which castrates all that enters into conflict with it (Icarus, Prometheus, the Mithraic bull). Politically the eagle is identified with imperialism, that is, with the unconstrained development of individual authoritarian power, triumphant over all obstacles. And metaphysically the eagle is identified with the *idea*, when, young and aggressive, it has not yet reached a state of pure abstraction, when it is still only the unbounded development of concrete fact disguised as divine necessity.

Revolutionary idealism tends to make of the revolution an eagle above eagles, a *supereagle* striking down authoritarian imperialism, an idea as radiant as an adolescent eloquently seizing power for the benefit of utopian enlightenment. This detour naturally leads to the failure of the revolution and, with the help of military fascism, the satisfaction of the elevated need for idealism. The Napoleonic epic represents its least ridiculous development: the castration of an Icarian revolution, shameless imperialism exploiting the revolutionary urge.

Meanwhile, brought back to the subterranean action of economic facts, the "old-mole" revolution hollows out chambers in a decomposed soil repugnant to the delicate nose of the utopians. "Old mole," Marx's resounding expression for the complete satisfaction of the revolutionary outburst of the masses, must be understood in relation to the notion of a geological uprising as expressed in the *Communist Manifesto*. Marx's point of departure has nothing to do with the heavens, preferred station of the imperialist eagle as of Christian or revolutionary utopias. He begins in the bowels of the earth, as in the materialist bowels of proletarians.

We should not be surprised to see such a general human contradiction as that between things low and things elevated represented here in the form of very particular psychological representations. It is true that philosophical usage excludes inverted reductions of this sort. But for this reason, philosophical usages themselves are in question. That is to say that to substitute endlessly and mutually reducible notions for the scandalous image of contingent nature making free determinations would only express the hatred of philosophers for those blind realities that are as insensitive to philosophical categories as rats gnawing books. The philosophers who work with obstinate patience to emasculate the representation of the world evidently would prefer to believe that a certain liberty of bearing, the provocative character of events, is superficial. Even in its most general form, the opposition which runs from the Very-High to the Very-Low has disappeared with the success of secular philosophy. At least it has ceased to occupy any specific position among other problems, for human vocabulary continues everywhere to maintain throughout a faithful memory of fundamental categories.

That this has been the fate of an essential problem, literally placed under a bushel, while evidence of it necessarily leaps forth every time a moral judgment is pronounced, is readily explained if we recognize that it was necessary at any cost to endow antinomies in general with a mechanical and abstract character (as with Kant or Hegel). It is true that it seems easy to characterize in this manner the antinomy of high and low, but this antinomy, more than any other, is thereby immediately deprived of interest and meaning. All of its interest and meaning are linked to the irreconcilable nature of its specific forms: the terrifying darkness of tombs or caves and the luminous splendor of heaven, the impurity of earth where bodies rot and the purity of lofty space; on the order of the individual the base and noble faculties, on the political order the imperialist eagle and the "old-mole" revolution, as on the universal order matter, vile and base reality, and elevated spirit. This language, unkown by philosophers (at least explicity), is nonetheless a universal language for the human race.

It is true that this language was provisionally rejected because of the mystical forms to which it gave rise. But it has been taken up again in our own day precisely for its material character. Whenever one has recourse to images, most often peremptory and provocative ones, borrowed from the most concrete of contradictions, it is reality on the material order, human physiology, that comes into play. A man is not so different from a plant, experiencing like a plant an urge that raises him perpendicular to the ground. It will not be difficult to show that human morality is linked to the urge to an erect posture that distinguishes the human being from the anthropomorphic ape. But on the other hand, a plant thrusts its obscene-looking roots into the earth in order to assimilate the putrescence of organic matter, and a man experiences, in contradiction to strict morality, urges that draw him to what is low, placing him in open antagonism to all forms of spiritual elevation. Such urges have always been eloquently rebuked, confused in their aggregate with the most immediately nefarious of specific passions: base and greedy for decomposition, they are no less the deep roots that give such a staggering sense to words as little acknowledged and allowing as little puerile hope to subsist as *human heart*.

If one now considers social strata, universally divided into upper and lower, it is impossible to deny that aspirations are produced within each class that head in one direction as well as in the other. Nevertheless the upper classes make almost exclusive use of ideas—i.e., the most elevated forms of human life—for even when those ideas have a low origin they are no less elaborated *in a high place*, in high intellectual spheres, before taking on universal value. On the other hand, the movements of the human heart, introducing with historical upheavals their immense disorder and their greedy vulgarity, are produced only within the proletariat, in the submerged masses dedicated to measureless agitation (even patriotic movements, directed and exploited by the dominant bourgeoisie, have consistency only insofar as they are supported by the deep eddies provoked in the lower social strata; meanwhile they are produced like the debauchery of minors for the benefit of bourgeois elegance and spiritual elevation, just as these authorize and organize capitalist exploitation).

III

Returning now to the particular case of the moral abnormalities that result when disheartened individuals betray their class, let us note first of all that hatred of bourgeois spiritual elevation, of fair words and empty promises, appeared for the first time with extraordinary acuteness and freshness in the writings of Nietzsche. An entire philosophy, neglected only for pragmatic reasons, has as its aim the establishing of values that would permit individuals to raise themselves above human class conditions. At the heart of Nietzsche's demands lies such flagrant disgust for the senile idealism of the establishment, such passionate revolt—so spiteful toward the hypocrisy and the moral shabbiness that presides over current world exploitation—that it is impossible to define his work as one of the ideological forms of the dominant class. Not that Nietzsche had anything whatsoever in common with the working proletariat: he was far from perceiving that there is only one solution to the difficulties that gave play to the violence of his language, namely the renunciation of all moral values associated with class superiority, the renunciation of all that deprives "distinguished' men of the virility of the proletarian. Nietzsche was condemned by circumstances to imagine his break with conformist ideology as an Icarian adventure. The urge that obliged him brutally to reject bourgeois tawdriness and conventional morality did not come from below, from the submerged upheaval of the human masses (by definition, bourgeois individuals can feel nothing directly of all that is overwhelming in those masses—an imperviousness to fact is undeniable); the only hope for emancipation for an individual of the bourgeois class derives from eventual action of an Icarian complex. It is impossible to betray one's class through friendship for the proletariat, but only through an inclination to seize what one must call, in accordance with Nietzsche's terminology, "fire from heaven,": and this is to be accomplished by simple subversion, for the pleasure of infringing supposedly intangible laws. But individuals only want to seize fire from heaven in order to annihilate themselves, like mites in the presence of an acetylene torch.

In effect, what can there be in the will to rise above social conditions, if one excludes the unconscious pathological desire to be struck down violently like Icarus and Prometheus. Current economic conditions force the ruling classes to rely upon undeniably less ethereal values than in the past. It is impossible to renew today the substitutions wrought during the Middle Ages; whereas the idealized Chivalry of the Holy Grail or an absurd knight errantry could buttress an exploitative and cynically self-serving "chivalric" class, present-day capitalism has been unable to invent any sublimation for the condition of a banker or captain of industry. The perfectly clear reason is that the category of the sublime, maintained in the development of a strictly military imperialism (with, for example, the eagle as moral emblem) has become useless to industrial and commercial development in ordinary times. Above all it has become irreconcilable with the practice of capitalist exploitation, which requires level-headedness, not foolish generosity, aptitude for mathematical speculation, nor the spirit of adventure. In capitalism power itself is carried to the highest abstraction of an idea (bank capital), and in order to exist, to attain selfhood, it suffices for the individual to participate regularly in this power (the least sensuous that has ever existed); however mundane its objective may be, this power constitutes a perfect incarnation of this idea, i.e., what is most elevated and free of the intervention of any values other than material utility. Under those conditions, what does the rage to resort to the elevated and sublime, to protests against the impoverishment of human nature, signify? A regression certainly.

It would be boorish today to neglect the frequency of the first reactionary movements, romanticisms, boorish to deny the reactionary and romantic character of Nietzschean morality. Doubtless it would be difficult to find in Nietzsche's work a shadow of the sentimental foolishness and the medieval awkwardness of the sentimental romantics (the French romantics or Wagner, for example). But it is Nietzsche's very awareness of the risk resulting from an exaltation literally unexpected—and lacking any object—that placed him in the classical rut of claims for a morality of the masters. It is not the masters who need such a morality: exploiters are not going to seek their values in unbalanced philosophy. When their values are given to them immediately by the economic conditions of exploitation, American bankers dispense with *The Will to Power*. Only\ the Nietzschean romantic exaltation required an improbably soaring of archaic values (rigorously exposed, it is true, by a philologist) borrowed from the dominant classes of primarily military epochs (Greek antiquity, the Italian Renaissance). And those values, if one provisionally sets aside the elimination of Christian elements and the introduction of moral cynicism, are reduced to the chivalric values on which modern society rested until the progressive introduction of bourgeois capitalist values.

But for a sick individual, isolated from his class and any social activity, what could the result finally be of these value substitutions? It is evident that a man like Nietzsche, wanting to assert the human splendor of people who really had exercised domination—a splendor determined by social forms that had disappeared—could only become aware, in the first place, of his ineptitude for current social forms, and, in the last, of the excessively derisive and even imbecilic character of this mental activity—brilliant or not.

Archaisms can be useful to conservatives. In the mind of a rebel, they represent no more than an Icarian illumination. Nietzsche was never attracted except by thoroughly defunct values that had become impractical and scandalous: values intended to ridicule prosaically—in their own eyes as well as in others—the adherents of a doctrine that is only a shattering provocation. Obviously if the man of genius admired by the mob is at bottom, as he admits, only a ludicrous and wretched creature, one has only to see things as they are: he only carries a splendid and intellectual nightmare to the sublime the better to offer his liver to the beak of simpletons and louts who lay down the law in contemporary society. And so he becomes the torn and at the same time insulting victim of unprecedented stupidity.

We must insist on the fact that there is no other *immediate* outcome for interior agitation resulting from an individual's inability to limit himself to the bourgeois ideal. Nietzsche revealed this primordial fact: once God had been killed by the bourgeoisie, the immediate result would be catastrophic confusion, emptiness, and even a sinister impoverishment. Therefore it was necessary not only to create new values, but more precisely values able to fill the void left by God: hence a series of antireligious and ethereal values.

Not that Nietzsche was altogether incapable of wallowing in the mud. Since the beginning of reactions against bourgeois mental forms, the tendency to see outmoded values as base has of necessity made way for itself, but only in the background. Zarathustra's "sense of the Earth" is a precise indication in that respect. Nor should one forget that Nietzsche already spoke of the sexual basis of higher psychic functions. He even went so far as to give greatest value from the perspective of philosophical truth to outbursts of laughter (may any truth that has not made you burst out laughing at least once be seen by you as false). It is nonetheless true that the opposing tendency quickly gained the upper hand, that laughter, brutal expression of the heart's baseness, became along with truth something elevated, weightless, Hellenic, etc.

IV

The same double tendency is found in contemporary surrealism, which maintains, of course, the predominance of higher ethereal values (clearly expressed by the addition of the prefix *sur*, the trap into which Nietzsche had already fallen with *superman*). More precisely, since surrealism is immediately distinguishable by the addition of low values (the unconscious, sexuality, filthy language, etc.), it invests these values with an elevated character by associating them with the most immaterial values.

The resulting adulterations matter little to the surrealists: that the unconscious is no more than a pitiable treasure-trove; that Sade, emasculated by his cowardly apologists, takes on the form of a moralising idealist . . . All claims from below have been scurrilously disguised as claims from above: and the surrealists, having become the laughing-stock of those who have seen close up a sorry and shabby failure, obstinately hold on to their magnificent Icarian pose.

In December 1929, M. Breton did not hesitate to make himself ridiculous by writing that "the simplest surrealist act consists of dashing down into the street, pistol in hand, and firing blindly, as fast as you can pull the trigger, into the crowd." He adds: "Anyone who, at least once in his life, has not dreamed of thus putting an end to the petty system of debasement and cretinization in effect has a well-defined place in that crowd, with his belly at barrel level."[1] That such an image should present itself so insistently to his view proves decisively the importance in his pathology of castration reflexes: such an extreme provocation seeks to draw immediate and brutal punishment. But the worst is not to be subject to reactions of this order (which no bourgeois rebel, it goes without saying, could have avoided); the *literary* use to which they are put is much more significant. Others instinctively know how blocked impulses are to be taken into account. The surrealists employ them in literature, in order to attain the displaced and pathetic grandeur that ridicules and strips them of relevance. For when bourgeois society refuses to take them seriously and to take up the challenge they offer, satisfied to isolate them in an impotent harangue that transforms them little by little into carnival puppets, the surrealists have found the destiny they were seeking, such that they would accept no other at any price. For them it was never a question of really terrifying: the intrinsic character of the bogeymen they play is sufficient, for they are eager to play the role of juvenile victims, despicable victims of a general incomprehension and degradation.

The transformations of Icarian reflexes into a pathetic-comic and gratuitous literature is doubtless surrealism's most striking characteristic. (With the apparent resolution to defend an increasingly mocking position, they have pushed an ill-considered provocation so far as to raise a hue and cry against those who would want speech to lead to action.) But interior moral activity, in all its forms, differs in no wise from this conspicuous literary exploitation. It is all too evident that the surrealists do not seek to achieve a contemptuous attitude through consciousness of their own moral integrity. On the contrary, a few radical principles serve only to enable them to feel their own life by contrast as a shabby joke, for they know too well their own lethargy and inertia, all too many haggling deals and petty compromises . . . But the Icarian movement consists precisely of acting and even thinking as if they had attained without laughter the violent spiritual elevation that is only the empty rumbling of their words. They heap uncompromising accusations upon dissident surrealists and experience at the same time the highest degree of bitter pleasure, because they feel obscurely, whatever their verbal arrogance, that their own fall is no less profound, nor even less apparent: how can they hide from themselves at bottom that certain of their accusations provoke only outbursts of laughter (or else imbecilic pity)?

Nevertheless one must pity those persons on whom a reading of the *Second Surrealist Manifesto* makes no strong impression—I say this without the least irony. Coming abruptly, after several prefaces of which the least one can say is that they betray a profound poverty of spirit, the *Second Manifesto* is without any doubt the most consequential work, the most consistent declaration, that the surrealists have attempted for a long time. Even its most radical implications have not yet been revealed, and perhaps it is useful that they are *here*, in the "remarkable garbage pail known," if one believes M. Breton, as *Bifur* . . . [2]

One could not repeat too much how childish it is to deny the *inevitable* spiritual upheavals and unrest that the surrealists have thought themselves able to express. This is why it is important to point out sharply the detour which the *Second Manifesto* resolutely executes with a dedication that rises to astonishing solemnity.

One can be grateful to M. Breton for several indications which recall the profound impulses that set things in motion at the beginnings of the surrealist movement. And we are not especially concerned here with what touches upon religion, family, or country: these, as it turns out, do not depend on the wrath of the surrealists to appear to us sticky with spittle. But without showing any respect for literary antiques, we can recognize that the ''unhealthy'' character of several works by Baudelaire, Rimbaud, Huysmans, and Lautréamont still remains the most that can be accomplished in this domain. Everything leads us to believe that surrealism still shares their obsession with unhealthiness, which is to say just how impossible it is at the present moment for anything human to arise, except in the cesspool of the heart; nonetheless it is regrettable that these unhealthy forms are limited to the poetic, and that, for M. Breton, to pass from brilliant shadow play to the *failed acts* that today underlie human existence, is to "hold any rung whatever of this *degraded* ladder . . . "³

It is regrettable, we say, that nothing can enter into M. Breton's confused head except in poetic form. All of existence, conceived as *purely* literary by M. Breton, diverts him from the shabby, sinister, or inspired events occurring all around him, from what constitutes the real decomposition of an immense world. Given the wrongs of the *times*, the confused and inert stupefaction of a collective bourgeois existence dedicated to nothing less than the mustiness of the balance sheet, the surrealists find no meaning in an ignoble rout save a pretext for tragic, headlong flight. Since "all that does not aim at the annihilation of being in an interior and blind radiance"⁴ is *vulgar* in his eyes, M. Breton seeks only, in sluggish confusion, raising on occasion some sad shreds of grandiloquence, to provoke a panic capable of justifying his willful aberrations. Unfortunately, even M. Breton has not managed so far to be frightened by his own phraseology . . .

Servile idealism rests precisely in this will to poetic agitation rather than in a strictly juvenile dialectic: a completely unhappy desire to turn to upper spiritual regions, a hatred of vulgarity, the base vulgarity that decomposes everything in a flash—leaving the pearls of wisdom to the mercy of the first swine. A peevish aristocracy, mental askesis—with such necessities, both puritanical and conventional, hypocrisy without the excuse of practical value begins. Where in it is the untrammeled frenzy of the heart, of a heart greedy for each contradiction crudely granted to solemn destiny, to each thing's *duty to be*—greedy, one must say with aggressive shame, to see its most touching and angelic flights of fancy sullied? . . . All this unhealthiness, vulgar or not, outside of which there is no life, but only the elements that provoke it (just as in the same street there is no love, but only beings brought together in their common greed by so little), this unhealthiness is perhaps no more than a literary last resort. For "everything tends to make us believe that there exists a certain point of the mind at which life and death, the real and the imagined, past and future, the communicable and the incommunicable, high and low, cease to be perceived as contradictions. One would search in vain for any motivation behind surrealist activity other than this point . . . "⁵ Nothing less is called for than the *annihilation* of healthy contingencies as well as the unhealthy contingencies of nature. But this enterprise, however surprising it may appear coming from a man who does not usually aspire to childishness (who would even appear, if one were to judge from several citations, not to be unaware of Hegel's *Logic*), this enterprise does not aim so much as one might think at the *empty abstraction* envisaged by Hegel, but rather, more exactly, at what M. Breton, with professional ease, himself calls "an interior and blind radiance . . . no more the soul of ice than of fire." Heaven's vault, still the Icarian illumination and the same flight toward the heavens from which it seems it will be easy to curse this base world (but from which we know above all with what derisive ease a man is cast)—it is into the *brilliant immensity of the sky*, not into the void of Hegelian being-nothingness, that M. Breton is constantly thrown by verbal momentum. M. Breton deludes himself, he abuses his mob like a priest when he undertakes to resolve contradictions so slippery for him as elevated and base. What need he has to make us believe that his preferred states are situated outside of everything, when every sentence he writes situates them *above*, when he is reduced to speak of nothing but "brief beauty concealed and of the long and accessible beauty that can be revealed."[6] From one who speaks across the heavens, full of aggressive respect for heaven and its lightning bolts, full of disgust for this too base world that he believes he scorns—scorns more than anyone has ever scorned it before him—after touching Icarian naiveté has betrayed his desire for the miraculous, we can only expect the sad but impotent will to provoke panic and the betrayal of the vulgar interests of the collectivity, which have become simply filth, a pretext to rise with cries of disgust.

Do not be shocked by the significance I place on the interpretation of an image (fundamental moreover in the *Second Manifesto*) as an equivalent of the Icarian celestial vault. An analysis of M. Breton's behavior permits us, moreover, to specify the sense of this psychological entity, to note in a general way the role of the sun in human impulses. Even though the blinding celestial vault, when it becomes a psychological obsession, implies spiritual elevation, this spiritual elevation fails to take on the value of steadfastness or conservation. In this case spiritual elevation is almost entirely determined by the conscious or unconscious desire for one of the basest forms of agitation, but this desire cannot be satisfied except by an elevation increasingly stripped of sense and purely aggressive, consequently tied to the most derisive, the most inane contempt for vulgar human nature. Placed in these conditions, a man comes to regard habitual vulgarity as a sign of guilt and punishment, for he is obliged to render himself guilty of extraordinary excesses in the most turbulent kind of exaltation, in order to regain this vulgarity, which has become for him a vertiginous consciousness of his fall. But when such a man begins to speak, he can arrange sentences in his mind only to condemn the entire earth, the base earth, domain of pure abjection. He even associates the image of the impending fall with this terrifying curse on the earth: "Let him," we read at the end of the *Second Manifesto*, "in spite of any restrictions, use the avenging arm of the *idea* against the bestiality of all beings and all things, and let him one day, vanquished—*but vanquished only if the world is world*—welcome the discharge of his sad rifles like a salvo fired in salute."[7]

In the conditions that have just been specified, it is evident at the very least that the implications of surrealism can be pursued only as negation (the provisional use of the Hegelian term is of little significance here). Only the rupture that eliminates the slightest concern for recognition, the slightest respect for persons (not even true contempt, hardly crass derision), allows this moral infantilism to pass to free subversion, the basest subversion. The passage from Hegelian philosophy to materialism (as from utopian or Icarian socialism to scientific socialism) makes explicit the necessary character of such a rupture. The forms of mental activity (in its most interior manifestations) do not have a development perceptibly different from the development of intellectual determinations concerning economic and social existence.

The earth is base, *the world is world*, human agitation is only vulgar and perhaps not acknowledgeable: this is the shame of Icarian despair. But to the *loss of the head* there is no other reply: a crass sneer, vile grimaces. For it is human agitation, with *all* the vulgarity of needs small and great, with its flagrant disgust for the police who repress it, it is the agitation of *all* men (except for this police and the friends of the police), that alone determines revolutionary mental forms, in opposition to bourgeois mental forms. In human terms no baseness values, at present, the rage of refined literati, lovers of an accursed poetry; what cannot move the heart of a ditchdigger already has the existence of shadows. There remains, it is true, the almost artificial lighting, which serves to display the ruins. And down with denigrators of an immediate "human interest," down with all the scribblers with their spiritual elevation and their sanctified disgust for material needs!

For those bourgeois who still exercise a certain mastery of their old intellectual domain, there is no possibility of instituting a culture, or even, more generally, purely proletarian principles of *mental* action. But there is no possibility for any class until bourgeois principles have become altogether and for everyone principles of derision and general disgust—including Icarian subterfuge, even if this subterfuge will be regarded someday as a kind of dawn of mental liberation, just as bourgeois revolutions represent the dawn of proletarian revolution. By excavating the fetid ditch of bourgeois culture, perhaps we will see open up in the depths of the earth immense and even sinister caves where force and human liberty will establish themselves, sheltered from the call to order of a heaven that today demands the most imbecilic elevation of any man's spirit.

Notes

1. [*The Second Surrealist Manifesto*, in André Breton, *Manifestoes of Surrealism*, trans. R. Seaver and H. R. Lane (Ann Arbor: The University of Michigan Press, 1969), p. 125. Tr.]

2. [Ibid, p. 166. Tr.]

3. [Ibid, p. 125. Tr.]

4. [Ibid, p. 124. Translation modified. Tr.]

5. [Ibid, p. 123. Translation modified. Tr.]

6. [Ibid, p. 187. Tr.]

7. [Ibid, p. 187. Tr.]

Base Materialism and Gnosticism

If one thinks of a particular object, it is easy to distinguish matter from form, and an analogous distinction can be made with regard to organic beings, with form taking on the value of the unity of being and of its individual existence. But if things as a whole are taken into account, transposed distinctions of this kind become arbitrary and even unintelligible. Two verbal entities are thus formed, explicable only through their constructive value in the social order: an abstract God (or simply the idea), and abstract matter; the chief guard and the prison walls. The variants of this metaphysical scaffolding are of no more interest than are the different styles of architecture. People become excited trying to know if the prison came from the guard or if the guard came from the prison; even though this agitation has had a primordial historical importance, today it risks provoking a delayed astonishment, if only because of the disproportion between the consequences of the debate and its radical insignificance.

It is nevertheless very remarkable that the only kind of materialism that up to now in its development has escaped systematic abstraction, namely dialectical materialism, had as its starting point, at least as much as ontological materialism, absolute idealism in its Hegelian form. (There is no need to go back on this method: materialism, whatever its scope in the positive order, necessarily is above all the obstinate negation of idealism, which amounts to saying, finally, of the very basis of *all* philosophy.) Now Hegelianism, no less than the classical philosophy of Hegel's period, apparently proceeded from very ancient metaphysical conceptions, conceptions developed by, among others, the Gnostics, in an epoch when metaphysics could still be associated with the most monstrous *dualistic* and therefore strangely abased cosmogonies.[1]

I admit that I have, in respect to mystical philosophies, only an unambiguous interest, analogous in practice to that of an uninfatuated psychiatrist toward his patients; it seems to me rather pointless to put one's trust in tendencies that, without meeting resistance, lead to the most pitiful dishonesty and bankruptcy. But it is difficult today to remain indifferent even to partly falsified solutions brought, at the beginning of the Christian era, to problems that do not appear noticeably different from our own (which are those of a society whose original principles have become, in a very precise sense, the *dead letter* of a society that must put itself in question and overturn itself in order to rediscover motives of force and violent agitation). Thus the adoration of an ass-headed god (the ass being the most hideously comic animal, and at the same time the most humanly virile) seems to me capable of taking on even today a crucial value: the severed ass's head of the acephalic personification of the sun undoubtedly represents, even if imperfectly, one of materialism's most virulent manifestations.

I will leave it to Henry-Charles Puech to explain here, in future articles,[2] the development of such myths, so suspect in this period, hideous as chancres and carrying the germs of a bizarre but mortal subversion of the ideal and of the order expressed today by the words "classical antiquity." Yet I think it would be neither vain nor impossible to simplify things extremely, first of all, and indicate the meaning that must be given to the mythological and philosophical disorders which at that time affected the representation of the world. Gnosticism, in fact, before and after the preachings of Christianity, and in an almost bestial way, no matter what were its metaphysical developments, introduced a most impure fermentation into Greco-Roman ideology, borrowed from everywhere, from the Egyptian tradition, from Persian dualism, from Eastern Jewish heterodoxy, elements that conformed the least to the established intellectual order; it added its own dreams, heedlessly expressing a few monstrous obsessions; it was not revolted, in its religious practices, by the basest (and thus most upsetting) forms of Greek or Chaldeo-Assyrian magic and astrology; and at the same time it utilized, but perhaps more exactly it compromised, newborn Christian theology and Hellenistic metaphysics.

It is not surprising that the protean character of this agitation has given rise to contradictory interpretations. It has even been possible to represent Gnosticism as a strongly Hellenized intellectual form of a primitive Christianity too popular and indifferent to metaphysical developments, a kind of superior Christianity elaborated by philosophers who had broken with Hellenistic speculation, and rejected by the uncultivated Christian masses.[3] Thus the principal protagonists of Gnosticism—Basilides, Valentinus, Bardesanes, Marcion—appeared to be great religious humanists and, from the point of view of traditional Protestantism, great Christians. Their bad name, the more or less suspect character of their theories, were supposedly explained by the fact that they were only known through the polemics of the church fathers, their violent enemies and obligatory slanderers.

The writings of the Gnostic theologians were systematically destroyed by the orthodox Christians (with few exceptions, nothing remains today of a considerable literature). Only the stones on which they engraved the figures of a provocative and especially indecent Pantheon permit one to comment at length on something other than diatribes: but they precisely confirm the bad opinion of the heresiologists. The most consistent modern exegesis admits, moreover, that the abstract forms of Gnostic entities evolved out of very crude myths, which correspond to the crudity of the images represented on the stones.[4] It establishes above all that Neoplatonism or Christianity must not be sought as the origin of Gnosticism, whose real foundation is Zoroastrian dualism.[5] A sometimes disfigured dualism, doubtless following Christian or philosophical influences, but a profound dualism and, at least in its specific development, not emasculated by an adaptation to social necessities, as in the case of the Iranian religion (on this subject, it is essential to observe that Gnosticism, and to the same degree Manicheanism, which in a way derived from it, never served any social organizations, never assumed the role of State religion).

In practice, it is possible to see as a *leitmotiv* of Gnosticism the conception of matter as an *active* principle having its own eternal autonomous existence as darkness (which would not be simply the absence of light, but the monstrous *archontes* revealed by this absence), and as evil (which would not be the absence of good, but a creative action). This conception was perfectly incompatible with the very principle of the profoundly monistic Hellenistic spirit, whose dominant tendency saw matter and evil as degradations of superior principles. Attributing the creation of the earth, where our repugnant and derisory agitation takes place, to a horrible and *perfectly illegitimate* principle evidently implies, from the point of view of the Greek intellectual construction, a nauseating, inadmissible pessimism, the exact opposite of what had to be established at all costs and made universally manifest. In fact the opposed existence of an excellent divinity, worthy of the absolute confidence of the human spirit, matters little if the baneful and odious divinity of this dualism is under no circumstances reducible to it, without any possibility of hope. It is true that even within Gnosticism things were not always so clear-cut. The fairly widespread doctrine of *emanation* (according to which the ignoble creator god, in other words the *cursed god*—sometimes associated with Jehovah of the Bible—emanated from the Supreme God) responded to a need for a palliative. But if we confine ourselves to the specific meaning of Gnosticism, indicated both by heresiological controversies

Figure 5. Archontes with duck heads. Cabinet des Médailles, 2108 B. Phot.
Bibl. nat. Paris. This stone bears on its reverse the inscription ABAATANAABA
(a variant of *abracadabra*).

and by carvings on stones, the despotic and bestial obsession with outlawed and
evil forces seems irrefutable, as much in its metaphysical speculation as in its
mythological nightmare.

It is difficult to believe that on the whole Gnosticism does not manifest above
all a sinister love of darkness, a monstrous taste for obscene and lawless
archontes, for the head of the solar ass (whose comic and desperate braying
would be the signal for a shameless revolt against idealism in power). The existence of a sect of *licentious Gnostics* and of certain sexual rites fulfills this obscure demand for a baseness that would not be reducible, which would be owed
the most indecent respect: black magic has continued this tradition to the present
day.

It is true that the supreme object of the spiritual activity of the Manicheans,
as of the Gnostics, was constantly the good and perfection: that was the way in
which their conceptions in themselves had a pessimistic meaning. But it is more
or less useless to take these appearances into account, and only the troubled concession to evil can in the end determine the meaning of these aspirations. If today
we overtly abandon the idealistic point of view, as the Gnostics and Manicheans
implicitly abandoned it, the attitude of those who see in their own lives an effect
of the creative action of evil appears even radically optimistic. It is possible in

Figure 6. Panmorphic Iao (?). Cabinet des Médailles. Phot. Bibl. nat. Paris. Agate. This representation, composed of a group of imaginary animals surrounded by seven planets, most likely represents the first of the seven planetary *archontes:* Iao, the *cursed* god, generally identified with the god of Genesis.

all freedom to be a plaything of evil if evil itself does not have to answer before God. Having had recourse to *archontes*, it does not appear that one has deeply desired the submission of things that belong to a higher authority, to an authority the *archontes* stun with an eternal bestiality.

Thus it appears—all things considered—that Gnosticism, in its psychological process, is not so different from present-day materialism, I mean a materialism not implying an ontology, not implying that matter is the thing-in-itself. For it

Figure 7. Acephalic god beneath two animal heads. Cabinet des Médailles, 2170. Phot. Bibl. nat. Paris. Lapis-lazuli. At the foot of the god, in a circle formed by a serpent biting its tail, Anubis, a woman, and a dog; below, a mummy. The acephalic god can be identified with the Egyptian god Bes.

is a question above all of not submitting oneself, and with oneself one's reason, to whatever is more elevated, to whatever can give a borrowed authority to the being that I am, and to the reason that arms this being. This being and its reason can in fact only submit to what is lower, to what can never serve in any case to ape a given authority. Also I submit entirely to what must be called matter, since *that* exists outside of myself and the idea, and I do not admit that my reason

Figure 8. God with the legs of a man, the body of a serpent, and the head of a cock. Cabinet des Médailles M. 8003. Phot. Bibl. nat. Paris. Red jasper.

becomes the limit of what I have said, for if I proceeded in that way matter limited by my reason would soon take on the value of a superior principle (which this *servile* reason would be only too happy to establish above itself, in order to speak like an authorized functionary). Base matter is external and foreign to ideal human aspirations, and it refuses to allow itself to be reduced to the great ontological machines resulting from these aspirations. But the psychological process brought to light by Gnosticism had the same impact: it was a question of disconcerting the human spirit and idealism before something base, to the extent that one recognized the helplessness of superior principles.

The interest of this juxtaposition is augmented by the fact that the specific reactions of Gnosticism led to the representation of forms radically contrary to the ancient academic style, to the representation of forms in which it is possible to see the image of this base matter that alone, by its incongruity and by an overwhelming lack of respect, permits the intellect to escape from the constraints of idealism. In the same way today certain plastic representations are the expression of an intransigent materialism, of a recourse to everything that compromises the powers that be in matters of form, ridiculing the traditional entities, naively rivaling stupefying scarecrows. This is no less important than general analytic interpretation, in the sense that only forms specific and meaningful to the same degree as language can give concrete and immediately perceptible expression to the psychological developments determined through analysis.

EXPLANATION OF THE ILLUSTRATIONS.—The stones published in this article are known by the traditional name of gnostic stones, or Basilidian stones, or *Abraxas*: their identification and nomenclature have as origin the name Abraxas, which is found in the legends and in the philosophy of the Gnostic philosopher Basilides. It is necessary however to indicate that this collection of stones, whose common character allows them to be grouped under the name of the Gnostics, does not necessarily come from Gnostic sects. Their origin could also be found in the practices of Greek or Egyptian magic. The majority of them are Gnostic, without it being possible to be more precise about each one of them. They present in any case the worst difficulties of interpretation because of the syncretism of their religious representations on the one hand and the frequent unintelligibility of their legends on the other.

The date is impossible to specify, but most of them belong to the third and fourth centuries. The origin is generally Eastern. Egypt in particular seems to have been an important center of production. Egyptian divinities or figures in an Egyptian style are frequently found on these stones. Thus the acephalic god and Anubis represented in Figure 7.

Notes

1. Since the Hegelian doctrine is above all an extraordinary and very perfect system of reduction, it is evident that it is only in a reduced and emasculated state that one finds there the *base elements* that are essential in Gnosticism.

However, in Hegel the role of these elements in thought remains one of destruction, just as destruction is given as necessary for the constitution of thought. This is why, when dialectical materialism was substituted for Hegelian idealism (through a complete overthrow of values, giving matter the role that thought had had), matter was no longer an abstraction but a source of contradiction; moreover, it was no longer a question of the providential character of contradiction, which became simply one of the properties of the development of material facts.

2. [See H.-C. Puech's "Le Dieu Besa et la magie hellénistique" in *Documents* 7 (1930), pp. 415-25. Tr.]

3. This interpretation has been developed in France by Eugène de Faye (cf. *Introduction à l'étude du gnosticisme*, Paris, 1903, taken from *Revue de l'histoire des religions*, vols. 45 and 46, and *Gnostiques et gnosticisme, Etude critique des documents du gnosticisme chrétien aux IIᵉ et IIIᵉ siecles*, Paris, 1913, in *Bibliothèque de l'Ecole des Hautes Etudes, Sciences religieuses*, vol. 27).

4. Wilhelm Bousset, *Hauptprobleme der Gnosis*, Göttingen, 1907.

5. Ibid, chapter 3, *Der Dualismus der Gnosis*.

The Deviations of Nature

Among all things that can be contemplated under the concavity of the heavens, nothing is seen that arouses the human spirit more, that ravishes the sense more, that horrifies more, that provokes more terror or admiration to a greater extent among creatures than the monsters, prodigies, and abominations through which we see the works of nature inverted, mutilated, and truncated.

This remark by Pierre Boaistuau can be found at the beginning of his *Histoires prodigieuses*, a work published in 1561,[1] in other words during a period of public calamities. Prodigies and monsters were regarded in the past as presages and, most often, as such, as birds of ill omen. Boaistuau had the merit of devoting his book to monsters without worrying about augury, and of recognizing to what extent men are eager for stupefaction.

The pleasure of going to see the "freaks" is today seen as a carnival pleasure, and characterizes the one who comes forward as a gawker. In the sixteenth century a kind of religious curiosity, due in part to the habit of living at the mercy of the most terrible scourges, was still mixed with curious silliness. Books devoted to Siamese twins and to two-headed calves were very common, and their authors did not hesitate to affect an elevated tone. In the eighteenth century the interest in monsters could be attributed to an alleged scientific curiosity. The luxurious album of engraved and colored illustrations by Regnault, which was first published in 1775 (and one of whose illustrations is reproduced here),[2] bears witness to a fairly superficial concern for information. It attests above all

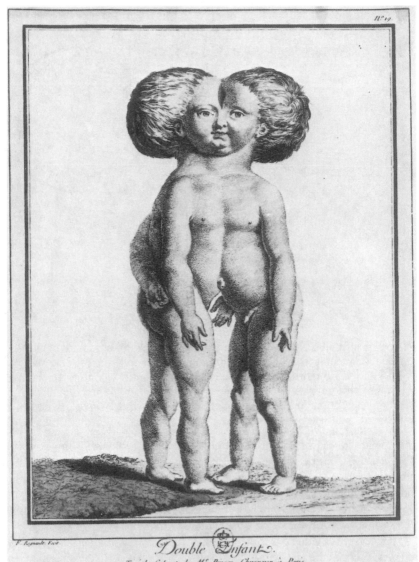

Figure 9. Regnault, *The Deviations of Nature*, 1775: "Double Child." Illustration of a wax figure in the *Cabinet Pinson*, today in the Museum of Natural History. Phot. Bibl. nat. Paris.

to the fact that, in one way or another, in one period or another, mankind cannot remain indifferent to its monsters.

I will not review here the system of anatomical classification, reprinted in all the dictionaries, from the treatises on teratology by Geoffroy-Saint-Hilaire or Guinard. It is of little importance, in fact, that the biologists have ended up classifying monsters in the same way as they do species. They remain, no less positively, anomalies and contradictions.

A "freak" in any given fair provokes a positive impression of aggressive incongruity, a little comic, but much more a source of malaise. This malaise is, in an obscure way, tied to a profound seductiveness. And, if one can speak of a *dialectic of forms*, it is evident that it is essential to take into account deviations for which nature—even if they are most often determined to be against nature— is incontestably responsible.

On a practical level this impression of incongruity is elementary and constant: it is possible to state that it manifests itself to a certain degree in the presence of any given human individual. But it is barely perceptible. That is why it is preferable to refer to monsters in order to determine it.

However, the common character of personal incongruity and the monster can be expressed with precision. The composite images that Galton achieved through successive exposures of analogous but different faces, on the same piece of photographic film, are well known. From the faces of four hundred male American students, one obtains the typical face of the American student. Georg Treu has defined in *Durschnittbild und Schönheit (The Composite Image of Beauty*, in *Zeitschrift für Aesthetik und Allgemeine Kunstwissenschaft*, 1914, IX, 3) the relation between the composite image and its components by showing that the first was necessarily more beautiful than an average example of the others; thus twenty mediocre faces constitute a beautiful face, and one obtains without difficulty faces whose proportions are very nearly those of the Hermes of Praxiteles. The composite image would thus give a kind of reality to the necessarily beautiful Platonic idea. At the same time, beauty would be at the mercy of a definition as classical as that of the common measure. But each individual form escapes this common measure and is, to a certain degree, a monster.

It is useful to observe here that the constitution of the perfect *type* with the aid of composite photography is not very mysterious. In fact, if one photographs a large number of similarly sized but differently shaped pebbles, it is impossible to obtain anything other than a sphere: in other words, a geometric figure. It is enough to note that a common measure necessarily approaches the regularity of geometric figures.

Monsters thus would be the dialectical opposites of geometric regularity, in the same manner as individual forms, but in an irreducible way. "Among all things that can be contemplated under the concavity of the heavens, nothing is seen that arouses the human spirit more . . . ''

The expression of the philosophical dialectic through forms, such as the maker of the film *Battleship Potemkin*, S. M. Eisenstein, intends to carry out in his next film (as he indicated in a lecture given at the Sorbonne on January 17), may take on the value of a revelation, and determine the most elementary, and thus consequential, human relations. Without broaching here the question of the metaphysical foundations of any given dialectic, one can affirm that the determination of a dialectical development of facts as *concrete* as visible forms would be literally overwhelming: ''Nothing is seen that arouses the human spirit more, that ravishes the senses more, that horrifies more, that provokes terror to a greater extent among creatures . . . ''

Notes

1. Pierre Boaistuau, called Launay, born in Nantes, died in Paris in 1566. His *Histoires prodigieuses* (first edition: Paris, 1561, in-8) was reprinted many times.

2. *Les Ecarts de la nature ou Recueil des principales monstruosités que la nature produit dans le monde animal*, painted after nature and published by Sr. and De Regnault, Paris, 1775, in-fol., 40 engraved plates.

Rotten Sun

The sun, from the human point of view (in other words, as it is confused with the notion of noon) is the most *elevated* conception. It is also the most abstract object, since it is impossible to look at it fixedly at that time of day. If we describe the notion of the sun in the mind of one whose weak eyes compel him to emasculate it, that sun must be said to have the poetic meaning of mathematical serenity and spiritual elevation. If on the other hand one obstinately focuses on it, a certain madness is implied, and the notion changes meaning because it is no longer production that appears in light, but refuse or combustion, adequately expressed by the horror emanating from a brilliant arc lamp. In practice the scrutinized sun can be identified with a mental ejaculation, foam on the lips, and an epileptic crisis. In the same way that the preceding sun (the one not looked at) is perfectly beautiful, the one that is scrutinized can be considered horribly ugly. In mythology, the scrutinized sun is identified with a man who slays a bull (Mithra), with a vulture that eats the liver (Prometheus): in other words, with the man who looks along with the slain bull or the eaten liver. The Mithraic cult of the sun led to a very widespread religious practice: people stripped in a kind of pit that was covered with a wooden scaffold, on which a priest slashed the throat of a bull; thus they were suddenly doused with hot blood, to the accompaniment of the bull's boisterous struggle and bellowing—a simple way of reaping the moral benefits of the blinding sun. Of course the bull himself is also an image of the sun, but only with his throat slit. The same goes for the cock, whose horrible and particularly solar cry always approximates the screams of a slaughter. One might add that the sun has also been mythologically expressed by a man slashing his own throat, as well as by an anthropomorphic being *deprived of a head*. All this leads one to say that the summit of elevation is in practice confused with a sudden fall of unheard-of violence. The myth of Icarus is particularly expressive from this point of view: it clearly splits the sun in two—the one that was shining at the moment of Icarus's elevation, and the one that melted the wax, causing failure and a screaming fall when Icarus got too close.

This human tendency to distinguish two suns owes its particular importance in this case to the fact that the psychological movements described are not ones that have been diverted, nor their urges attenuated, by secondary elements. But this also indicates that it would be ridiculous a priori to try to determine the precise equivalents of such movements in an activity as complex as painting. It is nevertheless possible to say that academic painting more or less corresponded to an elevation—without excess—of the spirit. In contemporary painting, however, the search for that which most ruptures the highest elevation, and for a blinding brilliance, has a share in the elaboration or decomposition of forms, though strictly speaking this is only noticeable in the paintings of Picasso.

Mouth

The mouth is the beginning or, if one prefers, the prow of animals; in the most characteristic cases, it is the most living part, in other words, the most terrifying for neighboring animals. But man does not have a simple architecture like beasts, and it is not even possible to say where he begins. He possibly starts at the top of the skull, but the top of the skull is an insignificant part, incapable of catching one's attention; it is the eyes or the forehead that play the meaningful role of an animal's jaws.

Among civilized men, the mouth has even lost the relatively prominent character that it still has among primitive men. However, the violent meaning of the mouth is conserved in a latent state; it suddenly regains the upper hand with a literally cannibalistic expression such as *mouth of fire* [*bouche à feu*], applied to the cannons men use to kill each other. And on important occasions human life is still bestially concentrated in the mouth: rage makes men grind their teeth, while terror and atrocious suffering turn the mouth into the organ of rending screams. On this subject it is easy to observe that the overwhelmed individual throws back his head while frenetically stretching his neck in such a way that the mouth becomes, as much as possible, an extension of the spinal column, *in other words, in the position it normally occupies in the constitution of animals.* As if explosive impulses were to spurt directly out of the body through the mouth, in the form of screams. This fact highlights both the importance of the mouth in animal physiology or even psychology, and the general importance of the superior or anterior extremity of the body, the orifice of profound physical impulses; one sees at the same time that a man can liberate these impulses in at least two different ways, in the brain or in the mouth, but that as soon as these impulses become violent, he is obliged to resort to the bestial way of liberating them. Whence the narrow constipation of a strictly human attitude, the magisterial look of the face with a *closed mouth*, as beautiful as a safe.

Sacrificial Mutilation and the Severed Ear of Vincent Van Gogh

The *Annales medico-psychologiques*[1] presents the following facts on the subject of "Gaston F . . . , age 30, embroidery designer, admitted to the Saint-Anne Hospital on January 25, 1924 . . . "

On the morning of December 11, he was walking on the Boulevard de Ménilmontant, and having arrived at the Père-Lachaise cemetery, *he stared at the sun, and, receiving from its rays the imperative order to tear off his finger*, without hesitation, without feeling any pain, he seized between his teeth his left index finger, successively broke through the skin, the flexor and extensor tendons, and the articular ligaments at the level of the phalangeal articulation; using his right hand, he then twisted the extremity of the dilacerated left index finger, severing it completely. He tried to flee from several policemen, who nevertheless succeeded in overpowering him, and took him to the hospital . . .

The young automutilator, beyond working as an embroidery designer, was a painter in his spare time. There are few details concerning the tendencies revealed in his painting, but we know that he had read the art criticism of Mirbeau. His anxieties also led him to such subjects as Hindu mysticism and the philosophy of Friedrich Nietzsche.

In the days that preceded the automutilation, he drank several glasses of rum or cognac. He still suspects that he was influenced by the biography of Van Gogh, in which he had read that the painter, during a spell of madness, had cut off his ear and sent it to a girl in a house of prostitution. It was then that, walking along the Boulevard de Ménilmontant on December 11, he "asked the sun for advice, got an idea into his head, stared at the sun to hypnotize himself, guessing that its answer was yes." He thereby seemed to receive approval. "Lazy man, get out of your sorry state" it seemed to be telling him, through thought transmission. "It did not seem very hard," he added, "after contemplating suicide, to bite off a finger. I told myself: I can always do that."

The fact that Gaston F. was influenced by Van Gogh is worth noting only for the sake of completeness. Once a decision is reached with the violence necessary for the tearing off of a finger, it entirely eludes the literary suggestions that may have preceded it; the order that the teeth had to carry out so brusquely must appear as a need that no one could resist. Moreover, the coincidence of the two painters' gestures regains its strange freedom at the moment when the same external force, independently chosen on both sides, intervenes in the activity of teeth or razor: no biography of Van Gogh could induce the Père-Lachaise mutilator's absurd recourse to the blinding rays of the sun, in order to carry out a sacrifice no one could bear to see without screaming . . .

It is relatively easy to establish the extent to which Van Gogh's life was dominated by the overwhelming relations he maintained with the sun, yet this question has never before been raised. The sun paintings by the Man with the Severed Ear are sufficiently well known and sufficiently unexpected to have disconcerted many; they only become intelligible when they are seen as the very expression of the personality (or, as some would say, of the sickness) of the painter.[2] Most were done after Van Gogh's mutilation (on Christmas night, 1888). The obsession, however, appears in two sketches (La Faille, 1374, 1375)[3] done during the Paris period (1886–88). The period of Arles is represented by the three *Sowers* (La Faille, 422, June 1888; 450 and 451, August 1888), but these three paintings still show only the sunset. The sun appears "in all its glory" only in 1889, during the painter's stay in the mental hospital in Saint-Rémy, in other words, after his mutilation (see La Faille, 617, June 1889; 628, September 1889 and 710, 713, 720, 729, 736, 737—all without an exact date). The correspondence of this period indicates that the solar obsession had finally reached its high point. It is at this time that he uses the expression "the sun in all its glory" in a letter to his brother and that he probably practiced staring at this blinding sphere from his window (which certain doctors in the past held to be a sign of incurable madness). After the departure from Saint-Rémy (January 1890) and until his suicide (July 1890) the sun disappears almost entirely from the paintings.

But in order to show the importance and the development of Van Gogh's obsession, it is necessary to link suns with sunflowers, whose large disk haloed with short petals recalls the disk of the sun, at which it ceaselessly and fixedly stares throughout the day. This flower is also simply known (in French) by the name "the sun"; in the history of painting it is linked to the name of Van Gogh, who wrote that he *had a little of the sunflower* (in the same way that Berne "has" the bear, or Rome "has" the she-wolf). As early as the Paris period, he had depicted a sunflower elevated on its stalk, isolated in a tiny garden; if most of the vases of sunflowers were painted at Arles in August 1888, at least two of the paintings date from the Paris period, and we also know that Gauguin, who at the time of the crisis of December 1888 was living with him, had just completed a portrait that shows Van Gogh painting sunflowers. It is probable that at this time Van Gogh was working on a variant of one of the paintings of August (he was working, as he often did, from memory, following Gauguin's example). The close association between the solar flower obsession and the most exasperated torment becomes all the more expressive when the heightened fancy of the painter sometimes leads to the representation of the flower as *withered and dead* (La Faille 452, 453 and fig. 1, p. 10). No one else, it seems, has ever painted wilted flowers, and Van Gogh himself painted all other flowers as fresh.

This double bond uniting the sun-star, the sun-flower, and Van Gogh can moreover be reduced to a normal psychological theme in which the star is opposed to the withered flower, as are the ideal term and the real term of the ego. This is what appears fairly regularly, it seems, in the different variants of the theme.

Speaking in a letter to his brother about a painting he liked, he expressed the wish that it be placed between two vases of sunflowers, like a clock between two candelabra. It is possible to see the painter himself as an overwhelming incarnation of the candelabrum of sunflowers, attaching to his hat a crown of lighted candles and going out under this halo at night in Arles (January or February 1889), under the pretext, as he said, of painting a countryside at night. The very fragility of this miraculous hat of flames without a doubt expresses the striving for dislocation that Van Gogh obeyed each time he came under the influence of a fiery focal point. For example when he represented a candlestick placed on the seat of Gauguin's empty chair . . .

A letter from the painter to his brother, dated December 1888 (*Brieven aan zijn Broeder*, no. 563) mentions for the first time "Gauguin's armchair, red and green night effect, walls and floor red and green again, on the seat two novels and a candle . . . "[4] Van Gogh adds in a second letter, written on January 17, 1890 (*Brieven aan zijn Broeder*, no. 571): "I should like De Haan to see a study of mine of a lighted candle and two novels (one yellow, the other pink) lying on an empty armchair (really Gauguin's chair), a size 30 canvas, in red and green. I have just been working again today on its pendant, my own empty chair,

Figure 10. Vincent Van Gogh, *The Chair and the Pipe.* December 1888-January 1889 (Arles). Reproduced by courtesy of the Trustees, The National Gallery, London.

a white deal chair with a pipe and a tobacco pouch. [This is the painting reproduced in La Faille as no. 498.] In these two studies, as in others, I have tried for an effect of light by means of clear color . . . "[5]

These two paintings are especially significant in that they date from the period of the mutilation. One need only look at the reproductions of the paintings to

Figure 11. Vincent Van Gogh, *The Armchair of Gauguin*, December 1888 (Arles). Stedelijk Museum, Amsterdam.

see that they represent not just an armchair or a chair, but the virile personae of the two painters.

Due to a lack of information, it is difficult to interpret these paintings with perfect certainty; one cannot, however, fail to be struck by a contrast to Gauguin's advantage: an unlit pipe (an extinguished and suffocating hearth) is opposed to a lit candle, a tawdry pouch of tobacco (a dessicated and calcified substance) is opposed to two novels covered with brightly colored paper. The difference is all the more charged with troubling elements in that it corresponds to the period in which Van Gogh's feelings of hatred for his friend were so extreme that they led to a definitive break, but the hatred directed against Gauguin is only one of the most bitter forms of an inner rending whose theme is generally found in all of Van Gogh's mental activity. Gauguin played for his friend the role of an ideal assuming the most exalted aspirations of Van Gogh's *ego*, even to the point of its most insane consequences: hateful and despairing humiliation, with its disconcerting counterpart, the close identification of the one who humiliates with the one who is humiliated. Even the ideal carries within itself something of the deformities of which it is the exasperated antithesis: the candle does not solidly adhere to the armchair, where its position is precarious and even shocking; the sun in its glory is doubtless opposed to the faded sunflower, but no matter how dead it may be this sunflower is also a sun, and the sun is in some way deleterious and sick: it is sulfur colored [*il a la couleur du soufre*], the painter himself writes twice in French.

This equivalence of opposing elements still characterizes, in *The Armchair of Gauguin*, the return of the theme in a new system of relations: in relation to the illuminated gas jet the unfortunate candle plays the same humiliating role that the dead pipe plays in relation to the candle; the upturned gas jet only elevates a little more a break that is, fundamentally, the sign of the irreducible heterogeneity of the lacerated (and unrestrained) elements of Van Gogh's personality.

The relations between this painter (identifying himself successively with fragile candles and with sometimes fresh, sometimes faded sunflowers) and an ideal, of which the sun is the most dazzling form, appear to be analogous to those that men maintained at one time with their gods, at least so long as these gods stupefied them; mutilation normally intervened in these relations as sacrifice: it would represent the desire to resemble perfectly an ideal term, generally characterized in mythology as a solar god who tears and rips out his own organs.

In this way the theme connects with Gaston F.'s mutilation, and its meaning can be emphasized through a third example, in which *a man of fire* orders a woman to tear off her ears in order to offer them to him.

A 34 year old woman, seduced and made pregnant by her employer, gave birth to an infant who died a few days after its birth. After this the unfortunate woman suffered from a persecution mania accompanied by uncontrollable body movements and religious hallucinations. She was placed in a mental hospital. One morning, a guard found her tearing out her right eye: the left ocular globe was completely removed, and in the empty socket shreds of the conjunctiva and cellular tissue could be seen, as well as adipose tissues; on the right there was a very pronounced exophthalmos . . . When interrogated as to the motive for her act, the patient stated that she had heard the voice of God and, some time later, had seen a man of fire: "Give me your ears, split open your head," the phantom told her. After hitting her head against the walls, she tried to tear off her ears, then decided to gouge out her eyes. The pain caused by her first efforts was extreme, but the voice urged her to overcome the pain and she did not give up. She claims to have lost consciousness at that point and cannot explain how she managed to completely tear out her left eye . . . [6]

This case is especially meaningful in that the substitution of eyes for ears, due to the lack of a sharp instrument, leads from the mutilation of relatively unimportant parts (such as a finger or an ear) to the Oedipal enucleation, in other words to the most horrifying form of sacrifice.

But how is it possible that gestures incontestably linked to mental disorder (even if they can never be seen as the symptoms of a specific mental illness)[7] may be spontaneously designated as the adequate expression of a veritable social function, of an institution as clearly defined, as generally human as sacrifice? The interpretation cannot, however, be contested when it is considered as an immediate association, entirely lacking any scientific elaboration. Even in antiquity, the insane were known to have characterized their mutilations in this way: Areteus[8] writes of sick people he saw tearing off their own limbs because of religious feelings and in order to pay homage to gods who demanded this sacrifice. But it is no less striking that, in our day, with the custom of sacrifice in full decline, the meaning of the word, to the extent that it implies a drive revealed by an *inner experience*,[9] is still as closely linked as possible to the notion of a *spirit of sacrifice*, of which the automutilation of madmen is only the most absurd and terrible example.

It is true that this demented part of the sacrificial domain, the only one that has remained accessible to us, to the extent that it belongs to our own pathological psychology, cannot simply be opposed to its counterpart, religious sacrifices of men and animals: the opposition even exists *within* religious practice, which itself confronts classic sacrifice with the most varied and insane forms of automutilation. In this respect it is the bloody orgies of Islamic sects[10] that appear at the present time with the most dramatic and significant forms: the participants, collectively raised to the height of religious frenzy, end up at the horrible omophagous sacrifice, as well as at direct or indirect mutilations, smashing each other on the head with clubs or axes, throwing themselves on swords, or gouging out their eyes. Whatever the role played by acquired skills, for example in enucleation, the necessity of throwing oneself or something of oneself *out of oneself* remains the psychological or physiological mechanism that in certain cases can have no other end than death. The celebrations held by fanatics moreover only reenact in an attenuated form, sometimes in the same regions, the gall-initiation rites of the priests of Cybele who, overcome by a fit of fury, were delirious for three days at a time, performing wild leaps and dances, brandishing weapons and cups, striking each other mercilessly, and arriving, while in an incredible exaltation, at the sacrifice of their own virility through the use of a razor, a shell, or a stone.[11]

The circumcision rite, in most cases, does not result in such scenes of delirium; it represents a less exceptional form of the religious ablation of a part of the body, and even though the patient himself does not act, this rite can be seen as a kind of collective automutilation. We know that it is practiced in more or less all parts of the world, by the Israelites, by Muslims, and by a very large number of the indigenous populations of Africa, Oceania, and America.[12] It is sometimes accompanied by real tortures that can result in death, as, for example, among the Becwanas of southern Africa.[13] Of course, any practice as difficult to explain rationally as this has given rise to numerous interpretations: the best known, which attributes a desire for hygiene to the primitive peoples who developed this innovation, has long since been discarded; on the other hand the one that presents this mutilation as sacrifice, even if such a generalization is debatable, is incontestably based on a number of positive examples.[14]

Besides, whatever may be the sacrificial nature of circumcision, it must be seen above all as an initiation rite, and as such it must be rigorously assimilated to other mutilations carried out in the same circumstances.[15] In particular, the tearing out of a tooth replaces circumcision in certain parts of New Guinea and Australia.[16] The rupture of personal homogeneity and the projection *outside the self* of a part of oneself, with their rage and pain, appear thus to be linked regularly to the expiations, periods of mourning, or debaucheries that are openly evoked by the ceremony marking the entry into adult society.

Less widespread than circumcision, the practice of the ablation of a finger is also much less well known; each example is quickly passed over by the different authors, who limit themselves in general to the indication, in a sentence, of the habitual occasions for the mutilation.[17] It is fairly frequently a matter of death and the manifestations of despair that follow it; however in India one finds it connected, for the woman, to the birth of a child, and sickness plays the same role in the Tonga Islands. Among Blackfoot Indians, the finger is offered to the morning star in a propitiation sacrifice. In the Fiji Islands the propitiation could even be addressed to a living man: when a subject gravely offended his chief, he cut off his little finger and presented it to the chief in a hollowed-out piece of bamboo, in order to obtain his pardon.[18] It is surprising that this form of mutilation is found in most parts of the world: in Australia, in New Guinea, in the Tonga and Fiji Islands; in Paraguay, in Brazil, and on the northwestern coast of North America; in Africa among the Pygmies of Lake Ngami, the Hottentots, the Bushmen. In Greece as well a stone finger set up over tumuli in the countryside indicated that even in the second century A. D. the custom might not have always been unknown there. "As you go from Megalopolis to Messene," writes Pausanias,

after advancing about seven stades, there stands on the left of the high-
way a sanctuary of the goddesses. They call the goddesses themselves,
as well as the district around the sanctuary, Maniae (*Madnesses*). In
my view this is a surname of the Eumenides; in fact they say that it
was here that madness overtook Orestes as punishment for shedding
his mother's blood. Not far from the sanctuary is a mound of earth, of
no great size, surmounted by a finger made of stone; the name, indeed, of the mound is the Tomb of the Finger. Here, it is said,
Orestes on losing his wits bit off one finger of one of his hands.
Adjoining this place is another, called Acé (*Remedies*) because in it
Orestes was cured of his malady. Here too there is a sanctuary for the
Eumenides. The story is that, when these goddesses were about to put
Orestes out of his mind, they appeared to him black; but when he had
bitten off his finger they seemed to him again to be white and he re-
covered his senses at the sight.[19]

The strange practice of the ablation of the finger seems to be particularly frequent in a region as archaic as Australia, which does not know sacrifice in the
classic sense of the word. And this fact is doubtless all the more remarkable in
that it is difficult to deny the existence of the same rite in the neolithic period:
in the *hand-patterns* obtained in caves by applying the hand to the wall and surrounding it with paint, one or several phalanges are missing.[20] Analogous practices found at the present time among the insane would thus appear to be not
only generally human, but also very primitive; madness would only remove
normal obstacles to an impulse as basic as its opposite, the impulse to eat.[21]

Even if there is an egoism that accompanies the appropriation of food and
wealth, the movement that pushes a man in certain cases to give himself (in other
words, to destroy himself) not only partially but completely, so that a bloody
death ensues, can only be compared, in its irresistible and hideous nature, to the
blinding flashes of lightning that transform the most withering storm into transports of joy. In ritual forms of communal sacrifice, in any case, an animal can
be substituted for the victim—a cowardly gesture. Only a pitiful, substituted victim "penetrates into the perilous domain of sacrifice; it dies there," according
to Hubert and Mauss,[22] "and indeed it is there in order to die. The sacrificer
remains protected." The freedom from "all selfish calculation," from all reserve, remains nevertheless at the limit of these efforts to remain outside sacrifice, to the extent that nightmare creatures, such as gods, are charged with carrying to the very end what ordinary men are happy to dream about: "the god who
sacrifices himself gives himself irrevocably," write Hubert and Mauss.[23] "This
time all intermediaries have disappeared. The god, who is at the same time the
sacrifier, is one with the victim and sometimes even with the sacrificer. All the
differing elements that enter into ordinary sacrifice here enter into each other
and become mixed together. But such mixing is possible only for mythical, that

is ideal, beings.'' Hubert and Mauss neglect here examples of the ''sacrifice of a god'' that they could have taken from cases of automutilation—and through which alone sacrifice loses its character as mere performance.

There is, in fact, no reason to separate Van Gogh's ear or Gaston F.'s finger from Prometheus's famous liver. If one accepts the interpretation that identifies the purveying eagle (the *aetos prometheus* of the Greeks) with the god who stole fire from the wheel of the sun, then the tearing out of the liver presents a theme in conformity with the various legends of the ''sacrifice of the god.''[24] The roles are normally shared between the human form of a god and his animal avatar; sometimes the man sacrifices the animal, sometimes the animal sacrifices the man, but each time it is a case of automutilation because the animal and the man form but a single being. The eagle-god who is confused with the sun by the ancients, the eagle who alone among all beings can contemplate while staring at ''the sun in all its glory,'' the Icarian being who goes to seek the fire of the heavens is, however, nothing other than an automutilator, a Vincent Van Gogh, a Gaston F. All the wealth he derives from the mythical delirium is limited to the incredible vomiting of the liver, ceaselessly devoured and ceaselessly vomited by the gaping belly of the god.

If one followed these associations, the use of the sacrificial mechanisms for various ends, such as propitiation or expiation, would be seen as secondary, and one would only retain the elementary fact of the radical *alteration* of the person which can be indefinitely associated with any other alteration that suddenly arises in collective life: for example, the death of a relative, initiation, the consumption of the new harvest . . . Such an action would be characterized by the fact that it would have the power to liberate heterogeneous elements and to break the habitual homogeneity of the individual, in the same way that vomiting would be opposed to its opposite, the communal eating of food. Sacrifice considered in its essential phase would only be the rejection of what had been appropriated by a person or by a group.[25] Because everything that is rejected from the human cycle is altered in an altogether troubling way, the sacred things that intervene at the end of the operation—the victim struck down in a pool of blood, the severed finger or ear, the torn-out eye—do not appreciably differ from vomited food. Repugnance is only one of the forms of stupor caused by a horrifying eruption, by the disgorging of a force that threatens to consume. The one who sacrifices is free—free to indulge in a similar disgorging, free, continuously identifying with the victim, to vomit his own being just as he has vomited a piece of himself or a bull, in other words free to throw himself suddenly *outside of himself*, like a gall or an aissaouah.

Still, one can doubt that even the most furious of those who have ever torn and mutilated themselves amid screams and to the beat of a drum have *abused* this marvelous freedom to the same extent as Vincent Van Gogh, who carried his severed ear to the place that most offends polite society. It is admirable that in this way he both manifested a love that refused to take anything into account and in a way spat in the faces of all those who have accepted the elevated and official idea of life that is so well known. Perhaps the practice of sacrifice has disappeared from the earth because it was not able to be sufficiently charged with this element of hate and disgust, without which it appears in our eyes as servitude. The monstrous ear sent in its envelope, however, abruptly leaves the magic circle where the rites of liberation stupidly aborted. It leaves along with the tongue of Anaxarchus of Abdera, bit off and spat bloody in the face of the tyrant Nicocreon, and with the tongue of a zeno of Elea spat in the face of Demylos . . . both of these philosophers having been subjected to atrocious tortures, the first crushed while still alive in a mortar.

Notes

1. H. Claude, A. Borel, and G. Robin, "Une automutilation révélatrice d'un état schizomaniaque" (*Annales médico-psychologiques*, 1924, vol. 1, pp. 331–39). Dr. Borel himself informed me of this case when I indicated to him the association I had been led to make between the obsession with the sun and the automutilation of Van Gogh. This report was therefore not the point of departure for this connection, but instead it was the confirmation of its interest.

2. On Van Gogh's sickness, see Jaspers, *Strindberg und Van Gogh*; W. Riese, "Ueber den Stilwandel bei Vincent Van Gogh," (*Zeitschrift für die Gesamte Neurologie und Psychiatrie*, 2 May 1925); W. Riese, *Vincent Van Gogh in der Krankheit*, 1926; and V. Doiteau and E. Leroy, *La Folie de Vincent Van Gogh*, 1928. The conclusions of these different authors are contradictory and inconclusive. They are not taken into account in the present article, which considers a psychological trait taking from sickness only its unbridled character.

3. J. B. de la Faille, *L'Oeuvre de Vincent Van Gogh*, 1928.

4. [See *The Complete Letters of Vincent Van Gogh* (Greenwich, Conn.: New York Graphic Society, 1958), vol. 3, p. 108. Tr.]

5. [*The Complete Letters of Vincent Van Gogh*, vol. 3, p. 121. Tr.]

6. After Ideler (*Allgemeine Zeitschrift für Psychiatrie*, vol. 27), quoted by M. Lorthiois, *De l'automutilation, Mutilations et suicides étranges*, Paris, 1909, p. 94, along with eleven other cases of voluntary enucleation. The work of Lorthiois gives an overview of automutilation, which is surprisingly frequent. Many of the mentally ill link their mutilation to a religious delirium or to feelings of guilt.

7. This is the clearly expressed opinion of Charles Blondel, in *Les Automutilateurs* (Paris, 1906). I do not think it possible to prove him wrong.

8. A famous Greek doctor of the first century A. D., the author of *De morborum diuturnorum et acutorum causis, signis et curatione*. The vocabulary of sacrifice is still used spontaneously by Montaigne when he reports a case of automutilation in chapter 4 of his *Essais*: mortified by an amorous adventure in which he behaved foolishly, a gentleman "mutilated himself and sent his mistress the organs that had disobeyed him in his desires, as a kind of *bloody victim* capable of *expiating* the offense he believed he had committed against her."

9. It is not a question here of the vulgar figurative sense of the word *sacrifice*, but rather of the facts with which it has remained unconsciously associated.

10. See J. Herber, *Les Hamadan et les Djoughiyyin* (Hesperis, 1923, pp. 217–36), which gives a bibliography of works on all sects; see also the extraordinary account of an Aissaouah celebration that ended with the death of a man, in E. Masquerey, *Souvenirs et visions d'Afrique*.

11. See C. Vellay, *Le Culte et les fêtes d'Adonis Thammouz*, Paris, 1905.

12. The ancient Egyptians also practiced circumcision; see the bibliography and the classificatory map in E. M. Loeb's *The Blood Sacrifice Complex*, 1923 (*Memoirs of the American Anthropological Association*, vol. 30).

13. See J. Brown, "Circumcision Rites of the Becwanas Tribes," (*Journal of the Royal Anthropological Institute of Great Britain and Ireland*, 1928).

14. See Henri Hubert and Marcel Mauss, *Mélanges d'histoire des religions*, 1909, pp. 125-26. [Bataille is referring to the *Essai sur la nature et la fonction du sacrifice* contained in this collection; English translation, *Sacrifice: Its Nature and Function*, trans. W. D. Halls (Chicago: The University of Chicago Press, 1964), pp. 98-99. Tr.] E. M. Loeb (op. cit.) examines the question and argues that it is a matter of sacrifice, citing a number of authors.

15. See, among others, Karsten, *The Civilisation of South American Indians*, London, 1926.

16. On the association made by frightened children between circumcision, the removal of a tooth, and castration, see Freud, *Totem and Taboo* (French translation), p. 410, note 1. [English translation: *Totem and Taboo*, trans. A. A. Brill (New York: Vintage Books, 1946), p. 197, note 87. Tr.]

17. See the bibliography in Loeb (op. cit.), pp. 39-40.

18. See H. Hale, *U. S. Exploring Expedition*, 1846, p. 66.

19. Pausanias, *Description of Greece*, book VIII, chapter 34. [We quote from the Loeb Classical Library translation by W. H. S. Jones (Cambridge: Harvard University Press, 1935), vol. 4, pp. 69-71. Tr.]

20. See Luquet, *L'Art et la religion des hommes fossiles*, Paris, 1926, p. 222, in which the thesis that the fingers were only concealed (folded over) is unconvincingly argued.

21. In omophagia and in the example of Oedipus eating his finger, the two impulses are produced simultaneously, but in both cases what is eaten normally is found repugnant, which changes completely the meaning of the appropriation.

22. *Mélanges d'histoire des religions*, Paris, 1909, p. 125. [*Sacrifice: Its Nature and Function*, p. 98. Tr.]

23. *Mélanges d'histoire* . . . , *p. 127.* [*Sacrifice: Its Nature and Function*, p. 101. Tr.] Of course, the general argument of Hubert and Mauss's essay is noticeably different from the one sketched out here; nevertheless it is to this work that an effort at interpretation, much too hastily presented in this article, refers. It is necessary to state here that Freud, in *Totem and Taboo*, referred to the earlier work of Robertson Smith (*Religion of the Semites* [Edinburgh: A. and C. Black, 1889]), and discounted the objections of Hubert and Mauss. [The "sacrifier," in the English translation of Hubert and Mauss we are quoting, refers to "the subject to whom the benefits of sacrifice accrue." Tr.]

24. See S. Reinach, "Aetos Prometheus" (*Cultes, mythes, et religions*, vol. 3, 1911, pp. 68-91). I cite the example of Prometheus here, in spite of the hypothetical nature of the interpretation, because of the particularly striking connection with Van Gogh and Gaston F. There are, other than Prometheus, numerous examples of the sacrifice of the God.

25. The drive behind such facts is eminently social in primitive societies, whereas it is hunger that seems to play the social role in current societies.

The Jesuve

I have acquired over what happens to me a power that overwhelms me; since everything that follows refers to the traditional practice of "sacrifice," I do not hesitate to write, even though in relation to me it is painfully comical, that it is a power analogous to that of a priest who slashes the throat of a cow. At the moment when the priest, armed with a knife (and with the priest, a dirty death) heads toward the cow, which is just a random animal, undifferentiated from any other cow that ruminates in a field, it becomes a divinity because of the circle traced around its legs. Thus the priest soon has the exorbitant possibility of opening the throat of the creature he had wanted to slash.

The practice of sacrifice has today fallen into disuse and yet it has been, due to its universality, a human action more significant than any other. Independently of each other, different peoples invented different forms of sacrifice, with the goal of answering a need as inevitable as hunger. It is therefore not astonishing that the necessity of satisfying such a need, under the conditions of present-day life, leads an isolated man into disconnected and even stupid behavior.

I thus allude to a series of trifles, of mean gestures, of errors, of a sort that no one would want to linger over, for fear of falling into a refinement of sensation or into intellectual complexities that apparently lead nowhere. From now on I must therefore insist upon the fact that in this order of things it is neither the singular character nor the exasperating minutiae of these stories that, it seems to me, are of interest to others than myself, but only a certain result foreseen with the aid of repellent detours. That which necessitates *in consciousness* mechanisms of an unparalleled complexity has a narrowly limited value, and it is almost odious that certain things have not remained in the unconscious state—but since it is not a question of sheepishly holding to what is already known, I see no reason not to provoke violently my comrades to perhaps unhoped-for excesses, even by entering into details that others, seemingly more virile, will judge tiresome and decadent.

The Pineal Eye

Given a certain latitude of interpretation, the entire conception—and at the same time the obsession—expressed by the image of the *pineal eye* and explained below goes back to the beginning of the year 1927, exactly during the period in which I wrote *The Solar Anus*, in other words a year before the *eye* appeared to me to be definitively linked to bullfighting images. I believe it necessary to furnish this chronological data before going on to considerations of a very general order, because those considerations present indissoluble links with facts as insignificant as a series of images.

The pineal eye probably corresponds to the anal (in other words nocturnal) conception that I initially had of the sun and that I then expressed in a phrase such as "the intact anus . . . to which nothing sufficiently blinding can be compared except the sun (even though the anus is the night)." I imagined the eye at the summit of the skull like a horrible errupting volcano, precisely with the shady and comical character associated with the rear end and its excretions. Now the eye is without any doubt the symbol of the dazzling sun and the one I imagined at the summit of my skull was necessarily on fire, since it was doomed to the contemplation of the sun at the apogee of its brilliance. The imagination of the ancients attributed to the eagle as solar bird the faculty of contemplating the sun face to face. In the same way an excessive interest in the simple represenation of the pineal eye is necessarily interpreted as an irresistible desire to become a *sun* oneself (a blind sun or a blinding sun, it hardly matters). In the case of the eagle, as in the case of my own imagination, the act of directly looking is the equivalent of identification. But the cruel and shattering character of this absurd desire soon appears, due to the fact that the eagle is cast down from the heights of the skies—and, as for the eye that opens in the middle of the skull, the result, even imaginary, is much more terrifying, though horribly ridiculous.

During this period, I did not hesitate to think seriously of the possibility that this extraordinary eye would finally really come to light through the bony roof of the head, because I believed it necessary that, after a long period of servility, human beings would have an eye just for the sun (whereas the two eyes in their sockets turn away from it with a kind of stupid obstinacy). I was not insane but I made too much of the necessity of leaving, in one way or another, the limits of our human experience, and I adapted myself in a fairly disordered way so that the most improbable thing in the world (the most overwhelming as well, something like foam on the lips) would at the same time appear to me to be necessary. I imagined on the one hand plants, which are uniformly animated by a vertical movement analogous to that of tides, which regularly elevate water, and on the other hand animals, which are animated by a horizontal movement analogous to that of the turning earth. Thus I arrived at reductions that were extremely simple and geometric but at the same time monstrously comic (for example, I saw that the alternating movement of all the coituses on the surface of the earth is similar to that of locomotive pistons, so that the continual movement of coituses on the surface of the earth is as closely tied to the earth's rotation as the movement of pistons is to that of wheels). Man appears in this brutal system as an animal exceptionally animated by the erection-movement that projects plants in a vertical direction, comparable to the male mammal who raises himself on his hind legs when mounting the female, but much more categorically erect, as erect as a penis.

Even today I do not hesitate to write that these first considerations on the positions of plants, animals, and men in a planetary system, far from appearing uniquely absurd to me, can be given as the basis for all considerations on human nature. And it is in fact from these that I undertake a certain preliminary exposition, whose meticulous elaboration is recent. In my opinion it is extremely curious to note that, in the course of the progressive erection that goes from the quadruped to *Homo erectus*, the aspect of ignominy grows to the point of reaching horrifying proportions—from the pretty lemur, still almost horizontal and scarcely baroque, to the gorilla. From there, on the contrary, primate evolution moves in the direction of a beauty whose appearance is more and more noble, through *Pithecanthropus erectus* and *Homo neanderthalensis*, primitive types whose erection is not yet complete, up to *Homo sapiens* who, alone among all the animals, attains a stiffness and a radical rectitude in military drill. If a race like the human race was not able to be born directly from a noble animal species, but only from a species whose origin was noble but which became repugnant trash in relation to the totality of mammals, it is perhaps not possible to look at the shit-smeared and obscene anuses of certain apes with the usual detachment. There is no child who has not at one time or another admired, in zoos, these filthy protuberances, dazzlingly colored excremental skulls, sometimes dappled, going from shocking pink to an extraordinarily horrible, pearly violet. It is likely that a certain potential for brilliance and dazzle proper to animal nature, which generally drifts toward the head (the buccal orifice), as much in man as in certain animals, was capable of drifting in apes toward the contrary extremity, in other words toward the anal orifice. This horrifying anomaly could even be represented, in a logical enough way, as the sign of an unbalanced nature (since the state of equilibrium is given by the common horizontal position). It is true that birds have found an equilibrium in an intermediary position, but it is fairly evident that that is a new equilibrium entirely different from that of the other animals, and determined by flight, in other words by a movement of displacement as continuous as that of the quadrupeds; the movement from branch to branch that determined the semivertical stance of apes implied, on the contrary, a movement of discontinuous displacement that never permitted a new harmony, and it developed little by little a manner of being and at the same time a monstrous appearance. Living in forests, more or less sheltered from the light of the sun, sometimes almost in the darkness of a cellar, clumsily swinging from one branch to another, apes are destined by a certain mode of life to a never-composed agitation, to a bizarre instability the very sight of which is extremely irritating; the obscene blossoming of their bald, haloed anuses, bursting like boils, is thus produced in a system denied any center of gravity and without resistance—perhaps because, there as elsewhere, the least rupture of equilibrium suffices for the liberation of the indecencies of nature, with the most shameful obscenity.

Anthropologists admit that the ancestors of man started to stand up straight from the moment they had to leave the forest (it is possible to imagine that the hideous animals were overcome by panic, for example, in the course of an immense fire). Deprived of the support of trees, but still used to moving around almost upright, they must have been reduced, fairly comically, to a stupid alternation between walking on four feet and walking vertically. But they could only keep themselves standing upright by gradually finding equilibrium, in other words, by giving some form of continuity and harmony to their movements. It appears plausible to admit, given the extraordinary difficulty represented by the vertical posture, that the early equilibrium of movements would have been precarious if it had not been developed—in other words, if it had not progressively led to the total equilibrium of forms to which we are habituated: phallic erection and regular beauty. Evolution up to the human form appears as a mechanically necessary return to a plastic harmony that had already been developed horizontally in the common ancestors of the monkey and the lemurs. Anthropologists, in spite of the extreme scarcity of data, have reconstituted the modalities of this evolution, above all in what concerns the bone structure of the head. The blossoming of the superior part of the skull starts with *Pithecanthropus erectus*, continues with *Homo neanderthalensis*, and is more or less perfectly accomplished in the different human types that exist today. The summit of the head has become—psychologically—the focal point of the new equilibrium. Everything in the bone structure that goes against the vertical impulse of the human being, such as the projection of the eye sockets and the jaws (a memory of the disorder and the urges of the ape and still half-horizontal), has almost entirely disappeared. But the reduction of the projection of the anal orifice is, to tell the truth, much more significant.

I am obliged to state that this account already raises numerous difficulties, and I hasten to add that, for the moment, I have no intention of resolving them as explicitly as is fitting. If I put forward here some conceptions, it is almost exclusively to characterize accidents, psychological or not, almost voluntary aberrations and insanities that carried them along or that they express or that they provoked. Thus I limit myself to indicating that the notion of equilibrium which plays such an important role in this account is in no way a hollow or arbitrary notion. It would probably be easy to study the more or less regular displacements of the center of gravity in the walking or running of various animals, and to show that what is called the beauty of forms is only an attribute of the continuous modes of displacement in which the equilibrium of the body in movement permits an important economy of force. Thus one understands that beauty, in the academic sense of the word, is reducible to a geometric simplification of lines (composite photographs permit one to obtain a human face of the Greek type with the aid of a certain number of irregular faces; the superimposed features, when mixed, allow only a regular constant to be seen). As brief and as insufficient as this allusion is, I think that it nevertheless permits one to represent as mechanically explicable the radical transformation of the hindquarters of the first men. Anal obscenity, pushed to such a point that the most representative apes even got rid of their tails (which hide the anuses of other mammals), completely disappeared from the fact of human evolution. The human anus secluded itself deep within flesh, in the crack of the buttocks, and it now forms a projection only in squatting and excretion. All the potential for blossoming, all the possibilities for the liberation of energy, now under normal conditions found the way open only toward the superor regions of the buccal orifices, toward the throat, the brain, and the eyes. The blossoming of the human face, gifted with the voice, with diverse modes of expression, and with the gaze, is like a conflagration, having the possibility of unleashing immense quantities of energy in the form of bursts of laughter, tears, or sobs; it succeeded the explosiveness that up to that point had made the anal orifice bud and flame.

Now I have given all these explanations only to say finally that when I imagined the disconcerting possibility of the pineal eye, I had no intention other than to represent discharges of energy at the top of the head—discharges as violent and as indecent as those that make the anal protuberances of some apes so horrible to see. I was not conscious of it originally, but my imagination did not go on without giving me horrible brain-transports, accompanied by an intense satisfaction; this eye that I wanted to have at the top of my skull (since I had read that its embryo existed, like the seed of a tree, in the interior of the skull) did not appear to me as anything other than a sexual organ of unheard-of sensitivity, which would have vibrated, making me let out atrocious screams, the screams of a magnificent but stinking ejaculation. Everything that I can recall of my reactions and my aberrations in this period, and moreover the normal symbolic value of a lightning-flash image, permits me today to characterize this pineal eye fantasy as an excremental fantasy. Besides, it would have been impossible for me to speak explicitly of it, to express totally what I felt so violently in early 1927 (and it still happens that I bitterly feel it) in any other way than by speaking of the nudity of an ape's anal projection, which on a day in July of the same year, in the Zoological Gardens of London, overwhelmed me to the point of throwing me into a kind of ecstatic brutishness. Today as I write, what I imagine of the pineal eye attains, through the course of a certain disorder, a brutality of erection so terrifying that I cannot imagine the enormous anal fruit of radial and shit-smeared raw pink meat (the one that struck me so in London) other than as an ignoble skull that I would smash with an axe blow, a rattled *grunt* deep in my throat. The axe blade would sink into this imaginary skull, like the cleavers of butchers that split in two, in a violent blow struck on the block, the sickening heads of skinned rabbits. For it is not self-evident that the noble parts of a human being (his dignity, the nobility that characterizes his face), instead of allowing only a sublime and measured flow of profound and tumultuous impulses, brusquely cease to set up the least barrier against a sudden, bursting eruption, as provocative and as dissolute as the one that inflates the anal protuberance of an ape . . .

The Pineal Eye

When my face is flushed with blood, it becomes red and obscene.

It betrays, at the same time, through morbid reflexes, a bloody erection and a demanding thirst for indecency and criminal debauchery.

For that reason I am not afraid to affirm that my face is a scandal and that my passions are only expressed by the Jesuve.

The terrestrial globe is covered with volcanoes, which serve as its anus.

Although this globe eats nothing, it often violently ejects the contents of its entrails.

These contents shoot out with a racket, and fall back, streaming down.

The Solar Anus

I. Scientific Anthropology and Mythical Anthropology

To the extent that a description of human life that goes back to the origins tries to represent what the formless universe has accomplished in producing man rather than something else, how it has been led to this useless production and by what means it made this creature something different from all the rest—to this extent it is necessary to abandon scientific anthropology, which is reduced to a babbling even more senile than puerile, reduced to giving answers that tend to make the questions put to it seem ludicrous, whereas these answers alone are miserably so when confronted with the inevitable and demanding brutality of an interrogation taking upon itself the very meaning of the life that this anthropology supposedly aims to describe.

But in the first phase, at least, philosophical speculation is rejected with no less impatience than the impotent theories of prehistory when this speculation, obeying the dictates of a guilty conscience, almost always kills itself or timidly prostrates itself before science. For even if this inhuman prostration can still be denounced, even if it is still possible for man to contrast his own cruelty and madness with a necessity that is crushing him, nothing of what is known of the means proper to philosophical investigation can inspire in him any confidence; philosophy has been, up to this point, as much as science, an expression of human subordination, and when man seeks to represent himself, no longer as a moment of a homogeneous process—of a necessary and pitiful process—but as a new laceration within a lacerated nature, it is no longer the leveling phraseology coming to him from the understanding that can help him: he can no longer recognize himself in the degrading chains of logic, but he recognizes himself, instead—not only with rage but in an ecstatic torment—in the virulence of his own phantasms.

Nevertheless, the introduction of a lawless intellectual series into the world of legitimate thought defines itself at the outset as the most arduous and audacious operation. And it is evident that if it were not practiced without equivocation, with a resolution and a rigor rarely attained in other cases, it would be the most vain operation.

Outside of a certain inaccessibility to fear—it is a question here essentially of undergoing, without being overwhelmed, the attraction of the most repulsive objects—two conditions thrust themselves on anyone whose object is to invest understanding with a content that will remain foreign to it, and they do so not only in a clear and distinct way, but as imperative prescriptions.

II. Conditions of Mythological Representation

In the first place, methodical knowledge can only be brushed aside to the extent that it has become an acquired faculty, since, at least in the present circumstances, without close contact with the homogeneous world of practical life, the free play of intelligible images would lose itself and would dissolve fatally in a region where no thought and no word would have the slightest consequence.

It is thus necessary to start by reducing science to a state that must be defined by the term subordination, in such a way that one uses it freely, like a beast of burden, to accomplish ends which are not its own. Left to itself, free in the poorest sense of the word (where liberty is only impotence), inasmuch as its legacy as the first condition of existence was the task of dissipating and annihilating mythological phantasms, nothing could keep science from blindly emptying the universe of its human content. But it is possible to use it to limit its own movement and to situate beyond its own limits what it will never attain, that before which it becomes an unsuccessful effort and a vague, sterile being. It is true that, posed in this way by science, these elements are still only empty terms and impotent paralogisms. It is only after having passed from these exterior limits of another existence to their mythologically lived content that it becomes possible to treat science with the indifference demanded by its specific nature, but this takes place only on condition that one has first enslaved science through the use of weapons borrowed from it, by making it itself produce the paralogisms that limit it.

The second condition is, first of all, only one of the forms of the first; here too science is utilized for a contrary end. The exclusion of mythology by reason is necessarily a rigorous one, on which there is no going back, and which, when required, must be made still more trenchant. But at the same time, it is necessary to overturn the values created by means of this exclusion; in other words, *the fact that reason denies any valid content in a mythological series is the condition of its most significant value.* For if the affective violence of human intelligence is projected like a specter across the deserted night of the absolute or of science, it does not follow that this specter has anything in common with the night in which its brilliance becomes glacial. On the contrary, a spectral content only truly exists as such from the moment when the milieu that contains it defines itself through its intolerance toward that which appears in it as a crime. The strongest repulsion by science that can be represented is necessary for the characterization of the excluded part. Such a characterization must be compared to the affective charge of an obscene element whose obscenity derives only from the prohibition leveled against it. So long as the formal exclusion has not taken place, a mythical statement can still be assimilated to a rational statement; the mythical can be described as real and can be methodically explained. But at the same time it loses its spectral characterization, its free falseness. It enters, as in the case of revealed imperative religions, into various mystical groupings that have as a goal the narrow enslavement of impoverished men to an economic necessity: in other words, in the last analysis, to an authority that exploits them.

It is true that such an operation would be inconceivable at the present time, due to the fact that the possibilities have been limited by the very development of science.

Science, proceeding on the basis of a mystical conception of the universe, has separated the constituent elements of the universe into two profoundly distinct classes: it has elaborated, through assimilation, the necessary and practical parts, transforming a mental activity, which previously was only an instrument of exploitation, into an activity useful for man's material life. At the same time, it has had to brush aside the delirious parts of the old religious constructions, in order to destroy them. But this act of destruction becomes, at the final point of development, an act of liberation: delirium escapes from necessity, casts off its heavy mantel of mystical servitude, and it is finally only then that, nude and lubricious, it plays with the universe and its laws as if they were toys.

III. The Pineal Eye

Starting from these two principles, and supposing that the first condition, which requires a scientific knowledge of the objects considered, has at least to a large extent been met, nothing stands in the way of a phantomlike and adventurous description of the universe. What remains to be said about the ways in which this description proceeds—and about the relations of the finished description with the object it describes—can only be a reflection on the realized experience.

The eye, at the summit of the skull, opening on the incandescent sun in order to contemplate it in a sinister solitude, is not a product of the understanding, but is instead an immediate existence; it opens and blinds itself like a conflagration, or like a fever that eats the being, or more exactly, the head. And thus it plays the role of a fire in a house; the head, instead of locking up life as money is locked in a safe, spends it without counting, for, at the end of this erotic metamorphosis, the head has received the *electric power of points*. This great burning head is the image and the disagreeable light of the *notion of expenditure*, beyond the still empty notion as it is elaborated on the basis of methodical analysis.

From the first, myth is identified not only with life but with the loss of life— with degradation and death. Starting from the being who bore it, it is not at all an external product, but the form that this being takes in his lubricious avatars, in the ecstatic gift he makes of himself as obscene and nude victim—and a victim not before an obscure and immaterial force, but before great howls of prostitutes' laughter.

Existence no longer resembles a neatly defined itinerary from one practical sign to another, but a sickly incandescence, a durable orgasm.

IV. The Two Axes of Terrestrial Life

No matter how blinding the mythical form, insofar as it is not a simple representation, but the exhausting consumption of being, it is possible, at its first indistinct appearance, to pass from a content to a container, to a circumstantial form that, although it is probably unacceptable from the point of view of science, does not seem different from the habitual constructs of the intellect.

The distribution of organic existence on the surface of the earth takes place on two axes: the first, vertical, prolongs the radius of the terrestrial sphere; the second, horizontal, is perpendicular to the first. Vegetation develops more or less exclusively on the vertical axis (which is also the axis of the fall of bodies); on the other hand, the development of animal life is situated, or tends to be situated, on the horizontal axis. But although, generally speaking, their movements are only slippages parallel to the lines described by the rotation of the terrestrial globe, animals are never completely foreign to the axis of vegetal life. Thus existence makes them raise themselves above the ground when they come into the world and, in a relatively stable way, when they exit from sleep or love (on the other hand, sleep and death abandon bodies to a force directed from high to low). Their skeleton, even in the most regular cases, is not perfectly adjusted to a horizontal trajectory: the skull and thus the orifice of the eyes are situated above the level of the anal vertebra. However, even if one refers to the position of the male in coitus, and to the structures of some birds, a complete verticality is never attained.

V. The Position of the Human Body and Eyes on the Surface of the Terrestrial Globe

Only human beings, tearing themselves away from peaceful animal horizontality, at the cost of the ignoble and painful efforts that can be seen in the faces of the great apes, have succeeded in appropriating the vegetal erection and in letting themselves be polarized, in a certain sense, by the sky.

It is thus that the Earth—whose immense regions are covered with plants that everywhere flee it in order to offer and destroy themselves endlessly, in order to project themselves into an alternately light and dark celestial void—releases to the disappointing immensity of space the totality of laughing or lacerated men.

But, in this liberation of man, which leads to a suffocating absence of limits on the surface of the globe, human nature is far from surrendering without resistance. For if it is true that his blood, bones, and arms, that the shuddering of his pleasure (or still more the silence of true dread)—if it is true that his senile laughter and his insipid hate are endlessly lost and rise toward a sky as beautiful as death, as pale and implausible as death, his eyes continue to fetter him tightly to vulgar things, in the midst of which necessity has determined his steps.

The horizontal axis of vision, to which the human structure has remained strictly subjected, in the course of man's wrenching rejection of animal nature, is the expression of a misery all the more oppressive in that it is apparently confused with serenity.

VI. The Vertigo-Tree

For the anthropologist who can only observe it, this contradiction of axes of the human structure is devoid of meaning. And if, without even being able to explain itself, anthropology underscored the importance of the axes, it would only betray an unjustifiable tendency toward mysticism. The description of the perpendicular axes only takes on its value once it becomes possible to construct on these axes the puerile play of a mythological existence, answering no longer to observation or deduction but to a free development of the relations between the immediate and varied consciousness of human life and the supposedly unconscious givens that constitute this life.

Thus the pineal eye, detaching itself from the horizontal system of normal ocular vision, appears in a kind of nimbus of tears, like the eye of a tree or, perhaps, like a human tree. At the same time this ocular tree is only a giant (ignoble) pink penis, drunk with the sun and suggesting or soliciting a nauseous malaise, the sickening despair of vertigo. In this transfiguration of nature, during which vision itself, attracted by nausea, is torn out and torn apart by the sunbursts into which it stares, the erection ceases to be a painful upheaval on the surface of the earth and, in a vomiting of flavorless blood, it transforms itself into a vertiginous fall in celestial space, accompanied by a horrible cry.

VII. The Sun

The sun, situated at the bottom of the sky like a cadaver at the bottom of a pit, answers this inhuman cry with the spectral attraction of decomposition. Immense nature breaks its chains and collapses into the limitless void. A severed penis, soft and bloody, is substituted for the habitual order of things. In its folds, where painful jaws still bite, pus, spittle, and larva accumulate, deposited by enormous flies: fecal like the eye painted at the bottom of a vase, this Sun, now borrowing its brilliance from death, has buried existence in the stench of the night.

VIII. The Jesuve

The terrestrial globe has retained its enormity like a bald head, in the middle of which the eye that opens on the void is both volcanic and lacustrine. It extends its disastrous countryside into the deep folds of hairy flesh, and the hairs that form its bush are inundated with tears. But the troubled feelings of a degradation even stranger than death do not have their source in a typical brain: heavy intestines alone press under this nude flesh, as charged with obscenity as a rear end—one that is just as satanic as the equally nude bottom a young sorceress raises to the black sky at the moment her fundament opens, to admit a flaming torch.

The love-cry torn from this comic crater is a feverish sob and a rattling blast of thunder.

The fecal eye of the sun has also torn itself from these volcanic entrails, and the pain of a man who tears out his own eyes with his fingers is no more absurd than this anal maternity of the sun.

IX. The Sacrifice of the Gibbon

The intolerable cry of cocks has a solar significance because of the pride and feeling of triumph of the man perceiving his own dejecta under the open sky. In the same way, during the night, an immense, troubled love, sweet as a young girl's spasm, abandons and throws itself into a giant universe, with the intimate feeling of having urinated the stars.

In order to renew this tender pact between belly and nature, a rotting forest offers its deceptive latrines, swarming with animals, colored or venomous insects, worms, and little birds. Solar light decomposes in the high branches. An Englishwoman, transfigured by a halo of blond hair, abandons her splendid body to the lubricity and the imagination (driven to the point of ecstasy by the stunning odor of decay) of a number of nude men.

Her humid lips open to kisses like a sweet swamp, like a noiseless flowing river, and her eyes, drowned in pleasure, are as immensely lost as her mouth. Above the entwined human beasts who embrace and handle her, she raises her marvelous head, so heavy with dazzlement, and her eyes open on a scene of madness.

Near a round pit, freshly dug in the midst of exuberant vegetation, a giant female gibbon struggles with three men, who tie her with long cords: her face is even more stupid than it is ignoble, and she lets out unbelievable screams of fear, screams answered by the various cries of small monkeys in the high branches. Once she is trussed up like a chicken—with her legs folded back against her body—the three men tie her upside down to a stake planted in the middle of the pit. Attached in this way, her bestially howling mouth swallows dirt while, on the other end, her huge screaming pink anal protrusion stares at the sky like a flower (the end of the stake runs between her belly and her bound paws): only the part whose obscenity stupefies emerges above the top level of the pit.

Once these preparations are finished, all the men and women present (there are, in fact, several other women, no less taken with debauchery) surround the pit: at this moment they are all equally nude, all equally deranged by the avidity of pleasure (exhausted by voluptuousness), breathless, at wits' end . . .

They are all armed with shovels, except the Englishwoman: the earth destined to fill the pit is spread evenly around it. The ignoble gibbon, in an ignoble posture, continues her terrifying howl, but, on a signal from the Englishwoman, everyone busies himself shoveling dirt into the pit, and then quickly stamps it down: thus, in the blink of an eye, the horrible beast is buried alive.

A relative silence settles: all the stupefied glances are fixed on the filthy, beautifully blood-colored solar prominence, sticking out of the earth and ridiculously shuddering with convulsions of agony. Then the Englishwoman with her charming rear end stretches her long nude body on the filled pit: the mucous-flesh of this bald false skull, a little soiled with shit at the radiate flower of its summit, is even more upsetting to see when touched by pretty white fingers. All those around hold back their cries and wipe their sweat; teeth bite lips; a light foam even flows from overly agitated mouths: contracted by strangulation, and even by death, the beautiful boil of red flesh is set ablaze with stinking brown flames. . . . .
. . . .
. . . .

Like a storm that erupts and, after several minutes of intolerable delay, ravishes in semidarkness an entire countryside with insane cataracts of water and blasts of thunder, in the same disturbed and profoundly overwhelming way (albeit with signs infinitely more difficult to perceive), existence itself shudders and attains a level where there is nothing more than a hallucinatory void, an odor of death that sticks in the throat.

In reality, when this puerile little vomiting took place, it was not on a mere carcass that the mouth of the Englishwoman crushed her most burning, her sweetest kisses, but on the nauseating JESUVE: the bizarre noise of kisses, prolonged on flesh, clattered across the disgusting noise of bowels. But these unheard-of events had set off orgasms, each more suffocating and spasmodic than its predecessor, in the circle of unfortunate observers; all throats were choked by raucous sighs, by impossible cries, and, from all sides, eyes were moist with the brilliant tears of vertigo. . . . .
. . . .

The sun vomited like a sick drunk above the mouths full of comic screams, in the void of an absurd sky . . . And thus an unparalleled heat and stupor formed an alliance—as excessive as torture: like a severed nose, like a torn-out tongue—and celebrated a wedding (celebrated it with the blade of a razor on pretty, insolent rear ends), the little copulation of the stinking hole with the sun . . .

X. The Bronze Eye

The little girls who surround the animal cages in zoos cannot help but be stunned by the ever-so lubricious rear ends of apes. To their puerile understanding, these creatures—who seem to exist only for the purpose of coupling with men—mouth to mouth, belly to belly—with the most doubtful parts of nature—propose enigmas whose perversity is barely burlesque. Girls cannot avoid thinking of their own little rear ends, of their own dejecta against which crushing interdictions have been leveled: but the image of their personal indecency, conveyed to them by the parti-colored, red, or mauve anal baldness of some apes, reaches, on the other side of the bars of the cage, a comic splendor and a suffocating atrocity. When the mythological deliria dissipate, after having fatigued the spirit through a lack of connections and through a disproportion to the real needs of life, the phantoms banished from all sides, abandoning the sun itself to the vulgarity of a nice day, make room for forms without mystery, through which one can easily make one's way, with no other goal than defined objects. But all it takes is an idiotic ape in his cage and a little girl (who blushes at seeing him take a crap), to rediscover suddenly the fleeing troop of phantoms, whose obscene sniggers have just charged a rear end as shocking as a sun.

What science cannot do—which is to establish the exceptional signification, the expressive value of an excremental orifice emerging from a hairy body like a live coal, as when, in a lavatory, a human rear end comes out of a pair of pants—the little girl achieves in such a way that there will be nothing left to do but stifle a scream. She drifts away, pressed on by a need; she trots in an alley where her steps make the gravel screech and where she passes her friends without seeing their multicolored balls, which are nevertheless well designed to attract eyes dazzled by any riot of color. Thus she runs to the foul-smelling place and locks herself in with surprise, like a young queen who, out of curiosity, locks herself in the throne room: obscurely, but in ecstasy, she has learned to recognize the face, the comic breath of death; she is unaware only of her own sobs of voluptuousness that will join, much later, this miraculous, sweet discovery . . .

In the course of the progressive erection that goes from the quadruped to *Homo erectus*, the ignominy of animal appearance grows to the point of attaining horrifying proportions, from the pretty and almost baroque lemur, who still moves on the horizontal plane, up to the gorilla. However, when the line of terminal evolution is directed toward the human being, the series of forms is produced, on the contrary, in the direction of a more and more noble or correct regularity. Thus at the present stage of development the automatic rectitude of a soldier in uniform, maneuvering according to orders, emerges from the immense confusion of the animal world and proposes itself to the universe of astronomy as its highest achievement. If, on the other hand, this mathematical military truth is contrasted with the excremental orifice of the ape, which seems to be its inevitable compensation, the universe that seemed menaced by human splendor in a pitifully imperative form receives no other response than the unintelligible discharge of a burst of laughter . . .

When the arboreal life of apes, moving in jerks from branch to branch, provoked the rupture of the equilibrium that resulted from rectilinear locomotion, everything that obscurely but ceaselessly sought to throw itself outside the animal organism was freely discharged into the region of the inferior orifice. This part, which had never been developed, and was hidden under the tails of other animals, sent out shoots and flowered in the ape; it turned into a bald protuberance and the most beautiful colors of nature made it dazzling. The tail, for a long time incapable of hiding this immense hernia of flesh, disappeared from the most evolved apes, those that carried on the genius of their species, in such a way that the hernia was able to blossom, at the end of the process, with the most hideous obscenity.

Thus the disappearance of the free caudal appendage with which, more than anything else, human pride is commonly associated, in no way signifies a regression of original bestiality, but rather a liberation of lubricious and absolutely disgusting anal forces, of which man is only the contradictory expression.

The earth, shaken to its foundations, answered this doubtful colic of nature—discharged, in the gluey penumbra of forests, through numberless flowers of flesh—with the noisy joy of entrails, with the vomiting of unbelievable volcanoes. In the same way that a burst of laughter provokes others, or a yawn provokes the yawns of a crowd, a burlesque fecal spasm had unleashed, under a black sky ravaged with thunder, a spasm of fire. In this wonderland, a wind, heavy with bloody smoke, broke down from time to time immense glowing trees, while tortuous rivers of red incandescent lava streamed from everywhere, as if from the sky. Victims of an insane terror, the giant apes fled, their flesh broiled, their mouths distorted by puerile screams.

Many of them were felled by fiery tree trunks, which laid them down, screaming, on their stomachs or backs; they soon caught fire and burned like wood. Occasionally, however, a few arrived on a treeless beach, spared by the fire, protected from the smoke by an opposing wind: they were nothing more than breathless lacerations, shapeless silhouettes, half eaten by fire, getting up or moaning on the ground, staggered by intolerable pain. Before a spectacle of red lava—as dazzling as a nightmare—of an apocalyptic lava that seemed to come bloody out of their own anuses (just as, originally, their own hairy bodies had thrust out and sadistically exhibited these vile anuses—as if all the more to insult and soil that which exists) these unfortunate creatures became like the wombs of women who give birth, something horrible . . .

It is easy, starting with the worm, to consider ironically an animal, a fish, a monkey, a man, as a tube with two orifices, anal and buccal: the nostrils, the eyes, the ears, the brain represent the complications of the buccal orifice; the penis, the testicles, or the female organs that correspond to them, are the complication of the anal. In these conditions, the violent thrusts that come from the interior of the body can be indifferently rejected to one extremity or the other, and they are discharged, in fact, where they meet the weakest resistance. All the ornaments of the head, of whatever type, mean the generalized privilege of the oral extremity; one can only contrast them with the decorative riches of the excremental extremity of apes.

But when the great anthropoid carcass found itself standing on the ground, no longer swinging from one tree to another, itself now perfectly straight and parallel to a tree, all the impulses that had up to that time found their point of free expulsion in the anal region ran up against a new barrier. Because of the erect posture, the anal region ceased to form a protuberance, and it lost the "privileged power of points": the erection could only be maintained on condition that a barrier of contracted muscles be regularly substituted for this "power of points." Thus the obscure vital thrusts were suddenly thrown back in the direction of the face and the cervical region: they were discharged in the human voice and in more and more fragile intellectual constructions (these new modes of discharge were not only adapted to the principle of the new structure, to the erection, but they even contributed to its rigidity and strength).

Beyond this, in order to consume an excess, the facial extremity assumed a part—relatively weak, but significant—of the excretory functions that up to that time had been routed in the opposite direction: men spit, cough, yawn, belch, blow their noses, sneeze, and cry much more than the other animals, but above all they have acquired the strange faculty of sobbing and bursting into laughter.

Alone, even though it may be substituted at the end of evolution for the mouth as the extreme point of the upper edifice, the pineal gland remains only in a virtual state and can only attain its meaning (without which a man spontaneously enslaves himself and reduces himself to the status of an employee) with the help of mythical confusion, as if better to make human nature a value foreign to its own reality, and thus to tie it to a spectral existence.

It is in relation to this last fact that the metamorphosis of the great ape must be seen as an *inversion*, having as its object not only the direction of the discharges thrust back through the head—transforming the head into something completely different from a mouth, making it a kind of flower blossoming with the most delirious richness of forms—but also the access of living nature (up to that point tied to the ground) to the unreality of solar space.

It is the inversion of the anal orifice itself, resulting from the shift from a squatting posture to a standing one, that is responsible for the decisive reversal of animal existence.

The bald summit of the anus has become the center, blackened with bushes, of the narrow ravine cleaving the buttocks.

The spectral image of this change of sign is represented by a strange human nudity—now obscene—that is substituted for the hairy body of animals, and in particular by the pubescent hairs that appear exactly where the ape was glabrous; surrounded by a halo of death, a creature who is too pale and too large stands up, a creature who, under a sick sun, is nothing other than the celestial eye it lacks.

The Use Value of D. A. F. de Sade
(An Open Letter to My
Current Comrades)

If I think it good to address this letter to my comrades, it is not because the propositions that it contains concern them. It will probably even appear to them that such propositions do not concern anyone in particular at all. But in this case I need to have at least a few people as witnesses to establish so complete a defection. There are, perhaps, declarations which, for lack of anything better, ridiculously need an Attic chorus, because they suppose, as their effect, in spite of everything, a minimum of astonishment, of misunderstanding, or of repugnance. But one does not address a chorus in order to convince it or rally it, and certainly one does not submit to the judgment of destiny without revolting, when it condemns the declarant to the saddest isolation.

This isolation, as far as I am concerned, is moreover in part voluntary, since I would agree to come out of it only on certain hard-to-meet conditions.

In fact even the gesture of writing, which alone permits one to envisage slightly less conventional human relations, a little less crafty than those of so-called intimate friendships—even this gesture of writing does not leave me with an appreciable hope. I doubt that it is possible to reach the few people to whom this letter is no doubt intended, over the heads of my present comrades. For—my resolution is all the more intransigent in that it is absurd to defend—it would have been necessary to deal not with individuals like those I already know, but only with men (and above all with masses) who are comparatively decomposed, amorphous, and even violently expelled from every form. But it is likely that such men do not yet exist (and the masses certainly do not exist).

All I can state is that, one day or another, they certainly will not fail to exist, given that current social bonds will inevitably be undone, and that these bonds cannot much longer maintain the habitual enslavement of people and customs. The masses will in turn be decomposed as soon as they see the prestige of industrial reality, to which they find themselves attached, disappear; in other words, when the process of material progress and rapid transformation in which they have had to participate (docile as well as in revolt) leads to a disagreeable and terminal stagnation.

My resolution thus cannot be defended only in that it eliminates—not without bitterness—every immediate satisfaction.

Outside of propositions that can only take on meaning through very general consequences, it so happens that it is high time for me to quell—at little cost—a part of this bitterness: it is possible at the very least to clear the narrow terrain— where from now on the debate will be carried out—of the intellectual bartering that usually goes on there. In fact it is obvious that if men incapable of histrionics succeed those of today, they will not be able to better represent the tacky phraseology now in circulation than by recalling the fate reserved, by a certain number of writers, for the memory of D. A. F. de Sade (moreover it will, perhaps, appear fairly quickly, in a very general way, that the fact of needlessly resorting to literary or poetic verbiage, the inability to express oneself in a simple and categorical way, not only are the result of a vulgar impotence, but always betray a pretentious hypocrisy).

Of course, I do not allude in this way to the various people who are scandalized by the writings of Sade, but only to his most open apologists. It has seemed fitting today to place these writings (and with them the figure of their author) above everything (or almost everything) that can be opposed to them, but it is out of the question to allow them the least place in private or public life, in theory or in practice. The behavior of Sade's admirers resembles that of primitive subjects in relation to their king, whom they adore and loathe, and whom they cover with honors and narrowly confine. In the most favorable cases, the author of *Justine* is in fact thus treated as any given *foreign body*; in other words, he is only an object of transports of exaltation to the extent that these transports facilitate his excretion (his peremptory expulsion).

The life and works of D. A. F. de Sade would thus have no other use value than the common use value of excrement; in other words, for the most part, one most often only loves the rapid (and violent) pleasure of voiding this matter and no longer seeing it.

I am thus led to indicate how, in a way completely different from this usage, the sadism which is not *completely different* from that which existed before Sade appears positively, on the one hand, as an irruption of excremental forces (the excessive violation of modesty, positive algolagnia, the violent excretion of the sexual object coinciding with a powerful or tortured ejaculation, the libidinal interest in cadavers, vomiting, defecation . . .)—and on the other as a corresponding limitation, a narrow enslavement of everything that is opposed to this irruption. It is only in these concrete conditions that sad social necessity, human dignity, fatherland and family, as well as poetic sentiments, appear without a mask and without any play of light and shadow; it is finally impossible to see in those things anything other than subordinate forces: so many slaves working like cowards to prepare the beautiful blustering eruptions that alone are capable of answering the needs that torment the bowels of most men.

But, given that Sade revealed his conception of terrestrial life in the most outrageous form (even given that it is not possible to reveal immediately such a conception other than in a terrifying and inadmissible form), it is perhaps not surprising that people have believed it possible to get beyond its reach. Literary men apparently have the best reason for not confirming a brilliant verbal and low-cost apology through practice. They could even pretend that Sade was the first to take the trouble to situate the domain he described outside of and above all reality. They could easily affirm that the brilliant and suffocating value he wanted to give human existence is inconceivable outside of fiction, that only poetry, exempt from all practical applications, permits one to have at his disposal, to a certain extent, the brilliance and suffocation that the Marquis de Sade tried so indecently to provoke.

It is right to recognize that, even practiced in the extremely implicit form it has retained up to this point, such a diversion discredits its authors (at the very least among those—even if, moreover, they are horrified by sadism—who refuse to become interested, for bad as well as for good reasons, in simple verbal prestidigitation).

The fact remains, unfortunately, that this diversion has been practiced for so long without denunciation, under cover of a fairly poor phraseology, simply because it takes place in an area where, it seems, everything slips away. . . . It is no doubt almost useless at the present time to set forth rational propositions, since they could only be taken up for the profit of some convenient and—even in an apocalyptic guise—thoroughly literary enterprise: in other words, on the condition that they be useful for ambitions calculated by the impotence of present-day man. The slightest hope, in fact, involves the destruction (the disappearance) of a society that has so ridiculously allowed the one who conceives that hope to exist.

The time has no less come, it seems to me—under the indifferent eyes of my comrades—to bet on a future that has, it is true, only an unfortunate, hallucinatory existence. At the very least the plan I think possible to sketch *intellectually* today of what will really exist later is the only thing that links the various preliminary propositions that follow to a still sickly will to *agitation*.

For the moment, an abrupt statement not followed by explanations seems to me to respond sufficiently to the intellectual disorientation of those who could have the opportunity to become aware of it. And (even though I am capable to a large extent of doing it now) I put off until later difficult and interminable explications, analogous to those of any other elaborated theory. At this point then I will set forth the propositions that, among other things, allow one to introduce the values established by the Marquis de Sade, obviously not in the domain of gratuitous impertinence, but rather directly in the very market in which, each day, the credit that individuals and even communities can give to their own lives is, in a way, registered.

Appropriation and Excretion

1. The division of social facts into religious facts (prohibitions, obligations, and the realization of sacred action) on the one hand and profane facts (civil, political, juridical, industrial, and commercial organization) on the other, even though it is not easily applied to primitive societies and lends itself in general to a certain number of confusions, can nevertheless serve as the basis for the determination of two polarized human impulses: EXCRETION and APPRO- PRIATION. In other words, during a period in which the religious organization of a given country *is developing*, this organization represents the freest opening for excremental collective impulses (orgiastic impulses) established in opposition to political, juridical, and economic institutions.

2. Sexual activity, whether perverted or not; the behavior of one sex before the other; defecation; urination; death and the cult of cadavers (above all, insofar as it involves the stinking decomposition of bodies); the different taboos; ritual cannibalism; the sacrifice of animal-gods; omophagia; the laughter of exclusion; sobbing (which in general has death as its object); religious ecstasy; the identical attitude toward shit, gods, and cadavers; the terror that so often accompanies involuntary defecation; the custom of making women both brilliant and lubricious with makeup, gems, and gleaming jewels; gambling; heedless expenditure and certain fanciful uses of money, etc. together present a common character in that the object of the activity (excrement, shameful parts, cadavers, etc.) is found each time treated as a foreign body (*daz ganz Anderes*); in other words, it can just as well be expelled following a brutal rupture as reabsorbed through the desire to put one's body and mind entirely in a more or less violent state of expulsion (or projection). The notion of the (heterogeneous) *foreign body* permits one to note the elementary *subjective* identity between types of excrement (sperm, mentrual blood, urine, fecal matter) and everything that can be seen as sacred, divine, or marvelous: a half-decomposed cadaver fleeing through the night in a luminous shroud can be seen as characteristic of this unity.[1]

3. The process of simple appropriation is normally presented within the pro-

cess of composite excretion, insofar as it is necessary for the production of an alternating rhythm, for example, in the following passage from Sade:

Verneuil makes someone shit, he eats the turd, and then he demands that someone eat his. The one who eats his shit vomits; he devours her puke.

The elementary form of appropriation is oral consumption, considered as communion (participation, identification, incorporation, or assimilation). Consumption is either sacramental (sacrificial) or not depending on whether the heterogeneous character of food is heightened or conventionally destroyed. In the latter case, the identification takes place first in the preparation of foods, which must be given an appearance of striking homogeneity, based on strict conventions. Eating as such then intervenes in the process as a complex phenomenon in that the very fact of swallowing presents itself as a partial rupture of physical equilibrium and is accompanied by, among other things, a sudden liberation of great quantities of saliva. Nevertheless, the element of appropriation, in moderate and rational form, in fact dominates, because cases in which eating's principal goal is physiological tumult (gluttony or drunkenness followed by vomiting) are no doubt unusual.

The process of appropriation is thus characterized by a homogeneity (static equilibrium) of the author of the appropriation, and of objects as final result, whereas excretion presents itself as the result of a heterogeneity, and can move in the direction of an ever greater heterogeneity, liberating impulses whose ambivalence is more and more pronounced. The latter case is represented by, for example, sacrificial consumption in the elementary form of the orgy, which has no other goal than the incorporation in the person of irreducibly heterogeneous elements, insofar as such elements risk provoking an increase of force (or more exactly an increase of *mana*).

4. Man does not only appropriate his food, but also the different products of his activity: clothes, furniture, dwellings, and instruments of production. Finally, he appropriates land divided into parcels. Such appropriations take place by means of a more or less conventional homogeneity (identity) established between the possessor and the object possessed. It involves sometimes a personal homogeneity that in primitive times could only be solemnly destroyed with the aid of an excretory rite, and sometimes a general homogeneity, such as that established by the architect between a city and its inhabitants.

In this respect, production can be seen as the excretory phase of a process of appropriation, and the same is true of selling.

5. The homogeneity of the kind realized in cities between men and that which surrounds them is only a subsidiary form of a much more consistent

homogeneity, which man has established throughout the external world by everywhere replacing *a priori* inconceivable objects with classified series of conceptions or ideas. The identification of all the elements of which the world is composed has been pursued with a constant obstinacy, so that scientific conceptions, as well as the popular conceptions of the world, seem to have voluntarily led to a representation as different from what could have been imagined *a priori* as the public square of a capital is from a region of high mountains.

This last appropriation—the work of philosophy as well as of science or common sense—has included phases of revolt and scandal, but it has always had as its goal the establishment of the homogeneity of the world, and it will only be able to lead to a terminal phase in the sense of excretion when the irreducible waste products of the operation are determined.

Philosophy, Religion, and Poetry in Relation to Heterology

6. The interest of philosophy resides in the fact that, in opposition to science or common sense, it must positively envisage the waste products of intellectual appropriation. Nevertheless, it most often envisages these waste products only in abstract forms of totality (nothingness, infinity, the absolute), to which it itself cannot give a positive content; it can thus freely proceed in speculations that more or less have as a goal, all things considered, the *sufficient* identification of an endless world with a finite world, an unknowable (noumenal) world with the known (phenomenal) world.

Only an intellectual elaboration in a religious form can, in its periods of autonomous development, put forward the waste products of appropriative thought as the definitively heterogeneous (sacred) object of speculation. But in general one must take into account the fact that religions bring about a profound separation within the sacred domain, dividing it into a superior world (celestial and divine) and an inferior world (demoniacal, a world of decomposition); now such a division necessarily leads to a progressive homogeneity of the entire superior domain (only the inferior domain resists all efforts at appropriation). God rapidly and almost entirely loses his terrifying features, his appearance as a decomposing cadaver, in order to become, at the final stage of degradation, the simple (paternal) sign of universal homogeneity.

7. In practice, one must understand by religion not really that which answers the need for the unlimited projection (expulsion or excretion) of human nature, but the totality of prohibitions, obligations, and partial freedom that socially channel and regularize this projection. Religion thus differs from a practical and theoretical *heterology*[2] (even though both are equally concerned with sacred or excremental facts), not only in that the former excludes the scientific rigor proper to the latter (which generally appears as different from religion

as chemistry is from alchemy), but also in that, under normal conditions, it betrays the needs that it was not only supposed to regulate, but satisfy.

8.   Poetry at first glance seems to remain valuable as a method of mental projection (in that it permits one to accede to an entirely heterogeneous world). But it is only too easy to see that it is hardly less debased than religion. It has almost always been at the mercy of the great historical systems of appropriation. And insofar as it can be developed autonomously, this autonomy leads it onto the path of a total poetic conception of the world, which ends at any one of a number of aesthetic homogeneities. The practical unreality of the heterogeneous elements it sets in motion is, in fact, an indispensable condition for the continuation of heterogeneity: starting from the moment when this unreality immediately constitutes itself as a superior reality, whose mission is to eliminate (or degrade) inferior vulgar reality, poetry is reduced to playing the role of the standard of things, and, in opposition, the worst vulgarity takes on an ever stronger excremental value.

The Heterological Theory of Knowledge

9.   When one says that heterology scientifically considers questions of heterogeneity, one does not mean that heterology is, in the usual sense of such a formula, the science of the heterogeneous. The heterogeneous is even resolutely placed outside the reach of scientific knowledge, which by definition is only applicable to homogeneous elements. Above all, heterology is opposed to any homogeneous representation of the world, in other words, to any philosophical system. The goal of such representations is always the deprivation of our universe's sources of excitation and the development of a servile human species, fit only for the fabrication, rational consumption, and conservation of products. But the intellectual process automatically limits itself by producing of its own accord its own waste products, thus liberating in a disordered way the heterogeneous excremental element. Heterology is restricted to taking up again, consciously and resolutely, this terminal process which up until now has been seen as the abortion and the shame of human thought.

In that way it [heterology] leads to the complete reversal of the philosophical process, which ceases to be the instrument of appropriation, and now serves excretion; it introduces the demand for the violent gratifications implied by social life.

10.   Only, on the one hand, the process of limitation and, on the other, the study of the violently alternating reactions of antagonism (expulsion) and love (reabsorption) obtained by positing the heterogeneous element, lie within the province of heterology as science. This element itself remains indefinable and

can only be determined through negation. The specific character of fecal matter or of the specter, as well as of unlimited time or space, can only be the object of a series of negations, such as the absence of any possible common denominator, irrationality, etc. It must even be added that there is no way of placing such elements in the immediate objective human domain, in the sense that the pure and simple objectification of their specific character would lead to their incorporation in a homogeneous intellectual system, in other words, to a hypocritical cancellation of their excremental character.

The objectivity of heterogeneous elements thus is of only purely theoretical interest, since one can only attain it on the condition that one envisage *waste products* in the total form of the infinite obtained by negation (in other words, objective heterogeneity's shortcoming is that it can only be envisaged in an abstract form, whereas the subjective heterogeneity of particular elements is, in practice, alone concrete).

11. Scientific data—in other words, the result of appropriation—alone retains an immediate and appreciable objective character, since immediate objectivity is defined by the possibilities of intellectual appropriation. If one defines real exterior objects it is necessary to introduce at the same time the possibility of a relation of scientific appropriation. And if such a relation is impossible, the element envisaged remains in practice unreal, and can only abstractly be made objective. All questions posed beyond this represent the persistence of a dominant need for appropriation, the sickly obstinacy of a will seeking to represent, in spite of everything, and through simple cowardice, a homogeneous and servile world.

12. It is useless to try to deny that one finds there—much more than in the difficulty (less embarrassing than facility) met with in the analysis of the process of excretion and appropriation—the weak point (in practice) of these conceptions, for one must generally take into account the unconscious obstinacy furnished by defections and complacency. It would be too easy to find in objective nature a large number of phenomena that in a crude way correspond to the human model of excretion and appropriation, in order to attain *once again* the notion of the unity of being, for example, in a dialectical form. One can attain it more generally through animals, plants, matter, nature, and being, without meeting really consistent obstacles. Nevertheless, it can already be indicated that as one moves away from man, the opposition loses its importance to the point where it is only a superimposed form that one obviously could not have discovered in the facts considered if it had not been borrowed from a different order of facts. The only way to resist this dilution lies in the practical part of heterology, which leads to an action that resolutely goes against this regression to homogeneous nature.

As soon as the effort at rational comprehension ends in contradiction, the practice of intellectual scatology requires the excretion of unassimilable elements, which is another way of stating vulgarly that a burst of laughter is the only imaginable and definitively terminal result—and not the means—of philosophical speculation. And then one must indicate that a reaction as *insignificant* as a burst of laughter derives from the extremely vague and distant character of the intellectual domain, and that it suffices to go from a speculation resting on abstract facts to a practice whose mechanism is not different, but which immediately reaches concrete heterogeneity, in order to arrive at ecstatic trances and orgasm.

Principles of Practical Heterology

13. Excretion is not simply a middle term between two appropriations, just as decay is not simply a middle term between the grain and the ear of wheat. The inability to consider in this latter case decay as an end in itself is the result not precisely of the human viewpoint but of the specifically intellectual viewpoint (to the extent that this viewpoint is in practice subordinate to a process of appropriation). The human viewpoint, independent of official declarations, in other words as it results from, among other things, the analysis of dreams, on the contrary represents appropriation as a means of excretion. In the final analysis it is clear that a worker works in order to obtain the violent pleasures of coitus (in other words, he accumulates in order to spend). On the other hand, the conception according to which the worker must have coitus in order to provide for the future necessities of work is linked to the unconscious identification of the worker with the slave. In fact, to the extent that the various functions are distributed among the various social categories, appropriation in its most overwhelming form historically devolves on slaves: thus in the past serfs had to accumulate products for knights and clerks, who barely took part in the labor of appropriation, and then only through the establishment of a morality that regularized for their own profit the circulation of goods. But as soon as one attacks the accursed exploitation of man by man, it becomes time to leave to the exploiters this abominable appropriative morality, which for such a long time has permitted their own orgies of wealth. To the extent that man no longer thinks of crushing his comrades under the yoke of morality, he acquires the capacity to link overtly not only his intellect and his virtue but his *raison d'être* to the violence and incongruity of his excretory organs, as well as to his ability to become excited and entranced by heterogeneous elements, commonly starting in debauchery.

14. The need—before being able to go on to radical demands and to the violent practice of a rigorous moral liberty—to abolish all exploitation of man

by man is not the only motive that links the practical development of heterology to the overturning of the established order.

In that they are manifested in a social milieu, the urges that heterology identifies *in practice* with the *raison d'être* of man can be seen in a certain sense as antisocial (to the same degree that sexual corruption or even pleasure is seen by certain individuals as a waste of strength, like, for example, the great ritual destructions of goods in British Columbia, or, among civilized peoples, the pleasure of crowds watching great fires at night). Nevertheless, the impulses that go against the interests of a society in a state of stagnation (during a phase of appropriation) have, on the contrary, social revolution (the phase of excretion) as their end: thus they can find, through the historical movements by means of which humanity spends its own strength freely and limitlessly, both total gratification and use in the very sense of general conscious benefit. Besides, whatever, the reality of this ulterior benefit might be, it is no less true that if one considers the submerged masses, doomed to an obscure and impotent life, the revolution by which these masses liberate force with a long-restrained violence is as much the practical *raison d'être* of societies as it is their means of development.

15. Of course the term *excretion* applied to the Revolution must first be understood in the strictly mechanical—and moreover etymological—sense of the word. The first phase of a revolution is *separation*, in other words, a process leading to the position of two groups of forces, each one characterized by the necessity of excluding the other. The second phase is the violent *expulsion* of the group that has possessed power by the revolutionary group.

But one also notes that each of the groups, by its very constitution, gives the opposing group an almost exclusively negative excremental character, and it is only because of this negativity that the sacrificial character of a revolution remains profoundly unconscious. The revolutionary impulse of the proletarian masses is, moreover, sometimes implicitly and sometimes openly treated as sacred, and that is why it is possible to use the word *Revolution* entirely stripped of its utilitarian meaning without, however, giving it an idealist meaning.

16. *Participation*—in the purely psychological sense as well as in the active sense of the word—does not only commit revolutionaries to a particular politics, for example, to the establishment of socialism throughout the world. It is also—and necessarily—presented as moral participation: immediate participation in the destructive action of the revolution (expulsion realized through the total shattering of the equilibrium of the social edifice), indirect participation in all equivalent destructive action. It is the very character of the revolutionary will to link such actions—not, as in the Christian apocalypse, to punishment—but to the enjoyment or the utility of human beings, and it is obvious that all destruction that is neither useful nor inevitable can only be the achievement of an exploiter

and, consequently, of morality as the principle of all exploitation.[3] But then it is easy to ascertain that the reality of such *participation* is at the very basis of the separation of the socialist parties, divided into reformists and revolutionaries.

Without a profound complicity with natural forces such as violent death, gushing blood, sudden catastrophes and the horrible cries of pain that accompany them, terrifying ruptures of what had seemed to be immutable, the fall into stinking filth of what had been elevated—without a sadistic understanding of an incontestably thundering and torrential nature, there could be no revolutionaries, there could only be a revolting utopian sentimentality.

17. The *participation* in everything that, among men, is horrible and allegedly sacred can take place in a limited and unconscious form, but this limitation and this unconsciousness obviously have only a provisional value, and nothing can stop the movement that leads human beings toward an ever more shameless awareness of the erotic bond that links them to death, to cadavers, and to horrible physical pain. It is high time that human nature cease being subjected to the autocrat's vile repression and to the morality that authorizes exploitation. Since it is true that one of a man's attributes is the derivation of pleasure from the suffering of others, and that erotic pleasure is not only the negation of an agony that takes place at the same instant, but also a lubricious participation in that agony, it is time to choose between the conduct of cowards afraid of their own joyful excesses, and the conduct of those who judge that any given man need not cower like a hunted animal, but instead can see all the moralistic buffoons as so many dogs.

18. As a result of these elementary considerations, it is necessary from now on to envisage two distinct phases in human emancipation, as undertaken successively by the different revolutionary surges, from Jacobinism to bolshevism.

During the revolutionary phase, the current phase that will only end with the world triumph of socialism, only the social Revolution can serve as an outlet for collective impulses, and no other activity can be envisaged in practice.

But the postrevolutionary phase implies the necessity of a division between the economic and political organization of society on one hand, and on the other, an antireligious and asocial organization having as its goal orgiastic participation in different forms of destruction, in other words, the collective satisfaction of needs that correspond to the necessity of provoking the violent excitation that results from the expulsion of heterogeneous elements.

Such an organization can have no other conception of morality than the one scandalously affirmed for the first time by the Marquis de Sade.

19. When it is a question of the means of realizing this orgiastic participa-

tion, [such] an organization will find itself as close to religions anterior *to the formations of autocratic States* as it is distant from religions such as Christianity or Buddhism.

One must broadly take into account, in such a forecast, the probable intervention of blacks in the general culture. To the extent that blacks participate in revolutionary emancipation, the attainment of socialism will bring them the possibility of all kinds of exchanges with white people, but in conditions radically different from those currently experienced by the civilized blacks of America. Now black communities, once liberated from all superstition as from all oppression, represent in relation to heterology not only the possibility but the necessity of an adequate organization. All organizations that have ecstasy and frenzy as their goal (the spectacular death of animals, partial tortures, orgiastic dances, etc.) will have no reason to disappear when a heterological conception of human life is substituted for the primitive conception; they can only transform themselves while they spread, under the violent impetus of a moral doctrine of white origin, taught to blacks by all those whites who have become aware of the abominable inhibitions paralyzing their race's communities. It is only starting from this collusion of European scientific theory with black practice that institutions can develop which will serve as the final outlets (with no other limitations than those of human strength) for the urges that today require worldwide society's fiery and bloody Revolution.

Notes

1. The identical nature, from the psychological point of view, of God and excrement should not shock the intellect of anyone familiar with the problems posed by the history of religions. The cadaver is not much more repugnant than shit, and the specter that projects its horror is *sacred* even in the eyes of modern theologians. The following passage from Frazer very nearly sums up the basic historical aspect of the question: " . . . These different categories of people differ, in our eyes, by virtue of their character and their condition: we should say that one group is sacred, the other filthy or impure. This is not the case for the savage, for his mind is much too crude to understand clearly what a sacred being is, and what an impure being is."

2. The science of what is completely other. The term *agiology* would perhaps be more precise, but one would have to catch the double meaning of *agio* (analogous to the double meaning of *sacer*), *soiled* as well as *holy*. But it is above all the term *scatology* (the science of excrement) that retains in the present circumstances (the specialization of the sacred) an incontestable expressive value as the doublet of an abstract term such as *heterology*.

3. For example, imperialist war.

II
(1932–1935)

The Critique of the Foundations
of the Hegelian Dialectic

The Marxist conception of the dialectic has often been challenged. Finally, Max Eastman considered it to be a form of religious thought. But the dialectic has only been the object of a negative critique. Those who criticized it acted as simple destroyers. They tried not to see that, by removing the dialectical method from proletarian ideology, they removed the blood from the body; they took no notice of that because Hegelianism, in whatever form it might take, was incompatible with their ordinary conceptions. Thus the Marxist dialectic was treated in the same way that the Hegelian dialectic in general was treated: it was pushed away with repugnance.

A new way of conceiving the Hegelian dialectic nevertheless starts with the critique of Nicolai Hartmann,[1] in which it is possible to find the elements of a true positive critique. The indications given by this German professor, in an article appearing in the *Revue de métaphysique et de morale*,[2] are sufficient in themselves: they express in concise form a direction that is, in our opinion, of the greatest interest to Marxist studies. Hartmann successively examines the different dialectical themes developed in Hegel's philosophy, and then compares them from the standpoint of their bases and forms. In this way he seeks to distinguish those that are justified by *experience*, founded in reality, from those that have only a verbal value. As an example of the latter he cites the famous theme of being and nothingness. "In the course of such an investigation," states Hartmann, "Hegel's *Logic* most seriously gives rise to the suspicion that, in its major part, it consists only of a dialectic lacking any foundation in reality. This is even more true," he adds, "in the *Philosophy of Nature* (this is obvious, it is true, and not unprecedented, as results already confirm).'"[3]

The profound difference between Hartmann's critique and the Marxist critique appears at the outset. For Marx and Engels, the dialectic is still—as it is for Hegel—the general law of a fundamental reality. Nature or matter has been substituted for logic, but the universe is nevertheless abandoned in its entirety to antithetical development. For Hartmann, on the other hand, the basic task lies in methodically testing the value of dialectical reasoning in its particular cases. And not only is universality set aside, but from the outset, more than any other element, nature is seen as a prohibited domain. The dialectical themes justified by Hartmann are borrowed neither from the *Logic* nor from the *Philosophy of Nature*, but from the *Philosophy of Right*, the *Philosophy of History*, and the *Phenomenology of Spirit*; and the first example Hartmann gives to found his conception has nothing to do with the grain of barley or with geological formations. It is, on the contrary, class struggle itself, the Hegelian theme of "master and slave." Thus a modern philosopher, wanting to found the dialectic in reality, immediately refers to the Marxist experience.[4]

One must recognize in any case that Marx and Engels themselves felt the necessity of a labor analogous—but only in its elementary principle—to the one that Hartmann has recently undertaken. The fact that they chose a domain of study different from that of Hartmann, that they had the ambition to give dialectical conceptions the character of general laws of nature in no way contradicts the fact that Engels tried, through a long study of the natural sciences, to give these laws an experimental value. But from the beginning we are led to differentiate between the domain admitted *a posteriori* by Hartmann and the one that Engels assigned himself *a priori*. Hartmann methodically seeks to recognize what, in the dialectical themes, can be seen as givens of lived experience, whereas Engels systematically imposed on himself the task of finding these laws in nature, in other words, in a domain that can at first appear to be closed to all antithetically developing rational conceptions.

Hartmann's attitude of indifference toward the *Philosophy of Nature* conforms to that of all the representatives of the natural sciences since Hegel. For scientists, a dialectical construction of the relations they study must seem incompatible with science: science must do as much as possible without the intervention of an element that is as foreign to it as is systematic contradiction—and in fact it *was* possible to do without it. The objection to the introduction of the dialectic was of a necessity so apparent to specialists that it was not even necessary to formulate it.

But the difficulty offered by nature to the dialectic is not only indicated by the history of all modern scientific research: Hegel himself was the first to indicate cautiously that it was precisely nature which by its "impotence [. . . to adhere strictly to the Notion . . .] sets limits to philosophy."[5] To philosophy: in other words, to the dialectical construction of the becoming of things. For him, nature is the *fall* of the idea; it is a negation, at the same time a revolt and an *absurdity*.

Even if he had set aside his idealist prejudices, nothing would have seemed more unreasonable to Hegel than looking for the foundations of the objectivity of dialectical laws in the study of nature. This effort would in fact lead again to basing the dialectical construction on its weakest part; it would lead to the paradox of the colossus with feet of clay. The very elements that suddenly become, for Marx and Engels, the method's foundations are precisely those that offer the most resistance to the application of this method, and not only by definition, but above all in practice. In spite of the trouble taken by Hegel to resolve the difficulties encountered in the *Philosophy of Nature*, this part of his work left even him unsatisfied. It must be recognized in principle that difficulties of this kind do not in any way permit Engels's efforts to be considered inherently untenable. Nevertheless, in fact, the failure of this effort was, in a way, given in its premises. The substitution of nature for logic is only the Scylla and Charybdis of post-Hegelian philosophy.

Today a new experimental justification of the dialectic has become necessary. It will be clear why this operation can only take place on the very terrain of its specific development, in other words on the immediate terrain of class struggle, in experience and not in an *a priori* fog of universal conceptions.

The failure of Engels, who worked for eight years preparing a dialectical theory of nature—which led only to the second preface of the *Anti-Dühring*[6] in 1885—has not yet been the object of the studies that the considerable efforts of this great pioneer of the Revolution so richly deserve. Many people prefer to speak of dialectical materialism as if it were not an incomplete project, but a constituted doctrine.[7] This carelessness is even more unjustifiable in that Engels's abandonment of the project was due neither to a lack of time, nor to any other circumstances external to the nature of the project itself. Engels invokes the death of Marx and the need to work on the edition of his friend's uncompleted works. He nevertheless wrote this second preface in which—after recognizing the insufficiency of the arguments in the *Anti-Dühring* that have to do with the dialectic—he gives a definition of the dialectic that is nothing more than an abandonment of his initial position. The immense and admirable effort of Engels, which we know of today due to the publications of Riazanov, therefore had this result: the change represented by the second preface in relation to the main text of the *Anti-Dühring*. This step backwards in itself accounts for the fact that Engels left unfinished a work to which, by his own account, he devoted the better part of eight years.

One still finds in 1881–82, in a note published by Riazanov,[8] an affirmation of the most suspect form of the dialectical conception. The "law" of the negation of the negation is cited there as one of the three essential dialectical laws of the history of nature. Nevertheless, the argument that follows stops at the transformation of quality into quantity.[9] No examples are given of the "negation of the negation." By 1885 this "negation of the negation" has disappeared from an account meant to remedy the insufficiencies of the *Anti-Dühring*, published in 1878.

It would, however, be easy to agree on this point: if any part of the *Anti-Dühring* can be criticized, it is the one that presents examples of the "negation of the negation"; the stories of grains of barley, butterflies, and geological strata. The insufficiency of this section is even more regrettable in that without this "negation of the negation" the dialectic loses its practical value in the realm of society. Nevertheless, instead of returning to this burning question, Engels in 1885 stops seeing the "negation of the negation" in the "essential of the dialectical conception of nature." The relevant passage from the second preface should be cited here in its entirety.

> It is however precisely the polar antagonisms put forward as irreconcilable and insoluble, the forcibly fixed lines of demarcation and class distinctions, that have given modern theoretical natural science its restricted, metaphysical character. The recognition that these antagonisms and distinctions, though to be found in nature, are only of relative validity, and that on the other hand their imagined rigidity and absolute validity have been introduced into nature only by our reflective minds—this recognition is the *kernel*[10] of the dialectical conception of nature.[11]

This declaration means nothing less than the renunciation of the hope of founding in nature the general law of which class struggle would only have been a particular case.

To link facts as different as the transformation of electricity into heat (or any other change in nature) and class struggle in fact makes no sense—and in fact no practical sense. Class struggle, which we cite as our most important example, is characterized first of all by the fact that the positive term, capitalism, necessarily implies the negative term, the proletariat; secondly, the realization of the negation implied in the second term implies, in turn, and with the same necessity, the negation of the negation (in this way the revolution has, at the same time, a negative and a positive sense). In other applications, this elementary schema can be altered; as Hartmann explains it,[12] dialectical themes can take a great number of forms, each one very different—but it is possible to admit such alteration while nevertheless refusing to recognize that this schema is the same when it reappears in a form so impoverished that one cannot imagine a greater impoverishment. If it is only a matter of recognizing diversity in identity, or identity in diversity, if it is only a matter of admitting that what is diversified does not necessarily remain identical to itself, then it is useless and even imprudent to invoke the authority of the Hegelian dialectic. For this dialectic is linked to a current of thought whose "long experimental history" is not exactly what Engels envisages when using this expression. Things must be looked at squarely, and it is necessary to admit that the dialectic had antecedents other than Heraclitus, Plato, or Fichte. It is linked even more essentially to currents of thought such as Gnosticism, Neoplatonic mysticism, and to philosophical phantoms such as Meister Eckhart, the Cardinal Nicholas of Cusa, and Jakob Boehme. Now it is no surprise that the thought of these phantoms as assimilated and adopted by Hegel is not applicable to the domain of natural science, or that if this thought seeks to wander in this domain, it only finds a place as a parasite, becoming ever poorer and finding itself reduced to the most miserable state. In fact, however, the same thought, conserved in its richest form, is adequate and, to a certain extent, alone is adequate, when it is a matter of representing the life and revolutions of societies.

But in order to conserve this adequacy, this thought must be conserved in its entirety, whatever its religious antecedents may have been. A justification of its attenuated form, based on the natural sciences, has revealed itself to be an insufficient effort, leaving the way open to analytical work established on the bases defined by Hartmann.

There remains the strangest element of Engels' *Weltanschauung*, his dialectical conception of mathematics,[13] which in certain ways recalls the mathematical idealism of Nicholas of Cusa, whom we have just cited as one of the mystical ancestors of the Hegelian dialectic.

Engels cannot be suspected of mathematical idealism, but his conception is even more strange in that it only differs from mathematical idealism to the extent that mathematics is assimilated to nature. This confusion is apparent in the following passage, which appears in the second preface to the *Anti-Dühring* (p. cvii; English translation, p. 17):

> It goes without saying that my recapitulation of mathematics and the natural sciences was undertaken in order to convince myself also in detail—of what in general I was not in doubt—that in *nature*,[14] amid the welter of innumerable changes, the same dialectical laws of motion [govern].

Beyond this, he gives mathematical examples of the negation of the negation that come from the history of geological movements and the history of the modes of property.

In any case, Engels saw in mathematics a kind of privileged domain of the conceptions he was trying to introduce: in this domain the dialectic had not only the most legitimate place, but the most privileged one as well. Mathematics furnished the convincing example of a science that had arrived at the dialectical stage.

For this reason it is all the more important to indicate here that this science rejected in its very development everything that could give rise to such an interpretation. What Engels considered a progress toward perfection[15] was considered by mathematicians a degeneration and an evil that had to be eliminated. [In its origins, infinitesimal calculus was in fact based on "contradictory" notions, and the demonstrations that were available were, in the words of Engels, "false from the point of view of elementary mathematics." Throughout the eighteenth century people worked without worrying about the logical difficulties presented by the use of the infinitely small, the passage to the limit, continuity, etc. "The simple question of proof is definitely pushed into the background, as compared with the manifold application of the method to new spheres of research."[16] But this sentence, which Engels put in the present tense, applied, in fact, only to a stage of analysis that had already been superseded. From the beginning of the nineteenth century, mathematicians such as Gauss, Abel, and Cauchy worked to give their demonstrations an absolute rigor and tried to revise, from this point of view, the demonstrations of their predecessors. Their successors continued this labor of purification and attacked the very principles of analysis: the passage to the limit, continuity, differentiation, integration, etc., were defined in such a way as to exclude all contradiction. In 1886, Jules Tannery,[17] summing up the mathematical activity of an entire century, could write:

> One can constitute analysis entirely with the notion of whole numbers and notions relative to the addition of whole numbers; it is useless to invoke any other postulate, or any other experiential given; the notion of infinity, which should not be seen as a mystery in mathematics, is reducible to this: after each whole number, there is another.

One cannot reproach Engels for his ignorance of the very latest scientific findings of his time, but when he writes of differentials:

> I only mention in passing that this ratio between two quantities that have disappeared, caught at the moment of their disappearance, is a contradiction; however, it cannot disturb us any more than it has disturbed the whole of mathematics for almost two hundred years.[18]

it is necessary to recognize that this contradiction finally not only troubled mathematicians, but even scandalized them, that they applied all their efforts to the task of eliminating it and—it would be vain to deny it—they succeeded. Today's analysis is presented with as much logical rigor as arithmetic or algebra. It is true that, even in elementary mathematics, Engels discovered examples of the negation of the negation or of dialectical thought. We cannot take up each example here; one can say, in a general way, that Engels' examples are all based on a certain "realistic" way of interpreting mathematical symbolism and logic. From the fact that the expression "first degree curve" designates a straight line, Engels believes it possible that there is identity between straight and curved; but is it not evident that the use of the word "curved" in this case is only a convention of language? In the same way, the fact that a root can be a power means nothing other than this: the sign designating the extraction of a root can be advantageously replaced by a factional number used as an exponent. Mathematical symbolism, translated into everyday language, can lead to contradictions; but these are, one might say, contradictions without reality, pseudocontradictions. A last example: imaginary quantities. Engels says they are in an "absurd contradiction . . . a real absurdity,"[19] but a mathematician would say that they are simply ordered couples of real numbers.

Thus mathematics—whether higher or not—underwent, during the nineteenth century, an evolution that in every way was contrary to Engels's program; it eliminated every appearance of a dialectic. Rigor in demonstrations, noncontradiction in principles, constant accord with logic; those are the ends pursued, and on the whole attained, by mathematics. One could object, certainly, that new difficulties reappeared with set theory and that the transfinite could give rise to developments having the appearance of the dialectic. But the mathematicians' attitude (their *practical* effort) toward these new paradoxes is the same as their attitude toward the old ones: far from seeing them as the result of a superior mode of thought, they examine them with horror. A new labor of logical reduction starts. We need mention here only the work of Hilbert and the Polish school.

If, in its origins, a mathematical theory can present a certain "floating" in its principles and can lack rigor in its demonstrations, that is a weakness–isn't it superfluous to say?—and not the proof] of the dialectical character of the object of science. It is true that mathematics is constructed through the denial of the degeneracies and weaknesses that its development introduces. But quite different are the completed domain of science and the detours that were necessary in order for the human mind to arrive at the point where this structure is found. The dialectic does not express the nature of mathematics; it applies to the agent and not to the object of scientific activity.

This last remark reintroduces the essential theme of this article. It is not a question of setting aside dialectical thought; one must instead try to know the limit beyond which its application in this direction is fruitful. It is useful to consider the following passage of Plekhanov: "There is not a single 'moral and political science,' as the French call them, that has not undergone the powerful and fruitful influence of Hegel."[20] This remark, which expresses the real thrust given to these sciences by the dialectic and which implies the sterility of this same method when applied to the natural sciences, coincides with the principles laid down in Hartmann's argument, which sought a domain of application for the dialectic. It is true that Plekhanov did not imagine a limit, but it is important to note that he recognized in his own way the striking privilege of the *moral and political sciences*. This is in any case a vague designation; Hartmann uses the more Hegelian expression "sciences of the spirit," which is relatively precise. But it should be understood that terminology must not prejudice anyone (in the final analysis) as to the nature of the object in question in a more or less homogeneous group of sciences, and furthermore that no precise limitation can be given in advance.

The publication of the detailed results of Hartmann's analysis will furnish the elements of a more exact labor of determination. This analysis has successively been applied to each of the numerous dialectical developments that make up the *oeuvre* of Hegel, and its preliminary goal has been to separate those developments representing a lived experience from those that are excrescences of dead flesh. But it is not necessary to wait for this publication in order to extend the domain of such investigations to include facts that were not integrated into Hegel's philosophy.

Starting from Hartmann's method, it is possible to analyze themes posed only by recent developments of science. And the fact must still be recognized that in the course of such analyses numerous subsidiary problems will necessarily be posed. From the outset this new investigation appears as an unlimited task, and it is even improbable that, starting from a comparable method imposing itself independently of the more or less open intentions to which, in Hartmann, it may correspond, the results of the two similar analyses will coincide at labor's end.

We will give here a few indications of the possibilities of a long systematic elaboration, which can lead to a readaptation of general conceptions. The precise point where introduced dialectical thought starts to express real relations must be determined in particular cases. For example, no opposition of terms can account for the biological development of a man who successively is an infant, an adolescent, an adult, and an old man. On the other hand, if one envisages the psychological development of the same man from a psychoanalytic point of view, one can say that the human being is first limited by the prohibitions that the father sets in opposition to his urges. In this precarious condition, he is reduced to unconsciously desiring the death of his father. At the same time, the wishes he directs against paternal power have their repercussions on the son's personality; he tries to bring castration down on himself, just as he brings on himself the shock of his death wishes. In most cases this negativity of the son does not express the entire real character of his life, which offers at the same time numerous and contradictory aspects. It is this negativity, however, that poses as a necessity the son's taking the place of his father, which he cannot accomplish without destroying the very negativity that had characterized him up to this point.

The importance of this theme comes from the fact that it constitutes an *experience lived* by each human being. Through this, the terms of dialectical development become elements of real existence.

Starting from this example we can moreover define the position of a certain number of problems, whereby it will be possible to indicate the orientation to which, in our opinion, the introduction of a dialectic of the real could correspond.

1. The theme of the father and son allows the demonstration of the fact that nature has not been left behind and replaced by a truly separate domain. In fact, the phenomena for which psychoanalysis accounts can be reduced in the final analysis to *drives* whose *goal* is expressed in psychological terms but whose source is of a somatic nature. There is no question here of a matter-spirit dualism; the objects of dialectical investigation represent only the most complex products of nature. The problem of their specific character can only be honestly posed if one sets aside from the outset the hateful and vulgar hypothesis of spiritualism, a move authorized precisely by psychoanalysis.

2. Not only has the domain of nature not been abandoned for phantoms that would be absolutely heterogenous to it, but the question remains whether a mode of thought founded neither directly on the study of nature nor on a work of pure logic but, as in the example we have just seen, on a *lived experience*—whether a mode of thought that seems to be directed by the very structure of the one who thinks is not susceptible to being applied, at least to a certain extent, to the understanding of nature. The first condition for whoever would attempt this application would be the awareness of the limits posed by the very origin of the method, which is another way of saying by the risky character of a hypothesis according to which the relatively simple forms of nature could be studied by using given facts furnished by the most complex.

3. Returning to the realm of practice, a last problem must be posed, which results from a difference that immediately appears between a method founded on the natural sciences and a dialectic recognizing its historical origins in lived experience. In the first, it is not possible to introduce a distinction between the opposing terms, which can be designated as positive or negative, but which are neither to the extent that these terms can be used indifferently for one or the other. Engels makes this observation himself in one of the notes published by Riazanov.[21] Very different are the examples that we consider truly valuable, in which negativity takes on a specific value. Now it would be easy to show that as a group the fundamental dialectical themes of the Marxist conception of history belong to this second category, and that their profound originality, and at

the same time their practical importance, consist precisely in the fact that they introduce into tactics a constant recourse to negative forces or actions, not as goals but as means demanded by historical development. The study of this characteristic of the dialectic is all the more important in that, surely, such methods determine both the suppleness and the power of Marxism, radically oppose it to reformist solutions,[22] and make it the living ideology of the modern proletariat, as the class condemned by the bourgeoisie to a negative existence, to the revolutionary activity that constitutes, from now on, the basis for a new society.

Notes

1. A study of this philosopher has appeared in Georges Gurvitch's *Les Tendances actuelles de la philosophie allemande*, Paris, 1930, pp. 187–206.

2. *Hegel et le problème de la dialectique du réel*, 1931, pp. 285–316.

3. *Hegel et le problème* . . . , p. 307.

4. Hartmann states: "The influence of the 'master/slave' dialectic seems less well known (than the dialectic of suffering), but its present usefulness is even greater, if that is possible; it suffices to recall that the Marxist theory of class struggle came out of it." *Revue de métaphysique*, 1931, p. 310.

5. *Encyclopedia*, section 250, Remark. [Hegel's *Philosophy of Nature*, Part II of the Encyclopedia of the Philosophical Sciences*, trans. A. V. Miller (Oxford: The Clarendon Press, 1970), pp. 23–24. Tr.]

6. We are following the translation of Laskine (Paris, 1911.) [The English translations here are from the *Anti-Dühring* (Moscow: Foreign Languages Publishing House, 1962). Tr.]

7. Lenin himself wrote of the insufficiency of works representing dialectical materialism: "The correctness of this side of the content of dialectics must be tested by the history of science. This side of dialectics as a rule receives inadequate attention (e. g., Plekhanov); the identity of opposites is taken as the sum total of *examples* ("for example, a seed," "for example, primitive communism"). The same is true of Engels. But with him it is "in the interests of popularization . . . " and not as a *law of knowledge* (and as a law of the objective world)." In "On Dialectics" (a text apparently written between 1912 and 1914), in *Materialism and Emperiocriticism* [English translation (New York: International Publishers, 1959), p. 377. Tr.]

8. *Archives Marx-Engels*, vol. 11, p. 54.

9. We will not speak here of the transformation of quantity into quality, a question that merits an in-depth study, but one that is distinct from the problems that we have wanted to consider in this article. What becomes of the value of this "law" once it is detached from its *a priori* justification? What then is its real meaning? What value should be attributed to the examples given, and to those that are not given? What are its connections with experimental laws? Can it, in the domain of the natural sciences, lead to new discoveries? These are methodological problems, which would demand a later study.

10. Our emphasis.

11. *Anti-Dühring*, p. cxii. [English translation, p. 21. Tr.]

12. *Revue de métaphysique*, 1931, pp. 289–90.

13. [For Hegel, on the contrary, mathematics is the work of abstract reason (*Verstand*) and not of concrete reason (*Vernünft*), i.e., the dialectical mode of thought.] [The long bracketed passage in the text, and note 13, were written by Raymond Queneau. Tr.]

14. Our emphasis.

15. *Anti-Dühring*, p. 148. [English translation, p. 185. Tr.]

16. *Anti-Dühring*, p. 148. [English translation, pp. 185–86. Tr.]

17. *Introduction à la théorie des fonctions*, Paris, 1886, p. viii.

18. *Anti-Dühring*, p. 172. [English translation, p. 189. Tr.]

19. *Anti-Dühring*, p. 148. [English translation, p. 167. Tr.]

20. *La Philosophie de Hegel*.

21. *Archives Marx-Engels*, 1925, vol. 2, p. 14.

22. In the *Communist Manifesto*, the revolutionary process is expressed by "measures . . . that appear economically insufficient and untenable, but that in the course of the movement, outstrip themselves . . . and are unavoidable as a means of entirely revolutionizing the mode of production." [English translation, *The Communist Manifesto* (New York: Monthly Review Press, 1964), p. 39. Tr.]

The Notion of Expenditure

I. The Insufficiency of the Principle of Classical Utility

Every time the meaning of a discussion depends on the fundamental value of the word *useful*—in other words, every time the essential question touching on the life of human societies is raised, no matter who intervenes and what opinions are expressed—it is possible to affirm that the debate is necessarily warped and that the fundamental question is eluded. In fact, given the more or less divergent collection of present ideas, there is nothing that permits one to define what is useful to man. This lacuna is made fairly prominent by the fact that it is constantly necessary to return, in the most unjustifiable way, to principles that one would like to situate beyond utility and pleasure: *honor* and *duty* are hypocritically employed in schemes of pecuniary interest and, without speaking of God, *Spirit* serves to mask the intellectual disarray of the few people who refuse to accept a closed system.

Current practice, however, is not deterred by these elementary difficulties, and common awareness at first seems able to raise only verbal objections to the principles of classical utility—in other words, to supposedly material utility. The goal of the latter is, theoretically, pleasure—but only in a moderate form, since violent pleasure is seen as *pathological*. On the one hand, this material utility is limited to acquisition (in practice, to production) and to the conservation of goods; on the other, it is limited to reproduction and to the conservation of human life (to which is added, it is true, the struggle against pain, whose importance itself suffices to indicate the negative character of the pleasure principle instituted, in theory, as the basis of utility). In the series of quantitative representations linked to this flat and untenable conception of existence only the question of reproduction seriously lends itself to controversy, because an exaggerated increase in the number of the living threatens to diminish the individual share. But on the whole, any general judgment of social activity implies the principle that all individual effort, in order to be valid, must be reducible to the fundamental necessities of production and conservation. Pleasure, whether art, permissible debauchery, or play, is definitively reduced, in the intellectual representations *in circulation*, to a concession; in other words it is reduced to a diversion whose role is subsidiary. The most appreciable share of life is given as the condition—sometimes even as the regrettable condition—of productive social activity.

It is true that personal experience—if it is a question of a youthful man, capable of wasting and destroying without reason—each time gives the lie to this miserable conception. But even when he does not spare himself and destroys himself while making allowance for nothing, the most lucid man will understand nothing, or imagine himself sick; he is incapable of a *utilitarian* justification for his actions, and it does not occur to him that a human society can have, just as he does, an *interest* in considerable losses, in catastrophes that, *while conforming to well-defined needs*, provoke tumultuous depressions, crises of dread, and, in the final analysis, a certain orgiastic state.

In the most crushing way, the contradiction between current social conceptions and the real needs of society recalls the narrowness of judgment that puts the father in opposition to the satisfaction of his son's needs. This narrowness is such that it is impossible for the son to express his will. The father's partially malevolent solicitude is manifested in the things he provides for his son: lodgings, clothes, food, and, when absolutely necessary, a little harmless recreation. But the son does not even have the right to speak about what really gives him a fever; he is obliged to give people the impression that for him no *horror* can enter into consideration. In this respect, it is sad to say that *conscious humanity has remained a minor*; humanity recognizes the right to acquire, to conserve, and to consume rationally, but it excludes in principle *nonproductive expenditure*.

It is true that this exclusion is superficial and that it no more modifies practical activities than prohibitions limit the son, who indulges in his unavowed pleasures as soon as he is no longer in his father's presence. Humanity can allow itself the pleasure of expressing, in the father's interest, conceptions marked with flat paternal sufficiency and blindness. In the practice of life, however, humanity acts in a way that allows for the satisfaction of disarmingly savage needs, and it seems able to subsist only at the limits of horror. Moreover, to the small extent that a man is incapable of yielding to considerations that either are official or are susceptible of becoming so, to the small extent that he is inclined to feel the attraction of a life devoted to the destruction of established authority, it is difficult to believe that a peaceful world, conforming to his interests, could be for him anything other than a convenient illusion.

The difficulties met with in the development of a conception that is not guided by the servile mode of father-son relations are thus not insurmountable. It is possible to admit the historical necessity of vague and disappointing images, used by a majority of people, who do not act without a minimum of error (which they use as if it were a drug)—and who, moreover, in all circumstances refuse to find their way in a labyrinth resulting from human inconsistencies. An extreme simplification represents, for the uncultivated or barely cultivated segments of the population, the only chance to avoid a diminution of aggressive force. But it would be cowardly to accept, as a limit to understanding, the conditions of poverty and necessity in which such simplified images are formed. And if a less arbitrary conception is condemned to remain esoteric, and if as such, in the present circumstances, it comes into conflict with an unhealthy repulsion, then one must stress that this repulsion is precisely the shame of a generation whose rebels are afraid of the noise of their own words. Thus one cannot take it into account.

II. The Principle of Loss

Human activity is not entirely reducible to processes of production and conservation, and consumption must be divided into two distinct parts. The first, reducible part is represented by the use of the minimum necessary for the conservation of life and the continuation of individuals' productive activity in a given society; it is therefore a question simply of the fundamental condition of productive activity. The second part is represented by so-called unproductive expenditures: luxury, mourning, war, cults, the construction of sumptuary monuments, games, spectacles, arts, perverse sexual activity (i.e., deflected from genital finality)—all these represent activities which, at least in primitive circumstances, have no end beyond themselves. Now it is necessary to reserve the use of the word *expenditure* for the designation of these unproductive forms, and not for the designation of all the modes of consumption that serve as a means to the end of production. Even though it is always possible to set the various forms of expenditure in opposition to each other, they constitute a group characterized by the fact that in each case the accent is placed on a *loss* that must be as great as possible in order for that activity to take on its true meaning.

This principle of loss, in other words, of unconditional expenditure, no matter how contrary it might be to the economic principle of balanced accounts (expenditure regularly compensated for by acquisition), only *rational* in the narrow sense of the word, can be illustrated through a small number of examples taken from common experience:

1. Jewels must not only be beautiful and dazzling (which would make the substitution of imitations possible): one sacrifices a fortune, preferring a diamond necklace; such a sacrifice is necessary for the constitution of this necklace's fascinating character. This fact must be seen in relation to the symbolic value of jewels, universal in psychoanalysis. When in a dream a diamond signifies excrement, it is not only a question of association by contrast; in the unconscious, jewels, like excrement, are cursed matter that flows from a wound: they are a part of oneself destined for open sacrifice (they serve, in fact, as sumptuous gifts charged with sexual love). The functional character of jewels requires their immense material value and alone explains the inconsequence of the most beautiful imitations, which are very nearly useless.

2. Cults require a bloody wasting of men and animals in *sacrifice*. In the etymological sense of the word, sacrifice is nothing other than the production of *sacred* things.

From the very first, it appears that sacred things are constituted by an operation of loss: in particular, the success of Christianity must be explained by the value of the theme of the Son of God's ignominious crucifixion, which carries human dread to a representation of loss and limitless degradation.

3. In various competitive games, loss in general is produced under complex conditions. Considerable sums of money are spent for the maintenance of quarters, animals, equipment, or men. As much energy as possible is squandered in order to produce a feeling of stupefaction—in any case with an intensity infinitely greater than in productive enterprises. The danger of death is not avoided; on the contrary, it is the object of a strong unconscious attraction. Besides, competitions are sometimes the occasion for the public distribution of prizes. Immense crowds are present; their passions most often burst forth beyond any restraint, and the loss of insane sums of money is set in motion in the form of wagers. It is true that this circulation of money profits a small number of professional bettors, but it is no less true that this circulation can be considered to be a real *charge* of the passions unleashed by competition and that, among a large number of bettors, it leads to losses disproportionate to their means; these even attain such a level of madness that often the only way out for gamblers is prison or death. Beyond this, various modes of unproductive expenditure can be linked, depending on the circumstances, to great competitive spectacles, just as elements moving separately are caught up in a mightier whirlwind. Thus horse races are associated with a sumptuary process of social classification (the existence of Jockey Clubs need only be mentioned) and the ostentatious display of the latest luxurious fashions. It is necessary in any case to observe that the complex of expenditure represented by present-day racing is insignificant when compared to the extravagance of the Byzantines, who tied the totality of their public activity to equestrian competition.

4. From the point of view of expenditure, artistic productions must be divided

into two main categories, the first constituted by architectural construction, music, and dance. This category is comprised of *real* expenditures. Nevertheless, sculpture and painting, not to mention the use of sites for ceremonies and spectacles, introduces even into architecture the principle of the second category, that of *symbolic* expenditure. For their part, music and dance can easily be charged with external significations.

In their major form, literature and theater, which constitute the second category, provoke dread and horror through symbolic representations of tragic loss (degradation or death); in their minor form, they provoke laughter through representations which, though analogously structured, exclude certain seductive elements. The term poetry, applied to the least degraded and least intellectualized forms of the expression of a state of loss, can be considered synonymous with expenditure; it in fact signifies, in the most precise way, creation by means of loss. Its meaning is therefore close to that of *sacrifice*. It is true that the word "poetry" can only be appropriately applied to an extremely rare residue of what it commonly signifies and that, without a preliminary reduction, the worst confusions could result; it is, however, impossible in a first, rapid exposition to speak of the infinitely variable limits separating subsidiary formations from the residual element of poetry. It is easier to indicate that, for the rare human beings who have this element at their disposal, poetic expenditure ceases to be symbolic in its consequences; thus, to a certain extent, the function of representation engages the very life of the one who assumes it. It condemns him to the most disappointing forms of activity, to misery, to despair, to the pursuit of inconsistent shadows that provide nothing but vertigo or rage. The poet frequently can use words only for his own loss; he is often forced to choose between the destiny of a reprobate, who is as profoundly separated from society as dejecta are from apparent life, and a renunciation whose price is a mediocre activity, subordinated to vulgar and superficial needs.

III. Production, Exchange, and Unproductive Activity

Once the existence of expenditure as a social function has been established, it is then necessary to consider the relations between this function and those of production and acquisition that are opposed to it. These relations immediately present themselves as those of an *end* with *utility*. And if it is true that production and acquisition in their development and changes of form introduce a variable that must be understood in order to comprehend historical processes, they are, however, still only means subordinated to expenditure. As dreadful as it is, human poverty has never had a strong enough hold on societies to cause the concern for conservation—which gives production the appearance of an end—to dominate the concern for unproductive expenditure. In order to maintain this preeminence, since power is exercised by the classes that expend, poverty was excluded from all social activity. And the poor have no other way of reentering the circle of power than through the revolutionary destruction of the classes occupying that circle—in other words, through a bloody and in no way limited social expenditure.

The secondary character of production and acquisition in relation to expenditure appears most clearly in primitive economic institutions, since exchange is still treated as a sumptuary loss of ceded objects: thus at its *base* exchange presents itself as a process of expenditure, over which a process of acquisition has developed. Classical economics imagined that primitive exchange occurred in the form of barter; it had no reason to assume, in fact, that a means of acquisition such as exchange might have as its origin not the need to acquire that it satisfies today, but the contrary need, the need to destroy and to lose. The traditional conceptions of the origins of economy have only recently been disproved—even so recently that a great number of economists continue arbitrarily to represent barter as the ancestor of commerce.

In opposition to the artificial notion of barter, the archaic form of exchange has been identified by Mauss under the name *potlatch*,[1] borrowed from the Northwestern American Indians who provided such a remarkable example of it. Institutions analogous to the Indian *potlatch*, or their traces, have been very widely found.

The *potlatch* of the Tlingit, the Haida, the Tsimshian, and the Kwakiutl of the northwestern coast has been studied in detail since the end of the nineteenth century (but at that time it was not compared with the archaic forms of exchange of other countries). The least advanced of these American tribes practice *potlatch* on the occasion of a person's change in situation—initiations, marriages, funerals—and, even in a more evolved form, it can never be separated from a festival; whether it provides the occasion for this festival, or whether it takes place on the festival's occasion. *Potlatch* excludes all bargaining and, in general, it is constituted by a considerable gift of riches, offered openly and with the goal of humiliating, defying, and *obligating* a rival. The exchange value of the gift results from the fact that the donee, in order to efface the humiliation and respond to the challenge, must satisfy the obligation (incurred by him at the time of acceptance) to respond later with a more valuable gift, in other words, to return with interest.

But the gift is not the only form of *potlatch*; it is equally possible to defy rivals through the spectacular destruction of wealth. It is through the intermediary of this last form that *potlatch* is reunited with religious sacrifice, since what is destroyed is theoretically offered to the mythical ancestors of the donees. Relatively recently a Tlingit chief appeared before his rival to slash the throats of some of his own slaves. This destruction was repaid at a given date by the slaughter of a greater number of slaves. The Tchoukchi of far northwestern Siberia, who have institutions analogous to *potlatch*, slaughter dog teams in order to stifle and humiliate another group. In northwestern America, destruction goes as far as the burning of villages and the smashing of flotillas of canoes. Emblazoned copper ingots, a kind of money on which the fictive value of an immense fortune is sometimes placed, are broken or thrown into the sea. The delirium of the festival can be associated equally with hecatombs of property and with gifts accumulated with the intention of stunning and humiliating.

Usury, which regularly appears in these operations as obligatory surplus at the time of the returned *potlatch*, gives rise to the observation that the loan with interest must be substituted for barter in the history of the origins of exchange. It must be recognized, in fact, that wealth is multiplied in *potlatch* civilizations in a way that recalls the inflation of credit in banking civilizations; in other words, it would be impossible to realize at once all the wealth possessed by the total number of donors resulting from the obligations contracted by the total number of donees. But this comparison applies only to a secondary characteristic of *potlatch*.

It is the constitution of a positive property of loss—from which spring nobility, honor, and rank in a hierarchy—that gives the institution its significant value. The gift must be considered as a loss and thus as a partial destruction, since the desire to destroy is in part transferred onto the recipient. In unconscious forms, such as those described by psychoanalysis, it symbolizes excretion, which itself is linked to death, in conformity with the fundamental connection between anal eroticism and sadism. The excremental symbolism of emblazoned coppers, which on the Northwest Coast are the gift objects *par excellence*, is based on a very rich mythology. In Melanesia, the donor designates as his excrement magnificent gifts, which he deposits at the feet of the rival chief.

The consequences in the realm of acquisition are only the unwanted result—at least to the extent that the drives that govern the operation have remained primitive—of a process oriented in the opposite direction. "The ideal," indicates Mauss, "would be to give a *potlatch* and not have it returned." This ideal is realized in certain forms of destruction to which custom allows no possible response. Moreover, since the yields of *potlatch* are in some ways pledged in advance in a new *potlatch*, the archaic principle of wealth is displayed with none of the attenuations that result from the avarice developed at later stages; wealth appears as an acquisition to the extent that power is acquired by a rich man, but it is entirely directed toward loss in the sense that this power is characterized as power to lose. It is only through loss that glory and honor are linked to wealth.

As a game, *potlatch* is the opposite of a principle of conservation: it puts an end to the stability of fortunes as it existed within the totemic economy, where possession was hereditary. An activity of excessive exchange replaced heredity (as source of possession) with a kind of deliriously formed ritual poker. But the players can never retire from the game, their fortunes made; they remain at the mercy of provocation. At no time does a fortune serve to *shelter its owner from need*. On the contrary, it functionally remains—as does its possessor—*at the mercy of a need for limitless loss*, which exists endemically in a social group.

The nonsumptuary production and consumption upon which wealth depends thus appear as relative utility.

IV. The Functional Expenditure of the Wealthy Classes

The notion of *potlatch*, strictly speaking, should be reserved for expenditures of an agonistic type, which are instigated by challenges and which lead to responses. More precisely, it should be reserved for forms which, for archaic societies, are not distinguishable from *exchange*.

It is important to know that exchange, at its origin, was *immediately* subordinated to a human *end*; nevertheless it is evident that its development, linked to progress in the modes of production, only started at the stage at which this subordination ceased to be immediate. The very principle of the function of production requires that products be exempt from loss, at least provisionally.

In the market economy, the processes of exchange have an acquisitive sense. Fortunes are no longer placed on a gambling table; they have become relatively stable. It is only to the extent that stability is assured and can no longer be compromised by even considerable losses that these losses are submitted to the regime of unproductive expenditure. Under these new conditions, the elementary components of *potlatch* are found in forms that are no longer as directly agonistic.[2] Expenditure is still destined to acquire or maintain rank, but in principle it no longer has the goal of causing another to lose his rank.

In spite of these attenuations, ostentatious loss remains universally linked to wealth, as its ultimate function.

More or less narrowly, social rank is linked to the possession of a fortune, but only on the condition that the fortune be partially sacrificed in unproductive social expenditures such as festivals, spectacles, and games. One notes that in primitive societies, where the exploitation of man by man is still fairly weak, the products of human activity not only flow in great quantities to rich men because of the protection or social leadership services these men supposedly provide, but also because of the spectacular collective expenditures for which they must pay. In so-called civilized societies, the fundamental *obligation* of wealth disappeared only in a fairly recent period. The decline of paganism led to a decline of the games and cults for which wealthy Romans were obliged to pay; thus it has been said that Christianity individualized property, giving its possessor total control over his products and abrogating his social function. It abrogated at least the obligation of this expenditure, for Christianity replaced pagan expenditure prescribed by custom with voluntary alms, either in the form of distributions from the rich to the poor, or (and above all) in the form of extremely significant contributions to churches and later to monasteries. And these churches and monasteries precisely assumed, in the Middle Ages, the major part of the spectacular function.

Today the great and free forms of unproductive social expenditure have disappeared. One must not conclude from this, however, that the very principle of expenditure is no longer the end of economic activity.

A certain evolution of wealth, whose symptoms indicate sickness and exhaustion, leads to shame in oneself accompanied by petty hypocrisy. Everything that was generous, orgiastic, and excessive has disappeared; the themes of rivalry upon which individual activity still depends develop in obscurity, and are as shameful as belching. The representatives of the bourgeoisie have adopted an effaced manner; wealth is now displayed behind closed doors, in accordance with depressing and boring conventions. In addition, people in the middle class—employees and small shopkeepers—having attained mediocre or minute fortunes, have managed to debase and subdivide ostentatious expenditure, of which nothing remains but vain efforts tied to tiresome rancor.

Such trickery has become the principle reason for living, working, and suffering for those who lack the courage to condemn this moldy society to revolutionary destruction. Around modern banks, as around the totem poles of the Kwakiutl, the same desire to dazzle animates individuals and leads them into a system of petty displays that blinds them to each other, as if they were staring into a blinding light. A few steps from the bank, jewels, dresses, and cars wait behind shop windows for the day when they will serve to establish the augmented splendor of a sinister industrialist and his even more sinister old wife. At a lower level, gilded clocks, dining room buffets, and artificial flowers render equally shameful service to a grocer and his wife. Jealousy arises between human beings, as it does among the savages, and with an equivalent brutality; only generosity and nobility have disappeared, and with them the dazzling contrast that the rich provided to the poor.

As the class that possesses the wealth—having received with wealth the obligation of functional expenditure—the modern bourgeoisie is characterized by the refusal in principle of this obligation. It has distinguished itself from the aristocracy through the fact that it has consented only to *spend for itself*, and within itself—in other words, by hiding its expenditures as much as possible from the eyes of the other classes. This particular form was originally due to the development of its wealth in the shadow of a more powerful noble class. The rationalist conceptions developed by the bourgeoisie, starting in the seventeenth century, were a response to these humiliating conceptions of restrained expenditure; this rationalism meant nothing other than the strictly economic representation of the world—economic in the vulgar sense, the bourgeois sense, of the word. The hatred of expenditure is the *raison d'être* of and the justification for the bourgeoisie; it is at the same time the principle of its horrifying hypocrisy. A fundamental grievance of the bourgeois was the prodigality of feudal society and, after coming to power, they believed that, because of their habits of accumulation, they were capable of acceptably dominating the poorer classes. And it is right to recognize that the people are incapable of hating them as much as their former masters, to the extent that they are incapable of loving them, for the bourgeois are incapable of concealing a sordid face, a face so rapacious and lacking in nobility, so frighteningly small, that all human life, upon seeing it, seems degraded.

In opposition, the people's consciousness is reduced to maintaining profoundly the principle of expenditure by representing bourgeois existence as the shame of man and as a sinister cancellation.

V. Class Struggle

In trying to maintain sterility in regard to expenditure, in conformity with a reasoning that balances *accounts*, bourgeois society has only managed to develop a universal meanness. Human life only rediscovers agitation on the scale of irreducible needs through the efforts of those who push the consequences of current rationalist conceptions as far as they will go. What remains of the traditional modes of expenditure has become atrophied, and living sumptuary tumult has been lost in the unprecedented explosion of *class struggle*.

The components of *class struggle* are seen in the process of expenditure, dating back to the archaic period. In *potlatch*, the rich man distributes products furnished him by other, impoverished, men. He tries to rise above a rival who is rich like himself, but the ultimate stage of his foreseen elevation has no more necessary a goal than his further separation from the nature of destitute men. Thus expenditure, even though it might be a social function, immediately leads to an agonistic and apparently antisocial act of separation. The rich man consumes the poor man's losses, creating for him a category of degradation and abjection that leads to slavery. Now it is evident that, from the endlessly transmitted heritage of the sumptuary world, the modern world has received slavery, and has reserved it for the proletariat. Without a doubt bourgeois society, which pretends to govern according to rational principles, and which, through its own actions, moreover, tends to realize a certain human homogeneity, does not accept without protest a division that seems destructive to man himself; it is incapable, however, of pushing this resistance further than theoretical negation. It gives the workers rights equal to those of the masters, and it announces this *equality* by inscribing that word on walls. But the masters, who act as if they were the expression of society itself, are preoccupied—more seriously than with any other concern—with showing that they do not in any way share the abjection of the men they employ. *The end of the workers' activity is to produce in order to live, but the bosses' activity is to produce in order to condemn the working producers to a hideous degradation*—for there is no disjunction possible between, on the one hand, the characterization the bosses seek through their modes of expenditure, which tend to elevate them high above human baseness, and on the other hand this baseness itself, of which this characterization is a function.

In opposition to this conception of agonistic social expenditure, there is the representation of numerous bourgeois efforts to ameliorate the lot of the workers—but this representation is only the expression of the cowardice of the modern upper classes, who no longer have the force to recognize the results of their own destructive acts. The expenditures taken on by the capitalists in order to aid the proletarians and give them a chance to pull themselves up on the social ladder only bear witness to their inability (due to exhaustion) to carry out thoroughly a sumptuary process. Once the loss of the poor man is accomplished, little by little the pleasure of the rich man is emptied and neutralized; it gives way to a kind of apathetic indifference. Under these conditions, in order to maintain a neutral state rendered relatively agreeable by apathy (and which exists in spite of troublesome elements such as sadism and pity), it can be useful to compensate for the expenditure that engenders abjection with a new expenditure, which tends to attenuate it. The bosses' political sense, together with certain partial developments of prosperity, has allowed this process of compensation to be, at times, quite extensive. Thus in the Anglo-Saxon countries, and in particular in the United States of America, the primary process takes place at the expense of only a relatively small portion of the population: to a certain extent, the working class itself has been led to participate in it (above all when this was facilitated by the preliminary existence of a class held to be abject by common accord, as in the case of the blacks). But these subterfuges, whose importance is in any case strictly limited, do not modify in any way the fundamental division between noble and ignoble men. The cruel game of social life does not vary among the different civilized countries, where the insulting splendor of the rich loses and degrades the human nature of the lower class.

It must be added that the attenuation of the masters' brutality—which in any case has less to do with destruction itself than with the psychological tendencies to destroy—corresponds to the general atrophy of the ancient sumptuary processes that characterizes the modern era.

Class struggle, on the contrary, becomes the grandest form of social expenditure when it is taken up again and developed, this time on the part of the workers, and on such a scale that it threatens the very existence of the masters.

VI. Christianity and Revolution

Short of revolt, it has been possible for the provoked poor to refuse all moral participation in a system in which men oppress men; in certain historical circumstances, they succeeded, through the use of symbols even more striking than reality, in lowering all of "human nature" to such a horrifying ignominy that the pleasure found by the rich in measuring the poverty of others suddenly became too acute to be endured without vertigo. Thus, independently of all ritual forms, an exchange of exasperated challenges was established, exacerbated above all by the poor, a *potlatch* in which real refuse and revealed moral filth entered into a rivalry of horrible grandeur with everything in the world that was rich, pure, and brilliant; and an exceptional outlet was found for this form of spasmodic convulsion in religious despair, which was its unreserved exploitation.

In Christianity, the alternations between the exaltation and dread, tortures and orgies constituting religious life were conjoined in a more tragic way and were merged with a sick social structure, which was tearing itself apart with the dirtiest cruelty. The triumphal song of the Christians glorifies God because he has entered into the bloody game of social war, and because he has "hurled the powerful from the heights of their grandeur and has exalted the miserably poor." Their myths associate social ignominy and the cadaverous degradation of the torture victim with divine splendor. In this way religion assumes the total oppositional function manifested by contrary forces, which up to this point had been divided between the rich and the poor, with the one group condemning the other to ruin. It is closely tied to terrestrial despair, since it itself is only an epiphenomenon of the measureless hate that divides men—but an epiphenomenon that tends to substitute itself for the totality of divergent processes it summarizes. In conformity with the words attributed to Christ, who said he came to divide and not to reign, religion thus does not at all try to do away with what others consider the scourge of man. On the contrary, in its immediate form, it wallows in a revolting impurity that is indispensable to its ecstatic torment.

The meaning of Christianity is given in the development of the delirious consequences of the expenditure of classes, in a mental agonistic orgy practiced at the expense of the real struggle.

However, in spite of the importance that it has had in human activity, Christian *humiliation* is only an episode in the historic struggle of the ignoble against the noble, of the impure against the pure. It is as if society, conscious of its own intolerable splitting, had become for a time dead drunk in order to enjoy it sadistically. But the heaviest drunkenness has not done away with the consequences of human poverty, and, with the exploited classes opposing the superior classes with greater lucidity, no conceivable limit can be assigned to hatred. In historical agitation, only the word Revolution dominates the customary confusion and carries with it the promise that answers the unlimited demands of the masses. As for the masters and the exploiters, whose function is to create the contemptuous forms that exclude human nature—causing this nature to exist at the limits of the earth, in other words in mud—a simple law of reciprocity requires that they be condemned to fear, to the *great night* when their beautiful phrases will be drowned out by death screams in riots. That is the bloody hope which, each day, is one with the existence of the people, and which sums up the insubordinate content of the class struggle.

Class struggle has only one possible end: the loss of those who have worked to lose "human nature."

But whatever form of development is foreseen, be it revolutionary or servile, the general convulsions constituted eighteen hundred years ago by the religious ecstasy of the Christians, and today by the workers' movement, must equally be represented as a decisive impulse *constraining* society to use the exclusion of one class by another to realize a mode of expenditure as tragic and as free as possible, and at the same time *constraining* it to introduce sacred forms so human that the traditional forms become relatively contemptible. It is the tropic character of such movements that accounts for the total human value of the workers' Revolution, a Revolution capable of exerting a force of attraction as strong as the force that directs simple organisms toward the sun.

VII. The Insubordination of Material Facts

Human life, distinct from juridical existence, existing as it does on a globe isolated in celestial space, from night to day and from one country to another—human life cannot in any way be limited to the closed systems assigned to it by reasonable conceptions. The immense travail of recklessness, discharge, and upheaval that constitutes life could be expressed by stating that life starts only with the deficit of these systems; at least what it allows in the way of order and reserve has meaning only from the moment when the ordered and reserved forces liberate and lose themselves for ends that cannot be subordinated to anything one can account for. It is only by such insubordination—even if it is impoverished—that the human race ceases to be isolated in the unconditional splendor of material things.

In fact, in the most universal way, isolated or in groups, men find themselves constantly engaged in processes of expenditure. Variations in form do not in any way alter the fundamental characteristics of these processes, whose principle is loss. A certain excitation, whose sum total is maintained at a noticeably constant level, animates collectivities and individuals. In their intensified form, the *states of excitation*, which are comparable to toxic states, can be defined as the illogical and irresistible impulse to reject material or moral goods that it would have been possible to utilize rationally (in conformity with the balancing of accounts). Connected to the losses that are realized in this way—in the case of the "lost woman" as well as in the case of military expenditure—is the creation of unproductive values; the most absurd of these values, and the one that makes people the most rapacious, is *glory*. Made complete through degradation, glory, appearing in a sometimes sinister and sometimes brilliant form, has never ceased to dominate social existence; it is impossible to attempt to do anything without it when it is dependent on the blind practice of personal or social loss.

In this way the boundless refuse of activity pushes human plans—including those associated with economic operations—into the game of characterizing universal matter; matter, in fact, can only be defined as the *nonlogical difference* that represents in relation to the *economy* of the universe what *crime* represents in relation to the law. The glory that sums up or symbolizes (without exhausting) the object of free expenditure, while it can never exclude crime, cannot be distinguished—at least if one takes into account the only characterization that has a value comparable to matter—from the *insubordinate characterization*, which is not the condition for anything else.

If in addition to one demonstrates the interest, concurrent with glory (as well as with degradation), which the human community necessarily sees in the qualitative change constantly realized by the movement of history, and if, finally, one demonstrates that this movement is impossible to contain or direct toward a limited end, it becomes possible, having abandoned all reserves, to assign a *relative* value to utility. Men assure their own subsistence or avoid suffering, not because these functions themselves lead to a sufficient result, but in order to accede to the insubordinate function of free expenditure.

Notes

1. On *potlatch*, see above all Marcel Mauss, ''Essai sur le don, form archaïque de l'échange'' in *Année sociologique*, 1925. [Translated as *The Gift: Forms and Functions of Exchange in Archaic Societies*, trans. I. Cunnison (New York: Norton, 1967). Tr.]

2. In other words: involving rivalry and struggle.

Sacrifices

I

Me,[1] I exist—suspended in a realized void—suspended from my own dread—different from all other being and such that the various events that can reach all other being and not *me* cruelly throw this *me* out of a total existence. But, at the same time, I consider my coming into the world—which depended on the birth and on the conjunction of a given man and woman, then on the moment of their conjunction. There exists, in fact, a unique moment in relation to the possibility of me—and thus the infinite improbability of this coming into the world appears. For if the tiniest difference had occurred in the course of the successive events of which I am the result, in the place of this *me*, integrally avid to be *me*, there would have been "an *other*."

The immense realized void is this infinite improbability and across it I, as imperative existence, play, because a simple presence suspended above such an immensity is comparable to the exercise of a dominion, as if the void in whose midst I am demands that I be *me* and the dread of this *me*. The immediate exigency of nothingness would thus imply not undifferentiated being but the painful improbability of the unique *me*.

The empirical knowledge of the structure this *me* has in common with the other *mes* has become an absurdity in this void where my dominion manifests itself, for the very essence of the *me* that I am consists in the fact that no other conceivable existence can replace it; the total improbability of my coming into the world poses, in an imperative mode, a total heterogeneity.

A fortiori a historical representation of the formation of *me* (considered as a part of everything that is an object of knowledge) and of its imperative or impersonal modes dissipates, and this allows only the subsistence of the violence and the avidity for the dominion of the *me* over the void in which it is suspended; at will, even in its prison, the *me* that I am realizes everything that preceded it or surrounds it, whether it exists as life or as simple being, as a void submitted to its anxious dominion.

The fact of supposing the existence of a possible and even necessary point of view that demands the inaccuracy of such a revelation (this supposition is implied by the recourse to expression) in no way invalidates the immediate reality of the experience lived by the imperative presence in the world of *me*; this lived experience *equally* constitutes an inevitable point of view, a direction of being required by the eagerness of its own movement.

II

A choice between opposing representations must be linked to the inconceivable solution to the problem of *that which exists*: *what exists* as profound existence liberated from the forms of *appearance*? Most often the hasty and ill-considered answer is given as if the question *what is there that is imperative*? (what is the moral value) and not *what exists*? had been posed. In other cases—where philosophy is deprived of its object—the no less hasty response is only the perfect and partial avoidance (and not the destruction) of the problem, if matter is represented as profound existence.

But from this it is possible to see—within the relatively clear given limits, beyond which doubt itself disappears with the other possibilities—that, while the meanings of all positive judgments on profound existence are not distinguishable from fundamental value judgments, thought remains free on the other hand to constitute the *me* as a foundation of all value without confusing this *me* (the value) with profound existence, and even without inscribing it within the framework of a reality that is manifest but hidden from plain sight.

The *me*, completely other due to its constitutive improbability, has been rejected in the course of the normal search for "that which exists" as the arbitrary but eminent image of nonexistence; it is as *illusion* that it responds to the extreme demands of life. In other words, the *me*, as an impasse outside of "that which exists"—and in which are found reunited, without any way out, all the extreme values of life—even though it is constituted in the presence of reality, does not belong in anyway to this reality, which it transcends. It neutralizes itself (ceases to be completely *other*) insofar as it ceases to be aware of the total improbability of its coming into the world, and consequently of its fundamental lack of relations with the world (to the extent that it is explicitly known—represented as the interdependence and chronological succession of objects—the world, as the integral development of that which exists, must in fact appear necessary or probable).

In an arbitrary order where each element of self-awareness escapes from the world (absorbed in the convulsive projection of the *me*), to the extent that philosophy, renouncing all hope of logical construction, arrives at—as at an end—a representation of relations defined as improbable (and which are only the middle terms of ultimate improbability), it is possible to represent the *me* in tears, or anxious; it can equally be thrown, in the case of a painful erotic choice, in the direction of a *me* other than itself but also other than any other. And thus the *me* can increase, as far as the eye can see, its painful awareness of its own escape out of the world—but it is only at the boundary of death that laceration, which constitutes the very nature of the immensely free *me*, transcending "that which exists," is revealed with violence.

In the coming of death, there appears a structure of the *me* that is entirely different from the "abstract me" (discovered, not through an active reflection reacting against all opposing limits, but through a logical investigation giving itself the form of its object in advance). This specific structure of the *me* is also distinct from the moments of personal existence, locked away due to practical activity and neutralized in the logical appearances of "that which exists." The *me* accedes to its specificity and to its integral transcendence only in the form of the "*me* that dies."

But this revelation of the *me* that dies is not given each time simple death is revealed to dread. It supposes the imperative completion and sovereignty of being at the moment it is projected into the unreal time of death. It supposes at once the exigency and the limitless breakdown of imperative life, the consequence of pure seduction and the heroic form of the *me*; it thus attains the rending subversion of the *god* that dies.

The death of the god is produced not as metaphysical alteration (concerning the common denominator of being), but as the absorption of a life avid for imperative joy in the heavy animality of death. The filthy aspects of the torn-apart body guarantee the totality of disgust where life subsides.

In this revelation of free, divine nature, the obstinate orientation of the avidity of life toward death (as it is given in every form of play or dream) no longer appears as a need for cancellation, but as the pure avidity to be *me*, death or the void being only the domain where—by its very breakdown—a dominion of the *me*, which must be represented as vertigo, infinitely raises itself up. This *me*, and this dominion, arrive at the purity of their desperate nature and thus realize the pure hope of the *me* that dies: it is the hope of a drunken man, pushing the boundaries of the dream beyond all conceivable limits.

At the same time the shadow of the divine person, laden with love, disappears—not exactly as vain appearance, but as dependence on a denied world that is founded on the reciprocal dependence of its parts.

It was the will to purify love of all preconditions that posed the unconditional existence of God as the supreme object of a rapturous escape from the self. But the conditional counterpart of divine majesty—the principle of political authority—leads the affective movement into the linkage of oppressed existences with moral imperatives; the affective movement is thrown back into the platitude of applied life, where the *me* as *me* withers away.

When the man-god appears and dies both as rottenness and as the redemption of the supreme person, revealing that life will answer avidity only on condition that it be lived as the *me* that dies, he nonetheless eludes the pure imperative of this *me*: he subjects it to the applied (moral) imperative of God and thus gives the *me* as existence *for others*, for God, and morality alone as existence *for itself*.

In an ideally brilliant and empty infinity, chaos to the point of revealing the absence of chaos, the anxious loss of life opens, but life only loses itself—at the limit of the last breath—*for this empty infinity*. The me raises itself to the pure imperative, living-dying for an abyss without walls or floor; this imperative is formulated as ''die like a dog'' in the strangest part of being. It abandons all applications in the world.

In the fact that life and death are passionately devoted to the subsidence of the void, the slave's subordinate relation to the master is no longer revealed, but life and void are confused and mingled like lovers, in the convulsive movements of the end. Burning passion is no longer acceptance and realization of nothingness: nothingness is still a cadaver; brilliance is the blood that flows and coagulates.

And just as the freed obscene nature of their organs more passionately connects embracing lovers, so too the nearby horror of the cadaver and the present horror of blood tie the *me* that dies more obscurely to an empty infinity—and this empty infinity is itself projected as cadaver and as blood.

III

In this hasty and still confused revelation of an ultimate region of being, at which philosophy, like all communal human determinations, only arrives in spite of itself (like a manhandled corpse), the fundamental problem of being was even suspended when the aggressive subversion of the *me* accepted illusion as the adequate description of its nature. In this way all possible mysticism was rejected, in other words, all particular revelation to which respect could have given form. Likewise, the imperative avidity for life, ceasing to accept as its domain the narrow circle of logically ordered appearances, had nothing more than an unknown death at the summit of its avid elevation and as object it had nothing more than the reflection of this death in deserted night.

Christian meditation before the cross was no longer rejected with simple hostility, but assumed in a total hostility that demanded embracing the cross—in hand-to-hand combat. And thus it must and it can be lived as death of the *me*, not as respectful adoration but with the avidity of sadistic ecstasy, the surge of a *blind* madness that alone accedes to the *passion* of the pure imperative.

In the course of the ecstatic vision, at the limit of death on the cross and of the blindly lived *lamma sabachtani*, the object is finally unveiled as *catastrophe* in a chaos of light and shadow, neither as God nor as nothingness, but as the object that love, incapable of liberating itself except outside of itself, demands in order to let out the scream of lacerated existence.

In this position of object as *catastrophe*, thought lives the annihilation that constitutes it as a vertiginous and infinite fall, and thus has not only catastrophe as its object; its very structure is *catastrophe*—it is itself absorption in the nothingness that supports it and at the same time slips away. Something immense is liberated from all sides with the magnitude of a cataract, surging forth from unreal regions of the infinite, sinking into them in a movement of inconceivable force. The mirror that, in the crash of telescoping trains, suddenly slashes open one's throat is the expression of this imperative—implacable—but already annihilated irruption.

In common circumstances, time appears locked—and practically annulled—in each permanent form and in each succession that can be grasped as permanence. Each movement susceptible of being inscribed in an order annuls time, which is absorbed in a system of measure and equivalence—thus time, having become virtually reversible, withers, and with time all existence.

However, burning love—consuming the existence exhaled with great screams—has no other horizon than a catastrophe, a scene of horror that releases time from its bonds.

Catastrophe—lived time—must be represented ecstatically not in the form of an old man, but as a skeleton armed with a scythe: a glacial and gleaming skeleton, to whose teeth adhere the lips of a severed head. As skeleton it is completed destruction, but armed destruction amounting to imperative purity.

Destruction gnaws deeply and thus purifies sovereignty itself. The imperative purity of time is opposed to God, whose skeleton is hidden behind gold draperies, under a tiara, and behind a mask: the divine mask and suavity express the application of an imperative form, giving itself as providence for the management of political oppression. But in divine love the freezing gleam of a sadistic skeleton is infinitely unveiled.

Revolt—its face distorted by amorous ecstasy—tears from God his naive mask, and thus oppression collapses in the crash of time. Catastrophe is that by which a nocturnal horizon is set ablaze, that for which lacerated existence goes into a trance—it is the Revolution—it is time released from all bonds; it is pure change; it is a skeleton that emerges from its cadaver as from a cocoon and that sadistically lives the unreal existence of death.

IV

Thus the nature of time as object of ecstasy reveals itself in accordance with the ecstatic nature of the *me* that dies. For the one and the other are pure change and both take place on the plane of an illusory existence.

But if the avid and obstinate question "what exists?" still traverses the immense disorder of living thought in the mode of the *me* that dies, what will be the meaning, at this moment, of the answer: "time is only an empty absurdity"?—or of all the other answers that refuse the being of time?

Or what will be the meaning of the opposite answer: "being is time"?

More clearly than in an order limited to the narrow realizations of order, the problem of the being of time can be elucidated in a disorder embracing the totality of conceivable forms. First of all the effort at a dialectical construction of contradictory answers is set aside insofar as it is a prejudice that would evade the rending implications of any problem.

Time is not the synthesis of being and nothingness if being or nothingness are only found in time and are only arbitrarily separated notions. There is, in fact, neither isolated being nor isolated nothingness; there is time. But to affirm the existence of time is an empty assertion in the sense that it gives less the vague attribute of existence to time than the nature of time to existence; in other words, it empties the notion of existence of its vague and limitless content, and at the same time it infinitely empties it of all content.

The existence of time does not even require the objective position of time as such; this existence, posed in ecstasy, means only the flight and the collapse of any object that understanding sought to give itself both as a value and as a fixed object. The existence of time projected arbitrarily into an objective region is only the ecstatic vision of a catastrophe destroying that which founds this region. Not because the region of objects is necessarily, like the *me*, infinitely destroyed by time itself, but because existence founded in the *me* suddenly looms there, destroyed, and because the existence of things is impoverished in comparison with that of the *me*.

The existence of things, assuming the value for *me*—projecting an absurd shadow—of the preparations for an execution, cannot enclose the death it brings, but is itself projected into this death, which encloses it.

To affirm the illusory existence of the *me* and of time (which is not only the structure of the me but the object of its erotic ecstasy) does not therefore mean that the illusion must be subjected to the judgment of things whose existence is profound, but that profound existence must be projected into the illusion that encloses it.

The being which, under a human name, is *me*, and whose coming into the world—across a space peopled with stars—was infinitely improbable, nevertheless encloses the world of the totality of things precisely because of its fundamental improbability (which is opposed to the structure of the real giving itself as such). The death that delivers me from the world that kills me *has* enclosed this real world in the unreality of the *me* that dies.

Note

1. ["Le moi," usually translated as "the I," "the Self," or (in psychoanalysis) "the ego," has been translated here as "the me" (or "me"), in order to remain faithful to Bataille's syntax. Tr.]

The Psychological Structure of Fascism

Having affirmed that the infrastructure of a society ultimately determines or conditions the superstructure, Marxism did not undertake any general elucidation of the modalities peculiar to the formation of religious and political society. While Marxism did acknowledge possible responses by the superstructure, it has not gone from mere assertion to scientific analysis. This essay attempts a rigorous (if not comprehensive) representation of the social superstructure and its relations to the economic infrastructure in the light of fascism. The fact that this is but a fragment of a relatively substantial whole explains a great number of lacunae, notably the absence of any methodological considerations;[1] it was even necessary to forego justifying the novelty of my point of view and to limit myself to the presentation of my basic position. However, the simple presentation of the structure of fascism had to be preceded by a description of the social structure as a whole.

It goes without saying that a study of the superstructure presupposes the development of a Marxist analysis of the infrastructure.

The Homogeneous Part of Society

A psychological description of society must begin with that segment which is most accessible to understanding—and apparently the most fundamental segment—whose significant trait is tendential *homogeneity*.[2] *Homogeneity* signifies here the commensurability of elements and the awareness of this commensurability: human relations are sustained by a reduction to fixed rules based on the consciousness of the possible identity of delineable persons and situations; in principle, all violence is excluded from this course of existence.

Production is the basis of a social *homogeneity*.[3] *Homogeneous* society is productive society, namely, useful society. Every useless element is excluded, not from all of society, but from its *homogeneous* part. In this part, each element must be useful to another without the *homogeneous* activity ever being able to attain the form of activity *valid in itself*. A useful activity has a *common denominator* with another useful activity, but not with activity *for itself*.

The common denominator, the foundation of social *homogeneity* and of the activity arising from it, is money, namely, the calculable equivalent of the different products of collective activity. Money serves to measure all work and makes man a function of measurable products. According to the judgment of *homogeneous* society, each man is worth what he produces; in other words, he stops being an existence *for itself*: he is no more than a function, arranged within measurable limits, of collective production (which makes him an existence *for something other than itself*).

But the *homogeneous* individual is truly a function of his personal products only in artisan production, where the means of production are relatively inexpensive and can be owned by the artisan. In industrial civilization, the producer is distinguished from the owner of the means of production, and it is the latter who appropriates the products for himself: consequently, it is he who, in modern society, is the function of the products; it is he—and not the producer—who founds social *homogeneity*.

Thus in the present order of things, the *homogeneous* part of society is made up of those men who own the means of production or the money *destined for their upkeep or purchase*. It is exactly in the middle segment of the so-called capitalist or bourgeois class that the tendential reduction of human character takes place, making it an abstract and interchangeable entity: a reflection of the *homogeneous things* the individual owns.

This reduction is then extended as much as possible to the so-called middle classes that variously benefit from realized profit. But the industrial proletariat remains for the most part irreducible. It maintains a double relation to homogeneous activity: the latter excludes it—not from work but from profit. As agents of production, the workers fall within the framework of the social organization, but the homogeneous reduction as a rule only affects their wage-earning activity; they are integrated into the psychological *homogeneity* in terms of their behavior on the job, but not generally as men. Outside of the factory, and even beyond its technical operations, a laborer is, with regard to a *homogeneous* person (boss, bureaucrat, etc.), a stranger, a man of another nature, of a non-reduced, nonsubjugated nature.

II. The State

In the contemporary period, social *homogeneity* is linked to the bourgeois class by essential ties: thus the Marxist conception is justified whenever the State is shown to be at the service of a threatened homogeneity.

As a rule, social *homogeneity* is a precarious form, at the mercy of violence and even of internal dissent. It forms spontaneously in the play of productive organization, but must constantly be protected from the various unruly elements that do not benefit from production, or not enough to suit them, or simply, that cannot tolerate the checks that homogeneity imposes on unrest. In such conditions, the protection of *homogeneity* lies in its recourse to imperative elements that are capable of obliterating the various unruly forces or bringing them under the control of order.

The State is not itself one of these imperative elements; it is distinct from kings, heads of the army, or of nations, but it is the result of the modifications undergone by a part of homogeneous society as it comes into contact with such elements. This part is an intermediary formation between the homogeneous classes and the sovereign agencies from which it must borrow its obligatory character, but whose exercise of sovereignty must rely upon it as an intermediary. It is only with reference to these sovereign agencies that it will be possible to envision the way in which this obligatory character is transferred to a formation that nevertheless does not constitute an existence valid in itself (*heterogeneous*), but simply an activity whose usefulness with regard to another part is manifest.

In practical terms, the function of the State consists of an interplay of authority and adaptation. The reduction of differences through compromise in parliamentary practice indicates all the possible complexity of the internal activity of adaptation required by *homogeneity*. But against forces that cannot be assimilated, the State cuts matters short with strict authority.

Depending on whether the State is democratic or despotic, the prevailing tendency will be either adaptation or authority. In a democracy, the State derives most of its strength from spontaneous homogeneity, which it fixes and constitutes as the rule. The principle of its sovereignty—the nation—providing both its end and its strength, is thus diminished by the fact that isolated individuals increasingly consider themselves as ends with regard to the State, which would thus exist *for them* before existing *for the nation*. And, in this case, personal life distinguishes itself from *homogeneous* existence as a value that presents itself as incomparable.

III. Dissociations, Critiques of Social Homogeneity and the State

Even in difficult circumstances, the State is able to neutralize those *heterogeneous* forces that will yield only to its constraints. But it can succumb to the internal dissociation of that segment of society of which it is but the constrictive form.

Social *homogeneity* fundamentally depends upon the homogeneity (in the general sense of the word) of the productive system. Every contradiction arising from the development of economic life thus entails a tendential dissociation of *homogeneous* social existence. This tendency towards dissociation exerts itself in the most complex manner, on all levels and in every direction. But it only reaches acute and dangerous forms to the extent that an appreciable segment of the mass of *homogeneous* individuals ceases to have an interest in the conservation of the existing form of homogeneity (not because it is *homogeneous*, but on the contrary, because it is in the process of losing that character). This part of society then spontaneously affiliates itself with the previously constituted *heterogeneous* forces and becomes indistinguishable from them.

Thus, economic circumstances act directly upon homogeneous elements and promote their disintegration. But this disintegration only represents the negative form of social effervescence: the dissociated elements do not act before having undergone the complete alteration that characterizes the positive form of this effervescence. From the moment that they rejoin the *heterogeneous* formations that already exist in either a diffuse or an organized state, they acquire from the latter a new character: the general positive character of *heterogeneity*. Furthermore, social *heterogeneity* does not exist in a formless and disoriented state: on the contrary, it constantly tends to a split-off structure; *and when social elements pass over to the* heterogeneous *side, their action still finds itself determined by the* actual structure *of that side*.

Thus, the mode of resolving acute economic contradictions depends upon both the historical state and the general laws of the *heterogeneous* social region in which the effervescence acquires its positive form; it depends in particular upon the relations established between the various formations of this region when *homogeneous* society finds itself materially dissociated.

The study of *homogeneity* and of the conditions of its existence thus necessarily leads to the essential study of *heterogeneity*. In fact, it constitutes the first phase of such study in the sense that the primary determination of *heterogeneity* defined as non-*homogeneous* supposes a knowledge of the *homogeneity* that delineates it by exclusion.

IV. Heterogeneous Social Existence

The entire problem of social psychology rests precisely upon that fact that it must be brought to bear on a form that is not only difficult to study, but whose existence has not yet been the object of a precise definition.

The very term *heterogeneous* indicates that it concerns elements that are impossible to assimilate; this impossibility, which has a fundamental impact on social assimilation, likewise has an impact on scientific assimilation. These two types of assimilation have a single structure: the object of science is to establish the *homogeneity* of phenomena; that is, in a sense, one of the eminent functions of *homogeneity*. Thus, the *heterogeneous* elements excluded from the latter are excluded as well from the field of scientific considerations: as a rule, science cannot know *heterogeneous* elements as such. Compelled to note the existence of irreducible facts—of a nature as incompatible with its own homogeneity as are, for example, born criminals with the social order—science finds itself *deprived of any functional satisfaction* (exploited in the same manner as a laborer in a capitalist factory, used without sharing in the profits). Indeed, science is not an abstract entity: it is constantly reducible to a group of men living the aspirations inherent to the scientific process.

In such conditions, the *heterogeneous* elements, at least as such, find themselves subjected to a *de facto* censorship: each time that they could be the object of a methodical observation, the functional satisfaction is lacking; and without some exceptional circumstances—like the intrusion of a satisfaction with a completely different origin—they cannot be kept within the field of consideration.

The exclusion of *heterogeneous* elements from the *homogeneous* realm of consciousness formally recalls the exclusion of the elements, described (by psychoanalysis) as *unconscious*, which censorship excludes from the conscious ego. The difficulties opposing the revelation of *unconscious* forms of existence are of the same order as those opposing the knowledge of *heterogeneous* forms. As will subsequently be made clear, these two kinds of forms have certain properties in common and, without being able to elaborate immediately upon this point, it would seem that the *unconscious* must be considered as one of the aspects of the *heterogeneous*. If this conception is granted, given what we know about repression, it is that much easier to understand that the incursions occasionally made into the *heterogeneous* realm have not been sufficiently coordinated to yield even the simple revelation of its positive and clearly separate existence.

It is of secondary importance to indicate here that, in order to avoid the internal difficulties that have just been foreseen, it is necessary to posit the limits of science's inherent tendencies and to constitute a knowledge of the *nonexplainable difference*, which supposes the immediate access of the intellect to a body of material prior to any intellectual reduction. Tentatively, it is enough to present the facts according to their nature and, with a view to defining the term *heterogeneous*, to introduce the following considerations:

1. Just as, in religious sociology, *mana* and *taboo* designate forms restricted to the particular applications of a more general form, the *sacred*, so may the *sacred* itself be considered as a restricted form of the *heterogeneous*.

Mana designates the mysterious and impersonal force possessed by individuals such as kings and witch doctors. *Taboo* indicates the social prohibition of contact pertaining, for example, to cadavers and menstruating women. Given the precise and limited facts to which they refer, these aspects of *heterogeneous* life are easy to define. However, an explicit understanding of the *sacred*, whose field of application is relatively vast, presents considerable difficulties. Durkheim faced the impossibility of providing it with a positive scientific definition: he settled for characterizing the sacred world negatively as being absolutely heterogeneous compared to the profane.[4] It is nevertheless possible to admit that the *sacred* is known positively, at least implicitly (since the word is commonly used in every language, that usage supposes a signification perceived by the whole of mankind). This implicit knowledge of a heterogeneous value permits a vague but positive character to be communicated to its description. Yet it can be said that the heterogeneous world is largely comprised of the sacred world, and that reactions analogous to those generated by sacred things are provoked by *heterogeneous* things that are not, strictly speaking, considered to be sacred. These reactions are such that the *heterogeneous* thing is assumed to be charged with an unknown and dangerous force (recalling the Polynesian *mana*) and that a certain social prohibition of contact (*taboo*) separates it from the *homogeneous* or ordinary world (which corresponds to the profane world in the strictly religious opposition);

2. Beyond the properly sacred things that constitute the common realm of religion or magic, the *heterogeneous* world includes everything resulting from *unproductive* expenditure[5] (sacred things themselves form part of this whole). This consists of everything rejected by *homogeneous* society as waste or as superior transcendent value. Included are the waste products of the human body and certain analogous matter (trash, vermin, etc.); the parts of the body; persons, words, or acts having a suggestive erotic value; the various unconscious processes such as dreams or neuroses; the numerous elements or social forms that *homogeneous* society is powerless to assimilate: mobs, the warrior, aristocratic and impoverished classes, different types of violent individuals or at least those who refuse the rule (madmen, leaders, poets, etc.);

3. Depending upon the person *heterogeneous* elements will provoke affective reactions of varying intensity, and it is possible to assume that the object of any affective reaction is necessarily *heterogeneous* (if not generally, at least with regard to the subject). There is sometimes attraction, sometimes repulsion, and in cerain circumstances, any object of repulsion can become an object of attraction and vice versa;

4. *Violence, excess, delirium, madness* characterize heterogeneous elements to varying degrees: active, as persons or mobs, they result from breaking the laws of social *homogeneity*. This characteristic does not appropriately apply to inert objects, yet the latter do present a certain conformity with extreme emotions (if it is possible to speak of the violent and excessive nature of a decomposing body);

5. The reality of *heterogeneous* elements is not of the same order as that of *homogeneous* elements. *Homogeneous* reality presents itself with the abstract and neutral aspect of strictly defined and identified objects (basically, it is the specific reality of solid objects). *Heterogeneous* reality is that of a force or shock. It presents itself as a charge, as a value, passing from one object to another in a more or less abstract fashion, almost as if the change were taking place not in the world of objects but only in the judgments of the subject. The preceding aspect nevertheless does not signify that the observed facts are to be considered as subjective: thus, the action of the objects of erotic activity is manifestly rooted in their objective nature. Nonetheless, in a disconcerting way, the subject does have the capacity to displace the exciting value of one element onto an analogous or neighboring one.[6] In heterogeneous reality, the symbols charged with affective value thus have the same importance as the fundamental elements, and the part can have the same value as the whole. It is easy to note that, since the structure of knowledge for a *homogeneous* reality is that of science, the knowledge of a *heterogeneous* reality as such is to be found in the mystical thinking of primitives and in dreams: it is identical to the structure of the *unconscious*;[7]

6. *In summary*, compared to everyday life, *heterogeneous* existence can be represented as something *other*, as *incommensurate*, by charging these words with the *positive* value they have in *affective* experience.

Examples of Heterogeneous Elements

If these suggestions are now brought to bear upon actual elements, the fascist leaders are incontestably part of heterogeneous existence. Opposed to democratic politicians, who represent in different countries the platitude inherent to *homogeneous* society, Mussolini and Hitler immediately stand out as something *other*. Whatever emotions their actual existence as political agents of evolution provokes, it is impossible to ignore the *force* that situates them above men, parties, and even laws: a *force* that disrupts the regular course of things, the peaceful but fastidious homogeneity powerless to maintain itself (the fact that laws are broken is only the most obvious sign of the transcendent, *heterogeneous* nature of fascist action). Considered not with regard to its external action but with regard to its source, the *force* of a leader is analogous to that exerted in hypnosis.[8] The affective flow that unites him with his followers—which takes the form of a moral identification[9] of the latter with the one they follow (and reciprocally)—is a function of the common consciousness of increasingly *violent* and excessive energies and powers that accumulate in the person of the leader and through him become widely available. (But this concentration in a single person intervenes as an element that sets the fascist formation apart within the *heterogeneous* realm: by the very fact that the affective effervescence leads to unity, it constitutes, as *authority*, an agency directed *against* men; this agency is an existence *for itself* before being useful; an existence *for itself* distinct from that of a formless uprising where *for itself* signifies "for the men in revolt.") This *monarchy*, this absence of all democracy, of all fraternity in the exercise of power—forms that do not exist only in Italy or Germany—indicates that the immediate natural needs of men must be renounced, under constraint, in favor of a transcendent principle that cannot be the object of an exact explanation.

In a quite different sense, the lowest strata of society can equally be described as heterogeneous, those who generally provoke repulsion and can in no case be assimilated by the whole of mankind. In India, these impoverished classes are considered *untouchable*, meaning that they are characterized by the prohibition of contact analogous to that applied to sacred things. It is true that the custom of countries in advanced civilizations is less ritualistic and that the quality of being *untouchable* is not necessarily hereditary; nevertheless, being destitute is all it takes in these countries to create between the self and others—who consider themselves the expression of normal man—a nearly insuperable gap. The nauseating forms of dejection provoke a feeling of disgust so unbearable that it is improper to express or even to make allusion to it. By all indications, in the psychological order of disfiguration, the material poverty of man has *excessive* consequences. And, in the event that *fortunate* men have not undergone *homogeneous* reduction (which opposes a legal justification to poverty), if we except those shameless attempts at evasion such as charitable pity, the hopeless violence of the reactions immediately takes on the form of a challenge to reason.

V. The Fundamental Dualism of the Heterogeneous World

The two preceding examples, taken from the broader domain of *heterogeneity*, and not from the sacred domain proper, nevertheless do present the specific traits of the latter. This is readily apparent with reference to the leaders who are manifestly treated by their followers as sacred persons. It is much less evident with reference to forms of poverty that are not the object of any cult.

But the revelation that such vile forms are compatible with the sacred character precisely marks the decisive headway made in the knowledge of the sacred as well as in that of the *heterogeneous* realm. The notion of the duality of sacred forms is one of the conclusive findings of social anthropology: these forms must be distributed among two opposing classes: *pure* and *impure* (in primitive religions certain impure things—menstrual blood, for example—are no less sacred than the divine nature; the awareness of this fundamental duality has persisted until relatively recent times: in the Middle Ages, the word *sacer* was used to designate a shameful illness—syphilis—and the deeper meaning of this usage was still intelligible.) The theme of sacred poverty—impure and untouchable—constitutes precisely the negative pole of a region characterized by the opposition of two extreme forms: in a certain sense, there is an identity of opposites between glory and dejection, between exalted and imperative (higher) forms and impoverished (lower) forms. This opposition splits the whole of the *heterogeneous* world and joins the already defined characteristics of *heterogeneity* as a fundamental element. (Undifferentiated *heterogeneous* forms are, in fact, relatively rare—at least in developed societies—and the analysis of the internal *heterogeneous* social structure is almost entirely reduced to that of the opposition between two contrary terms.)

VI. The Imperative Form of Heterogeneous Existence: Sovereignty

Heterogeneous fascist action belongs to the entire set of higher forms. It makes an appeal to sentiments traditionally defined as *exalted* and *noble* and tends to constitute authority as an unconditional principle, situated above any utilitarian judgment.

Obviously, the use of the words *higher, noble, exalted* does not imply endorsement. Here these qualities simply designate that something belongs to a category *historically* defined as *higher, noble,* or *exalted*: such particularized or novel conceptions can only be considered in relation to the traditional conceptions from which they derive; they are, furthermore, necessarily hybrid, without any far-reaching effect, and it is doubtless preferable, if possible, to abandon any representation of this order (for what admissible reasons would a man want to be noble, similar to a representative of the medieval, military caste and absolutely not ignoble, that is to say similar, in accordance with the judgment of history, to a man whose material destitution would have altered his human character, made him *something other*?).

Having formulated this reservation, the meaning of higher values must be clarified with the help of traditional qualifiers. *Superiority* (imperative sovereignty)[10] designates the entire set of striking aspects—affectively determining attraction or repulsion—characteristic of different human situations in which it is possible to dominate and even to oppress one's fellows by reason of their age, physical weakness, legal status, or simply of their necessity to place themselves under the control of one person: specific situations correspond to diverse circumstances, that of the father with regard to his children, that of the military leader with regard to the army and the civilian population, that of the master with regard to the slave, that of the king with regard to his subjects. To these real situations must be added mythological situations whose exclusively fictitious nature facilitates a condensation of the aspects characteristic of superiority.

The simple fact of dominating one's fellows implies the *heterogeneity* of the master, insofar as he is the master: to the extent that he refers to his nature, to his personal quality, as the justification of his authority, he designates his nature as *something other*, without being able to account for it rationally. But not only as *something other* with regard to the rational domain of the common denominator and the equivalent: the *heterogeneity* of the master is no less opposed to that of the slave. If the heterogeneous nature of the slave is akin to that of the filth in which his material situation condemns him to live, that of the master is formed by an act excluding all filth: an act pure in direction but sadistic in form.

In human terms, the ultimate imperative value presents itself in the form of royal or imperial authority in which cruel tendencies and the need, characteristic of all domination, to realize and idealize order are manifest in the highest degree. This double character is no less present in fascist authority, but it is only one of the numerous forms of royal authority, the description of which constitutes the foundation of any coherent description of fascism.

In opposition to the impoverished existence of the oppressed, political sovereignty initially presents itself as a clearly differentiated sadistic activity. In individual psychology, it is rare for the sadistic tendency not to be associated with a more or less manifest masochistic tendency. But as each tendency is normally represented in society by a distinct agency, the sadistic attitude can be manifested by an imperative person to the exclusion of any corresponding masochistic attitudes. In this case, the exclusion of the filthy forms that serve as the object of the cruel act is not accompanied by the positioning of these forms as a value and, consequently, no erotic activity can be associated with the cruelty. The erotic elements themselves are rejected at the same time as every filthy object and, as in a great number of religious attitudes, sadism attains a brilliant purity. The differentiation can be more or less complete—individually, sovereigns have been able to live power in part as an orgy of blood—but, on the whole, within the *heterogeneous* domain, the imperative royal form has historically effected an exclusion of impoverished and filthy forms sufficient to permit a connection with *homogeneous* forms at a certain level.

In fact, as a rule, *homogeneous* society excludes every *heterogeneous* element, whether filthy or noble; the modalities of the operation vary as much as the nature of each excluded element. For homogeneous society, only the rejection of impoverished forms has a constant fundamental value (such that the least recourse to the reserves of energy represented by these forms requires an operation as dangerous as *subversion*); but, given that the act of excluding impoverished forms necessarily associates *homogeneous* forms with imperative forms, the latter can no longer be purely and simply rejected. To combat the elements most incompatible with it, *homogeneous* society uses free-floating imperative forces; and, when it must choose the very object of its activity (the existence *for itself* in the service of which it must necessarily place itself) from the domain that it has excluded, the choice inevitably falls on those forces that have already proved most effective.

The inability of *homogeneous* society to find in itself a reason for being and acting is what makes it dependent upon imperative forces, just as the sadistic hostility of sovereigns toward the impoverished population is what allies them with any formation seeking to maintain the latter in a state of oppression.

A complex situation results from the royal person's modalities of exclusion: since the king is the object in which homogeneous society has found its reason for being, maintaining this relationship demands that he conduct himself in such a way that the *homogeneous* society can exist *for him*. In the first place, this requirement bears upon the fundamental *heterogeneity* of the king, guaranteed by numerous prohibitions of contract (taboos); this *heterogeneity*, however, is impossible to keep in a free state. In no case may *heterogeneity* receive its law from without, but its spontaneous movement can be fixed, at least tendentially, once and for all. Thus, the destructive passion (sadism) of the imperative agency is as a rule exclusively directed either toward foreign societies or toward the impoverished classes, toward all those external or internal elements hostile to *homogeneity*.

Historically, royal power is the form that results from such a situation. As for its positive function, a determining role is reserved for the very principle of unification, actually carried out in a group of individuals whose affective choice bears upon a single *heterogeneous* object. A shared orientation has, in itself, a constitutive value: it presupposes—vaguely, it is true—the imperative character of the object. Unification, the principle of *homogeneity*, is only a tendential fact, incapable of finding in itself a motive for requiring and imposing its existence; and, in most circumstances, the recourse to an external requirement has the value of a primary necessity. Yet, the pure *having to be*, the moral imperative, requires being *for itself*, namely, the specific mode of *heterogeneous* existence. But this existence precisely escapes the principle of having to be and can in no case be subordinated to it: it immediately accedes to *Being* (in other words it produces itself as the value *being or not being* and never as a value that has to be). The complex form in which the resolution of this incompatibility culminates poses the *having to be* of *homogeneous* existence in *heterogeneous* existences. Thus, imperative *heterogeneity* not only represents a differentiated form with regard to vague *heterogeneity*: it additionally supposes the structural modification of the two parts, *homogeneous* and *heterogeneous*, in contact with one another. On the one hand, the *homogeneous* formation akin to the royal agency, the State, derives its imperative character from this agency and seems to attain existence *for itself* by bringing about the barren and cold *having to be* of the whole of homogeneous society. But the State is in reality only the abstract, degraded form of the living *having to be* required, at the top, as an affective attraction and royal agency: it is simply vague *homogeneity* become a constraint. On the other hand, this mode of intermediary formation that characterizes the State penetrates imperative existence through reaction; but, in the course of this introjection, the proper form of *homogeneity* becomes—this time for real—existence *for itself* by denying itself: it becomes absorbed by *heterogeneity* and destroys itself as strictly *homogeneous* from the fact that, having become the negation of the principle of utility, it refuses all subordination. Although profoundly penetrated by the *reason of State*, the king nevertheless does not identify with the latter: he wholly maintains the separate character of divine supremacy. He is exempt from the specific principle of homogeneity, the compensation of rights and duties constituting the formal law of the State: the king's rights are unconditional.

There is hardly any need to suggest at this point that the possibility of such affective formations has brought about the infinite subjugation that degrades most forms of human life (much more so than abuses of power which, furthermore, are themselves reducible—insofar as the force in play is necessarily social—to imperative formations). If sovereignty is now considered in its tendential form—such as it has been lived historically by the subject to whom it owes its attractive value—yet independently of any particular reality, its nature appears, in human terms, to be the noblest—exalted to majesty—, pure in the midst of the orgy, beyond the reach of human infirmities. It constitutes the region formally exempt from self-interested intrigues to which the oppressed subject refers as to an empty but pure satisfaction. (In this sense the constitution of royal nature above an inadmissible reality recalls the fictions justifying eternal life.) As a tendential form, it fulfills the *ideal* of society and the course of things (in the subject's mind, this function is expressed naively: *if the king only knew . . .*). At the same time it is strict authority. Situated above *homogeneous* society, as well as above the impoverished populace or the aristocratic hierarchy that emanates from it, it requires the bloody repression of what is contrary to it and becomes synonymous in its split-off form with the heterogeneous foundations of the law: it is thus both the possibility of and the requirement for collective unity; it is in the royal orbit that the State and its functions of coercion and adaption are elaborated; the homogeneous reduction develops, both as destruction and foundation, to the benefit of royal greatness.

Posing itself as the principle for the association of innumerable elements, royal power develops spontaneously as an imperative and destructive force against every other imperative form that could be opposed to it. It thereby manifests, at the top, the fundamental tendency and principle of all authority: the reduction to a personal entity, the individualization of power. While impoverished existence is necessarily produced as a multitude and homogeneous society as a reduction to the common denominator, the imperative agency—the foundation of oppression—necessarily develops along the lines of a reduction to a unit in the form of a human being excluding the very possibility of a peer, in other words, as a radical form of exclusion requiring avidity.

VII. Tendential Concentration

This tendency toward concentration appears to be in contradiction, it is true, with the coexistence of distinct domains of power: the domain of royal sovereignty is different from military power and from the domain of religious authority. But taking note of this coexistence is precisely what draws attention to the composite character of royal power, in which it is easy to find the constitutive elements of the other two powers, the religious and the military.[11]

It thus becomes apparent that royal sovereignty should not be considered as a simple element having its own autonomous source, such as the army or the religious organization: it is exactly (and furthermore uniquely) the actualized concentration of these two elements formed in two different directions. The constant rebirth of military and religious powers in a pure state has never modified the principle of their tendential concentration in the form of a single sovereignty: even the formal refusal of Christianity has not prevented—to use vulgar symbolic terminology—the cross from lying on the steps of the throne with the saber.

Considered historically, this concentration can be achieved spontaneously: the head of the army succeeds in having himself crowned *king* through the use of force, or the established *king* takes hold of military power (in Japan, the emperor recently actualized this form, without, it is true, his own initiative having played a determining role). But each time, even in the case where royalty is *usurped*, the possibility of the uniting of powers depended upon their fundamental affinities and especially upon their tendential concentration.

The consideration of the principles governing these facts obviously becomes crucial from the moment that fascism renews their historical existence, that is, once again unites military and religious authority to effect a total oppression. (In this regard, it can be stated—without prejudicing any other political judgment—that any unlimited actualization of imperative forms amounts to a negation of humanity as a value that depends upon the play of internal oppositions.) Like Bonapartism, fascism (which etymologically signifies *uniting, concentration*) is no more than an acute reactivation of the latent sovereign agency, but with a character in a sense purified by the fact that paramilitary groups substituted for the army in the constitution of power immediately have that power as an object.

VIII. The Army and the Heads of the Army

As a rule, the army exists functionally because of war, and its psychological structure is entirely reducible to the exercise of that function. Thus, imperative character does not directly result from the social importance linked to the material power of controlling weapons: its internal organization—discipline and hierarchy—are what make it preeminently a noble society.

Obviously, the *nobility of arms* initially supposes an intense *heterogeneity*: discipline and hierarchy are themselves but forms and not the foundations of *heterogeneity*; bloodshed, carnage, and death alone are commensurate with the fundamental nature of weapons. But the ambiguous horror of war still has only a base *heterogeneity* (at best undifferentiated). The exalted, exalting control of weapons supposes the affective unification necessary to their cohesion, that is, to their effective value.

The affective character of this unification is manifest in the form of the soldier's attachment to the head of the army: it implies that each soldier equates the latter's glory with his own. This process is the intermediary through which disgusting slaughter is radically transformed into its opposite, glory—namely, into a pure and intense attraction. The glory of the chief essentially constitutes a sort of affective pole opposed to the nature of the soldiers. Even independently of their horrible occupation, the soldiers belong *as a rule* to a vile segment of the population; divested of its uniforms and wearing ordinary clothing, a professional army of the eighteenth century would have looked like a wretched populace. But even the elimination of enlistments from the lower classes would fail to change the deeper structure of the army; this structure would continue to base affective organization upon the social infamy of the soldiers. *Human beings* incorporated into the army are but negated elements, negated with a kind of rage (a sadism) manifest in the tone of each command, negated by the parade, by the uniform, and by the geometric regularity of cadenced movements. The chief, insofar as he is imperative, is the incarnation of this violent negation. His intimate nature, the nature of his glory, is constituted by an imperative act that annuls the wretched populace (which constitutes the army) as such (in the same way that the slaughter is annulled as such).

In social psychology, this imperative negation generally appears as the characteristic of *action*; in other words, every affirmed social action necessarily takes the unified psychological form of *sovereignty*; every lower form, every ignominy, being by definition passive, is transformed into its opposite by the simple fact of a transition to action. Slaughter, as an inert result, is ignoble; but, shifted onto the social action that caused it, the ignoble *heterogeneous* value thus established becomes noble (the action of killing and nobility are association by indefectible historical ties): all it takes is for the *action* to affirm itself effectively as such, to assume freely the imperative form that constitutes it.

This operation—the fact of assuming *in complete freedom* the imperative character of action—is precisely what characterizes the chief. It becomes possible to grasp here in an explicit form the role played by unification (individualization) in the structural modifications that characterize superior *heterogeneity*. Starting with formless and impoverished elements, the army, under the imperative impulse, becomes organized and internally achieves a *homogeneous* form on account of the negation directed at the disordered character of its elements:

in fact, the mass that constitutes the army passes from a depleted and ruined existence to a purified geometric order, from formlessness to aggressive rigidity. In actuality, this negated mass has ceased to be itself in order to become affectively ("affectively" refers here to simple psychological behaviors, such as *standing at attention* or *marching double time*) the chief's thing and like a part of the chief himself. A troop *at attention* is in a sense absorbed by the existence of the command and, thus, absorbed by the negation of itself. *Standing at attention* can be analogically considered as a tropic movement (a kind of negative geotropism) elevating not only the chief but all who follow his orders to the (geometrically) regular form of imperative sovereignty. Thus the implied infamy of the soldiers is only a basic infamy which, in uniform, is transformed into its opposite: order and glamour. The mode of *heterogeneity explicitly undergoes a thorough alteration, completing the realization of intense homogeneity* without a decrease of the fundamental *heterogeneity*. In the midst of the population, the army retains the distinction of being *wholly other*, but with a sovereignty linked to domination, to the imperative and separate character that the chief transmits to his soldiers.

Thus the dominant direction of the army, detached from its affective foundations (infamy and slaughter), depends upon the contrary *heterogeneity* of *honor* and *duty* incarnated in the person of the chief. (If the chief is not subordinate to a real agency or to an idea, duty is incarnated in his person in the same way as in that of the king.) Honor and duty, symbolically expressed by the geometry of the parades, are the tendential forms that situate military existence above *homogeneous* existence as imperative and as a pure reason for being. Having a limited bearing on certain levels of action, these forms, in their properly military aspect, are compatible with infinitely craven crimes, but they suffice to affirm the exalted value of the army and to make the internal domination characterizing its structure one of the fundamental elements of a supreme psychological authority instituted above the subjugated society.

Nevertheless, the immediate result of the power of the head of the army is only an internal homogeneity independent of social *homogeneity*, whereas specific royal power exists only in relation to *homogeneous* society. The integration of military power into social power therefore supposes a structural change: it supposes the acquisition of modalities characteristic of royal power in relation to the administration of the State, as they were described in relation to this power.

IX. Religious Power

It is granted in an implicit and vague manner that holding military power has been sufficient to exert a general domination. Nevertheless, with the exception of colonizations, which extend a preestablished power, examples of long-lasting, exclusively military dominations are hard to find. In fact, simple material armed force is incapable of founding any power: in the first place, such force depends on the internal attraction exerted by the chief (money is insufficient to constitute an army). And when the chief wants to use the force at his disposal to dominate society, he must further acquire the elements of an external attraction (of a *religious* attraction valid for the entire population).

It is true that the latter elements are sometimes at the disposal of force, yet, as the origin of royal power, military attraction probably has no primacy over religious attraction. To the extent that it is possible to formulate a valid judgment about the distant past of mankind, it seems fairly clear that religion—not the army—is the source of social authority. Furthermore, the introduction of heredity regularly marks the predominance of a religious form of power: it can rely upon its bloodlines, whereas military power depends first of all on personal value.

Unfortunately, it is difficult to ascribe a specific meaning to that which, in the blood or in the aspects of royalty, is characteristically religious: here one essentially confronts the bare and unlimited form of undifferentiated *heterogeneity*, before any of its perceptible elements (ones that can be made explicit) have been fixed by a still vague direction. This direction does exist nonetheless, but, in every causal state, the structural modifications that it introduces leave the field to a free projection of general affective forms, such as dread or sacred attraction. Furthermore, structural modifications are not what are immediately transmitted through physiological contact in heredity or by sacred rites, but rather a fundamental *heterogeneity*.

The (implicit) signification of the purely religious royal character can only be attained to the extent that its origin and structure appear to be shared with those of a divine nature. Though it is impossible, in such a cursory presentation, to present all of the affective movements involved in the establishment of mythical authorities (culminating in the positioning of a fictitious supreme authority), a simple juxtaposition is amply revealing. Unequivocal facts (identifications with the divine, mythical genealogies, the Roman or Shintoist imperial cults, the Christian theory of divine right) correspond to the shared structure of the two formations. One the whole, the king is considered in one form or another to be an emanation of a divine nature, along with everything that the principle of emanation entails in the way of identity when dealing with *heterogeneous* elements.

The notable structural modifications that characterize the evolution of the representation of the divine—starting with free and irresponsible violence—simply makes explicit those characterizing the formation of the royal nature. In both cases, the position of the sovereign is what directs the alteration of the *heterogeneous* structure. In both cases, we witness a concentration of attributes and forces; but, in the case of God, since the forces that he represents are only composed in a fictitious being (not subject to the limitation of having to be realized), it was possible to yield more perfect forms, more purely logical schemata.

The supreme being of theologians and philosophers represents the most profound introjection of the structure characteristic of *homogeneity* into *heterogeneous* existence: in his theological aspect, God preeminently fulfills the sovereign form. However, the counterpart to this possibility is implied by the fictitious character of divine existence, whose *heterogeneous* nature, lacking the limitative value of reality, can be overlooked in a philosophical conception (reduced to a formal affirmation that is in no way lived). In the order of free intellectual speculation, the idea can be substituted for God as supreme existence and power; this implies the admittedly partial revelation of a relative *heterogeneity* of the Idea (such as occurred when Hegel raised the Idea above the simple *having to be*).

X. Fascism as the Sovereign Form of Sovereignty

Stirring up such apparently anachronistic phantoms would surely be senseless if fascism had not, before our very eyes, reappropriated and reconstituted from the bottom up—starting, as it were, with nothing—the very process described above for the establishment of power. Until our times, there had only been a single historical example of the sudden formation of a total power, namely, the Islamic Khalifat. While both military and religious, it was principally royal, relying upon no prior foundation. Islam, a form comparable to fascism in its meager human wealth, did not even have recourse to an established nation, much less a constituted State. But it must be recognized that, for fascist movements, the existing State has first been something to conquer, then a means or a frame,[12] and that the integration of the nation does not change the schema of their formation. Just like early Islam, fascism represents the constitution of a total heterogeneous power whose manifest origin is to be found in the prevailing effervescence.

In the first place, fascist power is characterized by a foundation that is both religious and military, in which these two habitually distinct elements cannot be separated: it thus presents itself from the outset as an accomplished concentration.

It is true, however, that the military aspect is the predominant one. The affective relations that closely associate (identify) the leader to the member of the party (as they have already been described) are generally analogous to those uniting a chief to his soldiers. The imperative presence of the leader amounts to a negation of the fundamental revolutionary effervescence that he taps; the revolution, which is affirmed as a foundation is, at the same time, fundamentally negated from the moment that internal domination is militarily exerted on the militia. But this internal domination is not directly subordinated to real or possible acts of war: it essentially poses itself as the middle term of an external domination of society and of the State, as the middle term of a total imperative value. Thus, qualities characteristic of the two dominations (internal and external, military and religious) are simultaneously implied: qualities derived from the introjected *homogeneity*, such as duty, discipline, and obedience; and qualities derived from the essential *heterogeneity*, imperative violence, and the positioning of the chief as the transcendent object of collective affectivity. But the religious value of the chief is really the fundamental (if not formal) value of fascism, giving the activity of the militiamen its characteristic affective tonality, distinct from that of the soldier in general. The chief as such is in fact only the emanation of a principle that is none other than that of the glorious existence of a nation raised to the value of a divine force (which, superseding every other conceivable consideration, demands not only passion but ecstasy from its participants). Incarnated in the person of the chief (in Germany, the properly religious term, prophet, has sometimes been used), the nation thus plays the same role that Allah, incarnated in the person of Mahomet or the Khalif,[13] plays for Islam.

Fascism therefore appears first of all as a concentration and so to speak condensation of power[14] (a meaning actually indicated in the etymological value of the term). This general signification must furthermore be accepted in several ways. The accomplished uniting of imperative forces takes place at the top, but the process leaves no social faction inactive. In fundamental opposition to socialism, fascism is characterized by the uniting of classes. Not that classes conscious of their unity have adhered to the regime, but because expressive elements of each class have been represented in the deep movements of adherence that led to the seizing of power. Here the specific type of unification is actually derived from properly military affectivity, which is to say that the representative elements of the exploited classes have been included in the affective process only through the negation of their own nature (just as the social nature of a recruit is negated by means of uniforms and parades). This process, which *blends* the different social formations from the bottom up, must be understood as a fundamental process whose scheme is necessarily given in the very formation of the chief, who derives his profound meaning from the fact of having shared the dejected and impoverished life of the proletariat. But, as in the case of military organization, the affective value characteristic of impoverished existence is only displaced and transformed into its opposite; and it is its inordinate scope that gives the chief and the whole of the formation the accent of violence without which no army or fascism could be possible.

XI. The Fascist State

Fascism's close ties with the impoverished classes profoundly distinguish this formation from classical royal society, which is characterized by a more or less decisive loss of contact with the lower classes. But, forming in opposition to the established royal unification (the forms of which dominate society from too far above), the fascist unification is not simply a uniting of powers from different origins and a symbolic uniting of classes: it is also the accomplished uniting of the *heterogeneous* elements with the *homogeneous* elements, of sovereignty in the strictest sense with the State.

As a uniting, fascism is actually opposed as much to Islam as it is to traditional monarchy. In fact Islam was created from nothing, and that is why a form such as the State, which can only be the result of a long historical process, played no role in its immediate constitution; on the contrary, the existing State served from the outset as a frame for the entire fascist process of organic organization. This characteristic aspect of fascism permitted Mussolini to write that "everything is in the State," that "nothing human or spiritual exists nor *a fortiori* does it have any existence outside of the State."[15] But this does not necessarily imply an identity of the State and the imperative force that dominates the whole of society. Mussolini himself, who leaned toward a kind of Hegelian divinization of the State, acknowledges in willfully obscure terms a distinct principle of sovereignty that he alternatively designates as *the people, the nation*, and *the superior personality*, but that must be identified with the Fascist formation itself and its leader: "if the people . . . signifies the idea . . . that is incarnated in the people as the will of a few or even of a single person . . . It has to do," he writes, "neither with race nor with a determined geographical region, but with a grouping that is historically perpetuated, of a multitude unified by an idea that is a will to existence and to power: it is a self-consciousness, a personality."[16] The term *personality* must be understood as *individualization*, a process leading to Mussolini himself, and when he adds that "this superior personality is the nation as State. It is not the nation that creates the State . . . ,"[17] it must be understood that he has: 1) substituted the principle of the sovereignty of the individualized fascist formation for the old democratic principle of the sovereignty of the nation; 2) laid the groundwork for a conclusive interpretation of the sovereign agency and the State.

National Socialist Germany—which, unlike Italy (under the patronage of Gentile), has not officially adopted Hegelianism and the theory of the State as soul of the world—has not been afflicted with the theoretical difficulties resulting from the necessity of officially articulating a principle of authority: the mystical idea of race immediately affirmed itself as the imperative aim of the new fascist society; at the same time it appeared to be incarnated in the person of the Führer and his followers. Even though the conception of race lacks an objective base, it is nonetheless subjectively grounded, and the necessity of maintaining the racial value above all others obviated the need for a theory that made the State the principle of all value. The example of Germany thus demonstrates that the identity established by Mussolini between the State and the sovereign form of value is not necessary to a theory of fascism.

The fact that Mussolini did not formally distinguish the *heterogeneous* agency, the action of which he caused to penetrate deeply into the State, can equally be interpreted as an absolute seizure of the State and as a strained adaptation of the sovereign agency to the necessities of a regime of *homogeneous* production. It is in the development of these two reciprocal processes that fascism and the reason of the State came to appear identical. Nevertheless, the forms of life rigorously conserve a fundamental opposition when they maintain a radical duality of principles in the very person of the one holding power: the president of the Italian council and the German chancellor represent forms of activity radically distinct from those of the Duce or the Führer. Further, these two figures derive their fundamental power not from their official function in the State, like other prime ministers, but from the existence of a fascist party and from their personal position at the head of that party. In conjunction with the duality of *heterogeneous* and *homogeneous* forms, this evidence of the deep roots of power precisely maintains the unconditional supremacy of the *heterogeneous* form from the standpoint of the principle of sovereignty.

XII. The Fundamental Conditions of Fascism

As has already been indicated, *heterogeneous* processes as a whole can only enter into play once the fundamental *homogeneity* of society (the apparatus of production) has become dissociated because of its internal contradictions. Further, it can be stated that, even though it generally occurs in the blindest fashion, the development of heterogeneous forces necessarily comes to signify a solution to the problem posed by the contradictions of *homogeneity*. Once in power, developed *heterogeneous* forces have at their disposal the means of coercion necessary to resolve the differences that had arisen between previously irreconcilable elements. But it goes without saying that, at the end of a movement that excludes all subversion, the thrust of these resolutions will have been consistent with the general direction of the existing *homogeneity*, namely, with the interests of the capitalists.

The change resides in the fact that, having had recourse to fascist *heterogeneity*, these interests, from the moment of crisis on, are those of a group opposed to privately owned enterprises. As a result, the very structure of capitalism—the principle of which had been that of a spontaneous *homogeneity* of production based on competition, a *de facto* coincidence of the interests of the group of producers with the absolute freedom of each enterprise—finds itself profoundly altered. The awareness, developed in some German capitalists, of the peril to which this freedom subjected them in a critical period, must naturally be placed at the origin of the effervescence and triumph of National-Socialism. However, it is evident that this awareness did not yet exist for Italian capitalists who, from the moment of the march on Rome, were exclusively preoccupied with the irresolvability of their conflicts with the workers. It thus appears that the unity of fascism is located in its actual psychological structure and not in the economic conditions that serve as its base. (This does not contradict the fact that a general logical development of the economy retroactively provides the different fascisms with a common economic signification that they share, to be sure, with the political activity—absolutely foreign to fascism in the strictest sense—of the current government of the United States.)

Whatever the economic danger to which fascism responded, the awareness of this danger and the need to avoid it actually represent an as yet empty desire, which could be propped up by money. The realization of the force able to respond to the desire and to utilize the available monies takes place only in the *heterogeneous* region, and its possibility depends upon the actual structure of that region: on the whole, it is possible to consider this structure as variable depending on whether the society is democratic or monarchical.

Truly monarchial societies (as distinct from the adapted or bastardized political forms represented by England today or prefascist Italy) are characterized by the fact that a sovereign agency, having an ancient origin and an absolute form, is *connected* to the existing *homogeneity*. The constant evolution of the constitutive elements of this *homogeneity* can necessitate fundamental changes, but the need for change can become represented internally only in an altered minority: the whole of the *homogeneous* elements and the immediate principle of *homogeneity* remain committed to upholding the juridical forms and the existing administrative framework guaranteed by the authority of the king; the authority of the king coincides reciprocally with the upholding of these forms and this framework. Thus the upper part of the *heterogeneous* region is both immobilized and immobilizing, and only the lower part formed by the impoverished and oppressed classes is capable of entering into movement. But, for the latter, passive and oppressed by definition, the fact of entering into movement represents a profound alteration of their nature: in order to take part in a struggle against the sovereign agency and the legal homogeneity oppressing them, the lower classes must pass from a passive and diffuse state to a form of conscious activity; in Marxist terms, these classes must become aware of themselves as a revolutionary proletariat. This proletariat cannot actually be limited to itself: it is in fact only a point of concentration for every dissociated social element that has been banished to *heterogeneity*. It is even possible to say that such a point of concentration exists in a sense prior to the formation of what must be called the "conscious proletariat": the general description of the heterogeneous region actually implies it be posited as a constitutive element of the structure of a whole that includes not only imperative forms and impoverished forms but also *subversive forms*. These subversive forms are none other than the lower forms transformed with a view to the struggle against the sovereign forms. The necessity inherent to subversive forms requires that what is low become high, that what is high become low; this is the requirement in which the nature of subversion is expressed. In the case where the sovereign forms of a society are immobilized and bound, the diverse elements that have been banished to *heterogeneity* as a result of social decomposition can only ally themselves with the formations that result when the oppressed class becomes active: they are necessarily dedicated to subversion. The faction of the bourgeoisie that has become aware of the incompatibility with established social frameworks becomes united against figures of authority and blends in with the effervescent masses in revolt; and even in the period immediately following the destruction of the monarchy, social movements continued to be governed by the initial antiauthoritarian character of the revolution.

But in a democratic society (at least when such a society is not galvanized by the necessity of going to war) the *heterogeneous* imperative agency (nation in republican forms, king in constitutional monarchies) is reduced to an atrophied existence, so that its destruction no longer appears to be a necessary condition of change. In such a situation, the imperative forms can even be considered as a free field, open to all possibilities of effervescence and movement, just as subversive forms are in a democracy. And when *homogeneous* society undergoes a critical disintegration, the dissociated elements no longer necessarily enter the orbit of subversive attraction: in addition there forms at the top an imperative attraction that no longer immobilizes those who are subject to it. As a rule, until just recently, this imperative attraction only exerted itself in the direction of restoration. It was thus limited beforehand by the prior nature of the disappeared sovereignty, which most often implied a prohibitive loss of contact between the sovereign agency and the lower classes (the only spontaneous historical restoration, that of Bonapartism, must be put into relation with the manifest popular sources of Bonapartist power). In France, it is true, some of the constitutive forms of fascism were able to be elaborated in the formation— but especially in the difficulties of the formation—of an imperative attraction aimed at a dynastic restoration. The possibility of fascism nonetheless depended upon the fact that a reversion to vanished sovereign forms was out of the question in Italy, where the monarchy subsisted in a reduced state. Added to this subsistence, it was precisely the insufficiency of the royal formation that necessitated the formation of —and left the field open for—an entirely renewed imperative attraction with a popular base. Under these new conditions (with regard to the classical revolutionary dissociations in monarchical societies) the lower classes no longer exclusively experience the attraction represented by socialist subversion, and a military type of organization has in part begun to draw them into the orbit of sovereignty. Likewise, the dissociated elements (belonging to the middle or dominating classes) have found a new outlet for their effervescence, and it is not surprising that, given the choice between subversive or imperative solutions, the majority opted for the imperative.

An unprecedented situation results from the possibility of this dual effervescence. During the same period and in the same society, two competing revolutions, hostile to one another and to the established order, are being formed. There develop at the same time two segments that share a common opposition to the general dissociation of *homogeneous* society; this explains the numerous connections between them and even a kind of profound complicity. Furthermore, independently of their common origin, the success of one of the functions implies that of the opposing faction through a certain play of balance: it can cause it to occur (in particular, to the extent that fascism is an imperative response to the growing threat of a working class movement) and should be considered, in most cases, as the sign of that occurrence. But, unless it is possible to reestablish the disrupted *homogeneity*, it is evident that the simple formation of a situation of this order dictates its own outcome in advance: an increase in this effervescence is accompanied by a proportionate increase in the importance of the *dissociated elements* (bourgeois and petty bourgeois) as compared to that of the elements that had never been integrated (proletariat). Thus the chances for a working class revolution, a liberating subversion of society, disappear to the extent that revolutionary possibilities are affirmed.

As a rule, it seems therefore that revolutionary movements that develop in a democracy are hopeless, at least so long as the memory of the earlier struggles against the royal authority has been attenuated and no longer necessarily sets *heterogeneous* reactions in opposition to imperative forms. In fact, it is evident that the situation of the major democratic powers, where the fate of the Revolution is being played out, does not warrant the slightest confidence: it is only the very nearly indifferent attitude of the proletariat that has permitted these countries to avoid fascist formations. Yet it would be puerile to presume to enclose the world in such a neat construction: from the outset, the mere consideration of affective social formations reveals the immense resources, the inexhaustible wealth of the forms particular to affective life. Not only are the psychological situations of the democratic collectivities, like any human situation, transitory, but it remains possible to envision, at least as a yet imprecise representation, forms of attraction that differ from those already in existence, as different from present or even past communism as fascism is from dynastic claims. A system of knowledge that permits the anticipation of the affective social reactions that traverse the superstructure and perhaps even, to a certain extent, do away with it, must be developed from one of these possibilities. The fact of fascism, which has thrown the very existence of a workers' movement into question, clearly demonstrates what can be expected from a timely recourse to reawakened affective forces. Unlike the situation during the period of utopian socialism, morality and idealism are no more questions today than they are in fascist forms. Rather, an organized understanding of the movements in society, of attraction and repulsion, starkly presents itself as a weapon—at this moment when a vast convulsion opposes, not so much fascism to communism, but radical imperative forms to the deep subversion that continues to pursue the emancipation of human lives.

Notes

1. This is obviously the principal shortcoming of an essay that will not fail to astonish and shock those who are unfamiliar with French sociology, modern German philosophy (phenomenology), and psychoanalysis. As a piece of information, it can nevertheless be insisted upon that the following descriptions refer to *actual experiences* and that the psychological method used excludes any recourse to abstraction.

2. The words *homogeneous, heterogeneous*, and terms derived from them are stressed each time they are taken in a sense particular to this essay.

3. The most accomplished and expressive forms of social *homogeneity* are the sciences and the technologies. The laws founded by the sciences establish relations of identity between the different elements of an elaborated and measurable world. As for the technologies—which serve as a transition between production and science—, it is because of the very homogeneity of products and means that they are opposed, in underdeveloped civilizations, to religion and magic (cf. Hubert and Mauss, *Esquisse d'une theorie générale de la magie*, in *Année sociologique* 7, 1902–1903, p. 15).

4. *Formes élémentaires de la vie religieuse*, 1912, p. 53. [*The Elementary Forms of the Religious Life*, trans. J. W. Swain (London: Allen and Unwin, 1926), p. 38. Tr.] Following his analysis, Durkheim comes to identify the *sacred* and the *social*, but this identification necessitates the introduction of an hypothesis and, whatever its scope, does not have the value of an immediately significant definition (it actually represents the tendency of science to posit a *homogeneous* representation in order to avoid the discernible presence of fundamentally *heterogeneous* elements).

5. Cf. G. Bataille, "La notion de dépense," in *La critique sociale* 7, January 1933, p. 302. ["The Notion of Expenditure," above. Tr.]

6. It appears that the displacements are produced under the same conditions as are Pavlov's conditioned reflexes.

7. On the primitive mind, cf. Levy-Bruhl, *La mentalité primitive*; Cassirer, *Das mythische Denken*; on the unconscious, cf. Freud, *The Interpretation of Dreams*.

8. On the affective relations of the followers to the leader and on the analogy with hypnosis, cf. Freud, *Group Psychology and the Analysis of the "Ego"* (reprinted in *Essais de psychanalyse*, 1929).

9. Cf. W. Robertson Smith, *Lectures on the religion of the Semites*, first series, *The Fundamental Institutions*, Edinburgh, 1889.

10. The word *sovereign* comes from the lower Latin adjective *superaneus* meaning *superior*.

11. Freud, in *Group Psychology and the Analysis of the "Ego,"* studied precisely the two functions, military (army) and religious (church), in relation to the imperative form (unconscious) of individual psychology that he called the *Ego Ideal* or the *supergo*. If one refers to the whole of the elements brought together in the present study, that work, published in German in 1921, appears as an essential introduction of the understanding of fascism.

12. The modern Italian state is to a great extent a creation of fascism.

13. *Khalif* etymologically signifies *lieutenant* (standing in for [tenant lieu]; the full title is "lieutenant of the emissary of God."

14. Condensation of *superiority*, evidently related to a latent inferiority complex: such a complex has equally strong roots in both Italy and Germany; this is why, even if fascism develops subsequently in regions having attained a complete sovereignty and the awareness of the sovereignty, it is inconceivable that it could ever have been the autochthonous and specific product of such countries.

15. Mussolini, *Enciclopedia italiana*, article *Fascismo*.

16. Ibid.

17. Ibid.

Popular Front in the Street

Comrades:

I will speak on the question of the Popular Front.

However, I do not want to equivocate.

We are not politicians.

We want to express ourselves on the question of the Popular Front. It is necessary for us to define our position in relation to a new set of forces that at the present time dominates the political scene. But when we urge people to have confidence in us, we are not thinking of the kind of confidence that would be granted us because of more or less apt definitions derived, whether we wanted it or not, from political maneuvers.

We will not try to add new maneuvers to the already complex and often divergent maneuvers of the politicians.

When we speak to those who want to hear us, we do not essentially address their political finesse. The reactions we hope for from them are not calculations of positions, nor are they new political alliances. What we hope for is of a different nature.

We see that the human masses are at the disposition of blind forces which condemn them to inexplicable hecatombs, and which, while making them wait, give them a morally empty and materially miserable life.

What we have before our eyes is the horror of human impotence.

We want to confront this horror directly. We address ourselves to the direct and violent drives which, in the minds of those who hear us, can contribute to the surge of power that will liberate men from the absurd swindlers who lead them.

We know that such drives have little to do with the phraseology invented to maintain political positions. The will to be done with impotence implies, even in our eyes, scorn for this phrasemongering; the taste for verbal agitation has never passed for a mark of power.

On this point, we want to express ourselves in a precise way.

Derided humanity has already known surges of power. These chaotic but implacable power surges dominate history and are known as Revolutions. On many occasions entire populations have gone into the street and nothing has been able to resist their force. It is an incontestable fact that if men have found themselves in the streets, armed, in a mass uprising, carrying with them the tumult of the total power of the people, it has never been the consequence of a narrow and speciously defined political alliance.

What drives the crowds to the street is the emotion directly aroused by striking events in the atmosphere of a storm, it is the contagious emotion that, from house to house, from suburb to suburb, suddenly turns a hesitating man into a frenzied being.

It is evident that if, in general, insurrections had had to wait for learned disputes between committees and the political offices of parties, then there never would have been an insurrection.

Still, as astonishing as this may seem, one frequently notes, among militant revolutionaries, a complete lack of confidence in the spontaneous reactions of the masses.

The need to organize parties has resulted in unusual habits among the so-called revolutionary agitators, who confuse the entry of the Revolution into the street with their political platforms, with their well-groomed programs, with their maneuvers in the halls of Congress.

Amazingly, a distrust of the same order prevails against intellectuals. The distrust of intellectuals only apparently contradicts the one that underestimates the spontaneous movements of the masses.

As much as they can, certain professional revolutionary activists would like to eliminate, from the human tragedy that the Revolution necessarily is, all its emotional resources, the brutal convulsion of the masses, the atmosphere charged with hope, the rages and enthusiasms expressed in periods of crisis by those who write.

We are as far as we can be from the belief that a movement can do without its leaders, as far as we can be from the belief that this leadership can do without the resources of human knowledge contributed by the most recent advances of human understanding. But first of all we must protest against everything that is born in the poisoned atmosphere of professional congresses and committees, all of which are at the mercy of hallway maneuvers.

We do not think it possible to raise a political question without having a debate. And for us having the debate means having it in the street, it means having it where emotion can seize men and push them to the limit, without meeting the eternal obstacles that result from the defense of old political positions.

If we are to speak of the Popular Front, we must first identify what holds us firmly together, what links our origins to the emotions that constitute it, namely, the existence of the Popular Front in the street.

Comrades, we must say of the Popular Front that it was born on the Cours de Vincennes on the day of February 12, 1934, when for the first time the masses of workers gathered to demonstrate the strength of their opposition to fascism.

Most of us, comrades, were in the street that day and can recall the emotion that overcame us when the Communist marchers, coming out of the rue des Pyrénées, turned into the Cours de Vincennes and took up the entire width of the street: this massive group was preceded by a line of a hundred workers, shoulder to shoulder and arm in arm, marching with unprecedented slowness and singing the *Internationale*. Many among you, no doubt, can remember the huge old bald worker, with a reddish face and heavy white moustache, who walked slowly, one step at a time, in front of that moving human wall, holding high a red flag.

It was no longer a procession, nor anything poorly political; it was the curse of the working people, and not only in its rage, IN ITS IMPOVERISHED MAJESTY, which advanced, made greater by a kind of rending solemnity—by the menace of slaughter still suspended at that moment over all of the crowd.

Comrades, at that moment, on the Cours de Vincennes, the Communist masses marched in front of the Socialist masses, and a little later merged with them through an identical cry for unity of action. This was the period, however, when, in *L'Humanité*, professional politicians indulged in precise definitions of the situation: according to Marty, in an article whose delirium moreover must nevertheless be acknowledged, they had shot not fascists but workers on the Place de la Concorde. For the entire editorial board of *L'Humanité*, Daladier's government then became a government of executioners, and unity of action continued to be impossible with the Socialist traitors. On this question, the Central Committee of the party published, a few days after February 12, statements that clearly indicated their refusal.

This is how revolutionary activity can be expressed *in the street* with force and at the same time with an incomparable instinctive certainty, when from the poisoned atmosphere of committees and editorial offices nothing comes but political directives testifying to a scandalous blindness.

Political wrangling was again superseded by the reality of the street at the time of the definitive formation of the Popular Front.

The Popular Front was conceived by its founders as a defensive organization, reuniting all the forces hostile to fascism. It is impossible not to see that its birth coincided with the salvation of Stalin by the French Army. The grave, and perhaps even tragic, situation of the Soviets engaged them in a Franco-Russian political alliance, which then linked their interests to social conservatism in France. Clearly, from the moment that Soviet security depends on the French military forces, the Soviets cannot at the same time work to undermine these forces. In the spirit of its Communist founders, the Popular Front's goal was, without a doubt, the maintenance of a nonfascist, but strong, France, thus at the disposal of socially conservative elements.

In a certain sense, the Popular Front meant nothing more than the revolutionaries' abandonment of the anticapitalist offensive; the move to the defense of antifascism; the move to the simple defense of democracy; the abandonment, at the same time, of revolutionary defeatism.

Now comrades, what can we think of this abandonment of the anticapitalist offensive, at precisely the time when a great number of people, independently of their political tendencies, agreed upon the disastrous character of the capitalist system? From the revolutionary point of view, the abandonment of the anticapitalist offensive in the midst of the present crisis would represent the most scandalous possible weakness; isn't it incredible to leave to the worst slaves of capitalism, to the fascistic Croix de feu lackeys of the de Wendels, the rallying cry awaited by the anxious, disconcerted masses, the rallying cry to fight against a capitalism despised by the vast majority of men?

The default of the politicians thus would abandon the real world, the world of tragic sufferings and hopes, to the degrading verbal comedy of barracks-room thugs.

And at the same time, while dread mounts from day to day before the imminence of the physical extermination of men and human wealth, wouldn't it be incredible to anticipate a new conflict by giving the idea of antifascism a value on the level of military struggle, when we know, meanwhile, that stupid imperialism precisely engendered this fascism that we mean to fight while marching in the ranks assigned to us by generals and industrial magnates.

Comrades, if human reality, or to be more precise, human reality in the street—personally, it is in tying to it all the hope that stirs me that I use this term "street," which opposes life, real life, to the schemes as well as to the isolation of the absurdly involuted individual—if human reality did not in every possible way go beyond the mediocre conceptions and betrayals of conniving politicians, then the Popular Front would not have, for any of us, the profound meaning that it has acquired in the circumstances that we have lived and that we continue to live.

Even today, while many people—rightly or wrongly—are claiming that the Popular Front is falling apart at the top, that, beyond an antifascist defense it will be incapable of setting forth a plan for concerted action essential to the exercise of power, we continue to see growing among the masses who make up its strength, who were in the street yesterday, who will invade the street tomorrow, the agitation of the people's omnipotence.

Badly formed political conceptions have set these people in motion, but the Popular Front does not depend on the will of its founders to work exactly for their goals: the Popular Front is above all now a movement, an agitation, a crucible in which formerly separated political forces meld with an often tumultuous effervescence.

Now that the various social strata that constitute it have become conscious of the strength they represent when reunited, this strength, going to their heads, will attract them to each other and will break the chains meant to hold them.

Therefore, when our comrades of the revolutionary Socialist left call for the transformation of the defense against fascism into an anticapitalist offensive, of the Popular Front into the Popular Front of combat, they are only expressing the dynamic movement inherent in the makeup of forces in motion. Today it is not advisable for anyone to be opposed to the rise of the all-powerful populace.

We must not be unaware, however, that difficulties must be overcome, before the offensive can be realized, without which the party will find itself in the hands of those who are still criminally talking of the "lost victory."

We do not believe that organized parties should disappear, but we do not believe either that the masses can attain the power to put an end to domination by capitalist lackeys unless a movement appears that can escape the sterilizing control of these parties.

We must above all recognize as critical the period following the formation of a government that, without being the direct expression of the Popular Front, could nevertheless be brought to power by the parliamentarians who belonged to this Front.

From time to time the spokesmen of the Popular Front themselves are led to make statements that show an extreme uneasiness on this point. Concerning a Popular Front government, Pierre Jérôme, secretary-general of the Vigilance Committee, a few weeks ago expressed the fear that he could not cover budgetary expenditures with foreseen income: "In that case," Pierre Jérôme states, "we will see our enemies furnished with the best weapon they could hope for. To be sure, if panic sets in, we ourselves should not faint with fear . . . " Jérôme in any case sees a way out of this great difficulty: "In the end, all we need do is make the rich pay . . . "

In fact, nothing is more likely in the near future than a repeat of the disastrous events that sooner or later followed the electoral victories of the so-called Left of 1924 and 1932.

Without being able to have confidence in more or less arbitrary details, one can foresee, at one time or another, a serious crisis of the entire Left, a crisis that will not fail to seriously affect the Popular Front itself.

To tell the truth, those of us who see the Popular Front as a reality in motion have nothing to become excessively alarmed about in such a crisis. We must only foresee it, knowing full well that no development of forces and no great social transformation can take place without a crisis, knowing as well above all that the forces destined to prevail are those that not only overcome their crises, but are capable of profiting by them.

The Popular Front means for us the awareness the people first attained, in the days of February, of their strength in the face of Fascist thugs and lackeys. We do not believe that this awareness will allow itself to be shaken on the day miserable directors betray their own impotence.

These conditions are, on the contrary, in our opinion, necessary so that the masses, who have no desire for the reactionary solutions leading to poverty and war, this time can become aware of the inherent necessities of power. It is possible that a crisis is indispensable for the transformation—as indicated from the outset by the menacing attitude of the masses in the street—of the defensive Popular Front into the Popular Front of combat, and, of course, of combat for the anticapitalist dictatorship of the people.

It is clear from now on that, in order to have confidence in its own resources, the Popular Front must first lose the confidence it currently has in its principal leaders.

I do not think it necessary here to insist upon our reasons for having the greatest distrust and even the greatest contempt for given professional political parliamentarians, who tomorrow risk being entrusted with the position of leadership.

What interests us above all—the analysis of the economic bases of society having been accomplished, its results having proven, moreover, to be limited— are the emotions that give the human masses the surges of power that tear them away from the domination of those who only know how to lead them on to poverty and to the slaughterhouse.

But we would not want to suggest that we blindly abandon ourselves to the spontaneous reactions of the street.

We are led to make an essential distinction between the reactions that agitate men in the street and the phrasemongering of politicians, and all the teachings of the present period at the very least show that this distinction credits the men who have nothing going for them but their passions, to the detriment of those corrupted and often emptied of human content by the strategic task.

But we find no reason to renounce the decisive intervention of judgment and of the methodical understanding of the facts. We only wish to apply intelligence less to so-called political situations and to the logical deductions that ensue, than to the immediate comprehension of life. Even independently of the tragic events now taking place, we believe that there is more to learn in the streets of great cities, for example, than in political newspapers or books. For us a significant reality is the state of prostration and boredom expressed inside a bus by a dozen human faces, all of them complete strangers. For anyone not already hardened by the emptiness of life, there is in this world, which seems to have at its disposal limitless resources, a confusion remedied only by a kind of lazily accepted general imbecility. Even poverty seems at the very least less incurable than this stupid distress. A beggar whose broken voice cries out a song one can barely hear in the rear of a courtyard seems at times to have lost less in the game of life than the human matter arranged in buses and trains during rush hour.

Someone told me the other day, correctly, that the source of the Croix de Feu's might was very simple: the Croix de Feu, in general, are people who are bored. The minimum of contagious passion animating the Croix de Feu, the low budget exaltation—to tell the truth, an exaltation good for workrooms—maintained by this pillar of human boredom (family barracks) known as the Count Colonel de la Rocque, is somehow enough to maintain a vague gleam of life in empty brains, but no taste for what is burning or colorful in life grips them, and the sinister job of the Croix de Feu becomes their whole life.

The opium of the people in the present world is perhaps not so much religion as it is accepted boredom. Such a world is at the mercy, it must be known, of those who provide at least the semblance of an escape from boredom. Human life aspires to the passions, and again encounters its exigencies.

It can appear out of place and even absolutely absurd to those who worry about which platforms must serve as the basis for future actions, when we respond by saying that the world in which they bustle about is doomed to boredom.

This remark, however, has a very simple meaning: in the Communist opposition, I have personally known a great number of people for whom the definition of platforms has had an essential value. Their activity resulted only in stunning boredom, which they saw precisely as the mark of revolutionary seriousness.

We want to say that we oppose these preoccupations.

We believe that strength will belong not to those for whom action is a demand for morose and disagreeable work, but to those who, on the contrary, will deliver the world from its exhausting boredom.

We want to give precise answers to questions that demand precise answers, but we maintain that what is essential lies elsewhere.

We must contribute to the masses' awareness of their own power; we are sure that strength results less from strategy than from collective exaltation, and exaltation can come only from words that touch not the reason but the passions of the masses.

We want to hope that soon the masses will know how to gather and find together, in this reunion, the burning heat that attracts men from all sides and that will become the basis for an implacable popular domination.

We ask all those who, along with us, mean to pursue an action parallel to the one we see open before us how they hope to achieve the dictatorship of the working masses, how, first of all, they hope to realize the transformation of the defensive Popular Front into a Popular Front of combat.

As for us, we want to pose the question in a precise way. It seems to me personally that the only way to pose the question is the following: it is not really a question of knowing first of all what must be done, but what result must be envisioned. We know that the question of the takeover of power is now being posed. We know that, in all likelihood, the democratic regime, which struggles amidst mortal contradictions, cannot be saved.

The succession is open. We have many reasons to think that the Croix de Feu provide no response to the necessities resulting from the current situation— neither in their social content, the tenor of their program, nor in the personality of their chief. Their effective value seems to us in this respect to be situated far below that of the Italian Fascists or the German National Socialists.

The Popular Front in its present form is not, nor does it present itself, as an organized force within sight of taking power. It must thus be transformed, according to the plan of the socialist revolutionary Left, into a Popular Front of combat.

As for us, we say that this presupposes a renewal of political forms, a renewal possible in the present circumstances, when it seems that all revolutionary forces are called upon to fuse in an incandescent crucible. We are assured that insurrection is impossible for our adversaries. We believe that of the two hostile forces that will engage in the struggle for power, the fascists and the people, the force that gets the upper hand will be the one that shows itself most capable of dominating events and imposing an implacable power on its adversaries. What we demand is a coherent, disciplined organization, its entire will straining with enthusiasm toward popular power; this is the sense of responsibility that must devolve on those who tomorrow must be the masters, who must subordinate the system of production to human interests, who must impose silence, in their own country and at the same time throughout the world, on the nationalists' criminal and puerile passions.

. . . . .

After February 16.

500,000 workers, defied by little cockroaches, invaded the streets and caused an immense uproar.

Comrades, who has the right to lay down the law?

This ALL-POWERFUL multitude, thus HUMAN OCEAN . . .

Only this ocean of men in revolt can save the world from the nightmare of impotence and carnage in which it sinks!

III
(1936 – 1939)

The Labyrinth

Negativity, in other words, the integrity of determination.

Hegel

I. The Insufficiency of Beings

MEN ACT IN ORDER TO BE. This must not be understood in the negative sense of conservation (conserving in order not to be thrown out of existence by death), but in the positive sense of a tragic and incessant combat for a satisfaction that is almost beyond reach. From incoherent agitation to crushing sleep, from chatter to turning inward, from overwhelming love to hardening hate, existence sometimes weakens and sometimes accomplishes "being." And not only do states have a variable intensity, but different beings "are" unequally. A dog that runs and barks seems "to be" more than a mute and clinging sponge, the sponge more than the water in which it lives, an influential man more than a vacant passerby.

In the first movement, where the force that the master has at his disposal puts the slave at his mercy, the master deprives the slave of a part of his being. Much later, in return, the "existence" of the master is impoverished to the extent that it distances itself from the material elements of life. The slave enriches his being to the extent that he enslaves these elements by the work to which his impotence condemns him.

The contradictory movements of degradation and growth attain, in the diffuse development of human existence, a bewildering complexity. The fundamental

171

separation of men into masters and slaves is only the crossed threshold, the entry into the world of specialized functions where personal "existence" empties itself of its contents; a man is no longer anything but a part of being, and his life, engaged in the game of creation and destruction that goes beyond it, appears as a degraded particle lacking reality. The very fact of assuming that knowledge is a function throws the philosopher back into the world of petty inconsistencies and dissections of lifeless organs. Isolated as much from action as from the dreams that turn action away and echo it in the strange depths of animated life, he led astray the very being that he chose as the object of his uneasy comprehension. "Being" increases in the tumultuous agitation of a life that knows no limits; it wastes away and disappears if he who is at the same time "being" and knowledge mutilates himself by reducing himself to knowledge.

This deficiency can grow even greater if the object of knowledge is no longer being in general but a narrow domain, such as an organ, a mathematical question, a juridical form. Action and dreams do not escape this poverty (each time they are confused with the totality of being), and, in the multicolored immensity of human lives, a limitless insufficiency is revealed; life, finding its endpoint in the happiness of a bugle blower or the snickering of a village chair-renter, is no longer the fulfillment of itself, but is its own ludicrous degradation—its fall is comparable to that of a king onto the floor.

At the basis of human life there exists a *principle of insufficiency*. In isolation, each man sees the majority of others as incapable or unworthy of "being." There is found, in all free and slanderous conversation, as an animating theme, the awareness of the vanity and the emptiness of our fellowmen; an apparently stagnant conversation betrays the blind and impotent flight of all life toward an indefinable summit.

The sufficiency of each being is endlessly contested by every other. Even the look that expresses love and admiration comes to me as a doubt concerning my reality. A burst of laughter or the expression of repugnance greets each gesture, each sentence or each oversight through which my profound insufficiency is betrayed—just as sobs would be the response to my sudden death, to a total and irremediable omission.

This uneasiness on the part of everyone grows and reverberates, since at each detour, with a kind of nausea, men discover their solitude in empty night. The universal night in which everything finds itself—and soon loses itself—would appear to be existence for nothing, without influence, equivalent to the absence of being, were it not for human nature that emerges within it to give a dramatic importance to being and life. But this absurd night manages to empty itself of "being" and meaning each time a man discovers within it human destiny, itself locked in turn in a comic impasse, like a hideous and discordant trumpet blast. That which, in me, demands that there be "being" in the world, "being" and not just the manifest insufficiency of human or nonhuman nature, necessarily projects (at one time or another and in reply to human chatter) divine sufficiency across space, like the reflection of an impotence, of a servilely accepted malady of being.

II. The Composite Character of Beings and the Impossibility of Fixing Existence in Any Given *Ipse*

Being in the world is so *uncertain* that I can project it where I want—outside of me. It is a clumsy man, still incapable of eluding the intrigues of nature, who locks being in the me. Being in fact is found NOWHERE and it was an easy game for a sickly malice to discover it to be divine, at the summit of a pyramid formed by the multitude of beings, which has at its base the immensity of the simplest matter.

Being could be confined to the electron if *ipseity* were precisely not lacking in this simple element. The atom itself has a complexity that is too elementary to be determined *ipsely*.[1] The number of particles that make up a being intervene in a sufficiently heavy and clear way in the constitution of its *ipseity*; if a knife has its handle and blade indefinitely replaced, it loses even the shadow of *ipseity*; it is not the same for a machine which, after five or six years, loses each of the *numerous* elements that constituted it when new. But the *ipseity* that is finally apprehended with difficulty in the machine is still only shadowlike.

Starting from an extreme complexity, being imposes on reflection more than the precariousness of a fugitive appearance, but this complexity—displaced little by little—becomes in turn the labyrinth where what had suddenly come forward strangely loses its way.

A sponge is reduced by pounding to a dust of cells; this living dust is formed by a multitude of isolated beings, and is lost in the new sponge that it reconstitutes. A siphonophore fragment is by itself an autonomous being, yet the whole siphonophore, to which this fragment belongs, is itself hardly different from a being possessing unity. Only with linear animals (worms, insects, fish, reptiles, birds, and mammals) do the living individual forms definitively lose the faculty of constituting aggregates bound together in a single body. But while *societies* of nonlinear animals do not exist, superior animals form aggregates without ever giving rise to corporeal links; men as well as beavers or ants form societies of individuals whose bodies are autonomous. But in regard to being, is this autonomy the final appearance, or is it simply error?

In men, all existence is tied in particular to language, whose terms determine its modes of appearance within each person. Each person can only represent his total existence, if only in his own eyes, through the medium of words. Words spring forth in his head, laden with a host of human or superhuman lives *in relation* to which he privately exists. Being depends on the mediation of words, which cannot merely present it arbitrarily as "autonomous being," but which must present it profoundly as "being in relation." One need only follow, for a short time, the traces of the repeated circuits of words to discover, in a disconcerting vision, the labyrinthine structure of the human being. What is commonly called *knowing*—when a man *knows* his neighbor—is never anything but existence *composed* for an instant (in the sense that all existence composes itself—thus the atom composes its unity from variable electrons), which *once* made of these two beings a *whole* every bit as real as its parts. A limited number of exchanged phrases, no matter how conventional, sufficed to create the banal interpenetration of two existing juxtaposed regions. The fact that after this short exchange the man is aware of *knowing* his neighbor is opposed to a meeting without recognition in the street, as well as to the ignorance of the multitude of beings that one never meets, in the same way that life is opposed to death. The *knowledge* of human beings thus appears as a mode of biological connection, unstable but just as real as the connections between cells in tissue. The exchange between two human particles in fact possesses the faculty of surviving momentary separation.

A man is only a particle inserted in unstable and entangled wholes. These wholes are composed in personal life in the form of multiple possibilities, starting with a *knowledge* that is crossed like a threshold—and the existence of the particle can in no way be isolated from this composition, which agitates it in the midst of a whirlwind of ephemerids. This extreme instability of connections alone permits one to introduce, as a puerile but convenient illusion, a representation of isolated existence turning in on itself.

In the most general way, *every isolable element of the universe always appears as a particle that can enter into composition with a whole that transcends it. Being is only found as a whole composed of particles whose relative autonomy is maintained.* These two principles dominate the uncertain presence of an *ipse* being across a distance that never ceases to put *everything* in question. Emerging in universal play as unforeseeable chance, with extreme dread imperatively becoming the demand for universality, carried away to vertigo by the movement that composes it, the *ipse* being that presents itself as a universal is only a challenge to the diffuse immensity that escapes its precarious violence, the tragic negation of all that is not its own bewildered phantom's chance. But, as a man, this being falls into the meanders of the *knowledge* of his fellowmen, which absorbs his substance in order to reduce it to a component of what goes beyond the virulent madness of his autonomy in the total night of the world.

Abdication and inevitable fatigue—due to the fact that "being" is, *par excellence*, that which, desired to the point of dread, cannot be endured—plunge human beings into a foggy labyrinth formed by the multitude of "acquaintances" with which signs of life and phrases can be exchanged. But when he escapes the dread of "being" through this flight—a "being" that is autonomous and isolated in night—a man is thrown back into insufficiency, at least if he cannot find outside of himself the blinding flash that he had been unable to endure within himself, without whose intensity his life is but an impoverishment, of which he feels obscurely ashamed.

III. The Structure of the Labyrinth

Emerging out of an inconceivable void into the play of beings, as a lost satellite of two phantoms (one with a bristly beard, the other softer, her head decorated with a bun), it is in the father and mother who transcend him that the minuscule human being first encountered the illusion of sufficiency. In the complexity and entanglement of wholes, to which the human particle belongs, this satellite-like mode of existence never entirely disappears. A particular being not only acts as an element of a shapeless and structureless whole (a part of the world of unimportant "acquaintances" and chatter), but also as a peripheral element orbiting around a nucleus where being hardens. What the lost child had found in the self-assured existence of the all-powerful beings who took care of him is now sought by the abandoned man wherever knots and concentrations are formed throughout a vast incoherence. Each particular being delegates to the group of those situated at the center of the multitudes the task of realizing the inherent totality of "being." He is content to be a part of a total existence, which even in the simplest cases retains a diffuse character. Thus relatively stable wholes are produced, whose center is a city, in its early form a corolla that encloses a double pistil of sovereign and god. In the case where many cities abdicate their central function in favor of a single city, an empire forms around a capital where sovereignty and the gods are concentrated; the gravitation around a center then degrades the existence of peripheral cities, where the organs that constituted the totality of being wilt. By degrees, a more and more complex movement of group composition raises to the point of universality the human race, but it seems that universality, at the summit, causes all existence to explode and decomposes it with violence. The universal god destroys rather than supports the human aggregates that raise his ghost. He himself is only dead, whether a mythical delirium set him up to be adored as a cadaver covered with wounds, or whether through his very universality he becomes, more than any other, incapable of stopping the loss of being with the cracked partitions of *ipseity*.

IV. The Modalities of Composition
and Decomposition of Being

The city that little by little empties itself of life, in favor of a more brilliant and attractive city, is the expressive image of the play of existence engaged in composition. Because of the composing attraction, *composition empties elements of the greatest part of their being, and this benefits the center*—in other words, it benefits composite being. There is the added fact that, in a given domain, *if the attraction of a certain center is stronger than that of a neighboring center, the second center then goes into decline*. The action of powerful poles of attraction across the human world thus reduces, depending on their force of resistance, a multitude of personal beings to the state of empty shadows, especially when the pole of attraction on which they depend itself declines, due to the action of another more powerful pole. Thus if one imagines the effects of an influential current of attraction on a more or less arbitrarily isolated form of activity, a style of clothing created in a certain city devalues the clothes worn up to that time and, consequently, it devalues those who wear them within the limits of the influence of this city. This devaluation is stronger if, in a neighboring country, the fashions of a more brilliant city have already outclassed those of the first city. The objective character of these relations is registered in reality when the contempt and laughter manifested in a given center are not compensated for by anything elsewhere, and when they exert an effective fascination. The effort made on the periphery to "keep up with fashion" demonstrates the inability of the peripheral particles to exist by themselves.

Laughter intervenes in these value determinations of being as the expression of the circuit of movements of attraction across a human field. It manifests itself each time a change in level suddenly occurs: it characterizes all vacant lives as *ridiculous*. A kind of incandescent joy—the explosive and sudden revelation of the presence of being—is liberated each time a striking appearance is contrasted with its absence, with the human void. Laughter casts a glance, charged with the mortal violence of being, into the void of life.

But laughter is not only the composition of those it assembles into a unique convulsion; it most often decomposes without consequence, and sometimes with a virulence that is so pernicious that it even puts in question composition itself, and the wholes across which it functions. Laughter attains not only the peripheral regions of existence, and its object is not only the existence of fools and children (of those who remain vacant); through a necessary reversal, it is sent back from the child to its father and from the periphery to the center, each time the father or the center in turn reveals an insufficiency comparable to that of the particles that orbit around it. Such a central insufficiency can be ritually revealed (in saturnalia or in a festival of the ass as well as in the puerile grimaces of the father amusing his child). It can be revealed by the very action of children or the "poor" each time exhaustion withers and weakens authority, allowing its precarious character to be seen. In both cases, a dominant necessity manifests itself, and the profound nature of being is disclosed. Being can complete itself and attain the menacing gradeur of imperative totality; this accomplishment only serves to project it with a greater violence into the vacant night. The relative insufficiency of peripheral existences is absolute insufficiency in total existence. Above knowable existences, laughter traverses the human pyramid like a network of endless waves that renew themselves in all directions. This reverberated convulsion chokes, from one end to the other, the innumerable being of man— opened at the summit by the agony of God in a black night.

V. The Monster in the Night of the Labyrinth

Being attains the blinding flash in tragic annihilation. Laughter only assumes its fullest impact on being at the moment when, in the fall that it unleashes, a representation of death is cynically recognized. It is not only the composition of elements that constitutes the incandescence of being, but its decomposition in its mortal form. The difference in levels that provokes common laughter—which opposes the lack of an absurd life to the plenitude of successful being—can be replaced by that which opposes the summit of imperative elevation to the dark abyss that obliterates all existence. Laughter is thus assumed by the totality of being. Renouncing the avaricious malice of the scapegoat, being itself, to the extent that it is the sum of existences at the limits of the night, is spasmodically shaken by the idea of the ground giving way beneath its feet. It is in *universality* (where, due to solitude, the possibility of facing death through war disappears) that the necessity of engaging in a struggle, no longer with an equal group but with nothingness, becomes clear. THE UNIVERSAL resembles a bull, sometimes absorbed in the nonchalance of animality and abandoned to the secret paleness of death, and sometimes hurled by the rage of ruin into the void ceaselessly opened before it by a skeletal torero. But the void it meets is also the nudity it espouses TO THE EXTENT THAT IT IS A MONSTER lightly assuming many crimes, and it is no longer, like the bull, the plaything of nothingness, because nothingness itself is its plaything; it only throws itself into nothingness in order to tear it apart and to illuminate the night for an instant, with an immense laugh—a laugh it never would have attained if this nothingness had not totally opened beneath its feet.

Note

1. See Paul Langevin, *La Notion de corpuscules et d'atomes* (Paris: Hermann, 1934), p. 35.

The Sacred Conspiracy

An already old and corrupt nation, courageously shaking off the yoke of its monarchical government in order to adopt a republican one, can only maintain itself through many crimes; for it is already in crime, and if it wants to move from crime to virtue, in other words from a violent state to a peaceful one, it would fall into an inertia, of which its certain ruin would soon be the result.

Sade

What looks like politics, and imagines itself to be political, will one day unmask itself as a religious movement.

Kierkegaard

Today solitary, you who live apart, you one day will be a people. Those who have designated themselves will one day be a designated people, and from this people will be born the life that goes beyond man.

Nietzsche

What we have started must not be confused with anything else, cannot be limited to the expression of a thought, and still less to what is rightly considered art.

It is necessary to produce and to eat: many things are necessary that are still nothing, and so it is with political agitation.

Who dreams, before having struggled to the end, of relinquishing his place to men it is impossible to look at without feeling the need to destroy? If nothing can be found beyond political activity, human avidity will meet nothing but a void.

WE ARE FEROCIOUSLY RELIGIOUS and, to the extent that our existence is the condemnation of everything that is recognized today, an inner exigency demands that we be equally imperious.

What we are starting is a war.

It is time to abandon the world of the civilized and its light. It is too late to be reasonable and educated—which has led to a life without appeal. Secretly or not, it is necessary to become completely different, or to cease being.

The world to which we have belonged offers nothing to love outside of each individual insufficiency: its existence is limited to utility. A world that cannot be loved to the point of death—in the same way that a man loves a woman—represents only self-interest and the obligation to work. If it is compared to worlds gone by, it is hideous, and appears as the most failed of all. In past worlds, it was possible to lose oneself in ecstasy, which is impossible in our world of educated vulgarity. The advantages of civilization are offset by the way men profit from them: men today profit in order to become the most degraded beings that have ever existed.

Life has always taken place in a tumult without apparent cohesion, but it only finds its grandeur and its reality in ecstasy and in ecstatic love. He who tries to ignore or misunderstand ecstasy is an incomplete being whose thought is reduced to analysis. Existence is not only an agitated void, it is a dance that forces one to dance with fanaticism. Thought that does not have a dead fragment as its object has the inner existence of flames.

It is necessary to become sufficiently firm and unshaken so that the existence of the world of civilization finally appears uncertain.

It is useless to respond to those who are able to believe in the existence of this world and who take their authority from it; if they speak, it is possible to look at them without hearing them and, even when one looks at them, to "see" only what exists far behind them. It is necessary to refuse boredom and live only for fascination.

On this path, it is vain to become restless and seek to attract those who have idle whims, such as passing the time, laughing, or becoming individually bizarre. It is necessary to go forward without looking back and without taking into account those who do not have the strength to forget immediate reality.

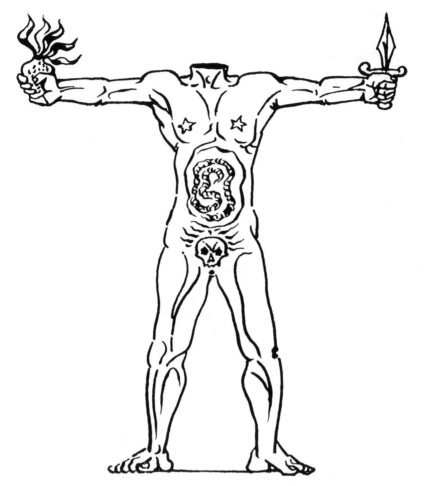

Figure 12. André Masson, *Acéphale.* © by ADAGP, Paris, 1985.

Human life is exhausted from serving as the head of, or the reason for, the universe. To the extent that it becomes this head and this reason, to the extent that it becomes necessary to the universe, it accepts servitude. If it is not free, existence becomes empty or neutral and, if it is free, it is in play. The Earth, as long as it only gave rise to cataclysms, trees, and birds, was a free universe; the fascination of freedom was tarnished when the Earth produced a being who demanded necessity as a law above the universe. Man however has remained free not to respond to any necessity; he is free to resemble everything that is not himself in the universe. He can set aside the thought that it is he or God who keeps the rest of things from being absurd.

Man has escaped from his head just as the condemned man has escaped from his prison. He has found beyond himself not God, who is the prohibition against crime, but a being who is unaware of prohibition. Beyond what I am, I meet a being who makes me laugh because he is headless; this fills me with dread because he is made of innocence and crime; he holds a steel weapon in his left hand, flames like those of a Sacred Heart in his right. He reunites in the same eruption Birth and Death. He is not a man. He is not a god either. He is not me but he is more than me: his stomach is the labyrinth in which he has lost himself, loses me with him, and in which I discover myself as him, in other words as a monster.

What I have thought or represented, I have not thought or represented alone. I am writing in a little cold house in a village of fishermen; a dog has just barked in the night. My room is next to the kitchen where André Masson is happily moving around and singing; at this very moment, as I write, he has just put on the phonograph a recording of the overture to *Don Giovanni*; more than anything else, the overture to *Don Giovanni* ties my lot in life to a challenge that opens me to a rapturous escape from the self. At this very moment, I am watching this acephalic being, this intruder composed of two equally excited obsessions, become the "Tomb of Don Giovanni." When, a few days ago, I was with André Masson in this kitchen, seated, a glass of wine in my hand, he suddenly talked of his own death and the death of his family, his eyes fixed, suffering, almost screaming that it was necessary for it to become a tender and passionate death, screaming his hatred for a world that weighs down even on death with its employee's paw—and I was no longer able to doubt that the lot and the infinite tumult of human life were open to those who could no longer exist as empty eye sockets, but as seers swept away by an overwhelming dream they could not own.

Tossa, April 29, 1936

Nietzsche and the Fascists

Elisabeth Judas-Förster

The Jew Judas betrayed Jesus for a small sum of money—after that he hanged himself. The betrayal carried out by those close to Nietzsche does not have the brutal consequences of Judas's, but it sums up and makes intolerable all the betrayals that deform the teachings of Nietzsche (betrayals that put him on the level of the most shortsighted of current enthusiasms). The anti-Semitic falsifications of Frau Förster, Nietzsche's sister, and of Herr Richard Oehler, his cousin, are in some ways even more vulgar than Judas's deal—beyond all reckoning, they give the force of a whiplash to the maxim in which Nietzsche expressed his horror of anti-Semitism:

DO NOT BEFRIEND ANYONE INVOLVED IN THIS IMPUDENT HOAX, RACISM![1]

The name of Elisabeth Förster-Nietzsche,[2] who died on November 8, 1935, after living a life devoted to a very narrow and degrading form of family-worship, has not yet become an object of aversion . . . On November 2, 1933 Elisabeth Förster-Nietzsche had not forgotten the difficulties that came up between her and her brother over her marriage, in 1885, to the anti-Semite Bernhard Förster. A letter in which Nietzsche reminds her of his ''repulsion''—''as pronounced as possible'' for her husband's party—which he specifically mentions with bitterness—was published through her own efforts.[3] On November 2, 1933, receiving Adolf Hitler at Weimar, in the *Nietzsche-Archiv*,

Elisabeth Förster testified to Nietzsche's anti-Semitism by reading a text by Bernhard Förster.

> Before leaving Weimar to go to Essen [reports the *Times* of November 4, 1933], Chancellor Hitler went to visit Frau Elisabeth Förster-Nietzsche, the sister of the famous philosopher. The aged lady gave him a sword cane that had belonged to her brother. She led him on a tour of the Nietzsche archives.
> Herr Hitler listened to a reading of a statement, addressed to Bismarck, written in 1879 by Dr. Förster, an anti-Semitic agitator, which protests against the "Jewish spirit's invasion of Germany." Holding Nietzsche's cane, Herr Hitler walked through the cheering crowd and got back into his car in order to go to Erfurt, and from there to Essen.

Nietzsche, writing in 1887 a scorning letter to the anti-Semite Theodor Fritsch,[4] ends it with these words:

> BUT FINALLY, WHAT DO YOU THINK I FEEL WHEN ZARATHUSTRA'S NAME COMES OUT OF THE MOUTH OF AN ANTI-SEMITE!

The Second Judas of the *Nietzsche-Archiv*

Adolf Hitler, in Weimar, had himself photographed before a bust of Nietzsche. Herr Richard Oehler, Nietzsche's cousin and a collaborator of Elisabeth Förster at the archives, had the photograph reproduced as the frontispiece of his book *Nietzsche and the Future of Germany*.[5] In this work, he tried to show the profound kinship of Nietzsche's teachings and those of *Mein Kampf*. He recognizes, it is true, the existence of passages in Nietzsche that are not hostile to the Jews, but he concludes:

> Most important for us is this warning:
> "Admit no more Jews! And especially close the doors to the east!" . . . "That Germany has amply *enough* Jews, that the German stomach, the German blood has trouble (and will still have trouble for a long time) digesting even this quantum of 'Jew'—as the Italians, French, and English have done, having a stronger digestive system— that is the clear testimony and language of a general instinct to which one must listen, in accordance with which one must act. 'Admit no more Jews! And especially close the doors to the east (also to Austria!' thus commands the instinct of a people whose type is still weak and indefinite, so it could easily be blurred or extinguished by a stronger race."

It is not only a case here of an "impudent hoax," but of a crudely and consciously fabricated falsehood. This text appears, in fact, in *Beyond Good and Evil* (section 251), but the opinion it expresses is not that of Nietzsche, but that of the anti-Semites, taken up by Nietzsche in order to mock it.

I have not met a German yet who was well disposed toward the Jews; and however unconditionally all the cautious and politically minded repudiated real anti-Semitism, even this caution and policy are not directed against the species of this feeling itself but only against its dangerous immoderation, especially against the inspired and shameful expression of this immoderate feeling—about this, one should not deceive oneself. That Germany has amply *enough* Jews, etc.

After this comes the passage attributed by the fascist forger to Nietzsche! A little further on a practical conclusion is, moreover, given to these considerations: "it might be useful and fair to expel the anti-Semite screamers from the country." This time Nietzsche speaks in his own name. The aphorism as a whole favors the assimilation of the Jews by the Germans.

Do Not Kill:
Reduce to Slavery

DOES MY *LIFE* MAKE IT LIKELY THAT I COULD ALLOW ANYONE AT ALL TO "CLIP MY WINGS"?[6]

The tone Nietzsche used during his lifetime to answer obnoxious anti-Semites excludes the possibility of treating the question lightly, and of considering the Weimar Judases' treason to be venial: he appears there with "clipped wings."

Nietzsche's relatives have attempted nothing less base than the reduction to degrading slavery of the one who intended to disprove servile morality. Is it possible that there is no gnashing of teeth in the world, and doesn't this absence become so obvious that, in the ever-growing confusion, it makes one silent and violent? How, when one is in a rage, could this not be blindingly clear: when all of humanity is rushing toward slavery, there exists something that must not be enslaved, that cannot be enslaved?

NIETZSCHE'S DOCTRINE CANNOT BE ENSLAVED.

It can only be followed. To place it behind or in the service of *anything else* is a betrayal deserving the kind of contempt that wolves have for dogs.

DOES NIETZSCHE'S LIFE MAKE IT SEEM LIKELY THAT HE CAN HAVE HIS "WINGS CLIPPED" BY ANYONE AT ALL?

Whether it be anti-Semitism, fascism—or socialism—there is only *use*. Nietzsche addressed *free spirits*, incapable of letting themselves be used.

The Nietzschean Left and Right

The very movement of Nietzsche's thought implies a destruction of the different possible foundations of current political positions. Groups of the right base their action on an emotional attachment to the past. Groups of the left on rational principles. Now attachment to the past and to rational principles (justice, social equality) are both rejected by Nietzsche. Thus it would have to be impossible to use his teachings in any given orientation.

But his teachings represent an incomparable seductive force, and consequently quite simple a "force," that politicians are tempted to enslave, or at the very least to agree with, in order to benefit their enterprises. The teachings of Nietzsche "mobilize" the will and the aggressive instincts; it was inevitable that existing activities would try to draw into their movement these now mobile and still *unemployed* wills and instincts.

The absence of all possible adaptation to one or the other of these political orientations has had, under these conditions, only one result. Since Nietzschean exaltation can be solicited only because of a misunderstanding of its nature, it has been solicited in both directions at once. To a certain extent, a Nietzschean left and right have appeared, just as, in the past, a Hegelian left and right appeared.[7] But Hegel located himself in the political sphere, and his dialectical conceptions explain the formation of the two opposed tendencies of his doctrine that developed after his death. It is a question in one case of logical and well-thought-out developments, in the other of irrationality, of frivolity, or of betrayal. On the whole, the demands put forward by Nietzsche, far from being understood, have been treated like everything else in a world in which a servile attitude and *use value* alone appear admissible. On a global scale, the transvaluation of values, even if it has been the object of real attempts at understanding, has remained so generally unintelligible that the treasonous and platitudinous interpretations of which it has been the object very nearly pass unnoticed.

"Remarks for Asses"

Nietzsche himself said that he felt only repugnance for the political parties of his day, but ambiguity remains on the subject of fascism, which only developed long after his death and which, in addition, is the only political movement that has consciously and systematically used Nietzschean criticism. According to the Hungarian Georg Lukács (one of the few, it seems, among current Marxist theorists to have a profound awareness of the essence of Marxism—but ever since he has had to take refuge in Moscow he has been morally broken; he is now nothing more than a shadow of his former self)—according to Lukács "the very clear difference between the ideological level of Nietzsche and that of his fascist successors cannot hide the fundamental historical fact that makes Nietzsche one of the principle ancestors of fascism" (*Littérature Internationale* 9, 1935, p. 79). The analysis on which Lukács bases this conclusion is sometimes perhaps refined and clever, but it is only an analysis that dispenses with a consideration of the whole, in other words, of what alone is "existence." Fascism and Nietzscheanism are mutually exclusive, and are even violently mutually exclusive, as soon as each of them is considered in its totality: on one side life is tied down and stabilized in an endless servitude, on the other there is not only a circulation of free air, but the wind of a tempest; on one side the charm of human culture is broken in order to make room for vulgar force, on the other force and violence are tragically dedicated to this charm. How can one not see the abyss that separates a Cesare Borgia, a Malatesta, from a Mussolini? The former were insolent scorners of tradition and of all morality, making use of bloody and complex events to benefit a greed for life that exceeded them; the latter has been slowly enslaved by everything he was able to set in motion only by paralyzing, little by little, his earliest impulses. Already, in Nietzsche's eyes, Napoleon appeared "corrupted by the means he *had to* employ"; Napoleon "*lost noblesse* of character."[8] An infinitely more burdensome constraint no doubt weighs on modern dictators, reduced to finding their force by identifying themselves with all the impulses that Nietzsche scorned in the masses, in particular, "mendacious racial self-admiration and racial indecency."[9] There is a corrosive derision in imagining a possible agreement between Nietzschean demands and a political organization which impoverishes existence at its summit, which imprisons, exiles, or kills everything that could constitute an aristocracy[10] of "free spirits." As if it were not blindingly obvious that when Nietzsche demands a love corresponding to the sacrifice of life, it is for the "faith" that he communicates, for the values that his own existence makes real, and obviously not for a fatherland . . .

"Remarks for asses" wrote Nietzsche himself, already fearing a confusion of the same type, and one just as wretched.[11]

The Nietzschean Mussolini

Insofar as fascism values a philosophical source, it is attached to Hegel and not to Nietzsche.[12] One should read the article, in the *Enciclopedia Italiana*, that Mussolini himself devoted to the movement he created;[13] the vocabulary, and even more than the vocabulary the spirit, are Hegelian and not Nietzschean. Mussolini twice is able to use the expression "will to power," but it is no coincidence that this will is only an attribute of the idea that unifies the crowd . . . [14]

The red agitator underwent the influence of Nietzsche; the unitarist dictator has remained aloof. The regime itself has spoken on the question. In an article in *Fascismo*, July 1933, Cimmino denies any ideological filiation linking Nietzsche and Mussolini. Only the will to power would connect their doctrines. But Mussolini's will to power "is not selfish"; it is preached to all Italians, whom *Il Duce* "wants to make supermen." For, affirms the author, "even if we were all supermen, we would still only be men. . . . There is nothing more natural than the fact that, in other respects, Nietzsche pleases Mussolini:

Nietzsche will always belong to all men of action and will . . . The profound difference between Nietzsche and Mussolini lies in the fact that power, insofar as it is will, force, and action, is the product of instinct—I would say almost of physical nature. It can belong to the most incompatible people: one can use it for the most varied ends. On the other hand, ideology is a spiritual factor: it is ideology that really unites men. . . . '' It is not useful to insist on the overt idealism of this text, which has the merit of being honest, if one compares it to the German writings. It is more remarkable to see *Il Duce* cleared of a possible accusation of Nietzschean selfishness. The ruling circles of Fascism seem to have stopped at the Stirnerian interpretation of Nietzsche, expressed around 1908 by Mussolini himself.[15]

> For Stirner, for Nietzsche [the revolutionary wrote at the time], and for all those whom Turk, in his *Geniale Mensch*, calls the antisophs of selfishness, the State is oppression organized to the detriment of the individual. But nevertheless, even for animals of prey there exists a principle of solidarity. . . . The instinct of sociability, according to Darwin, is inherent in man's very nature. It is impossible to imagine a human being living outside the infinite chain of his fellow men. Nietzsche felt profoundly the ''fatality'' of this law of universal solidarity. The Nietzschean superman tries to escape the contradiction: he lets loose his will to power and directs it against the mob outside, and the tragic grandeur of his labors furnishes the poet—for yet a little while—with a subject worthy of being sung.

One can see, then, why Mussolini, stressing the non-Italian influences that helped form early Fascism, speaks of Sorel, Péguy, and Lagardelle, and not of Nietzsche. Official Fascism has been able to use invigorating Nietzschean maxims, displaying them on walls; its brutal simplifications must nevertheless be sheltered from the too-free, too-complex, and too-rending Nietzschean world. This prudence seems to be based, it is true, on an outmoded interpretation of Nietzsche's attitude, but this interpretation has been carried out, and it has been because the movement of Nietzsche's thought constitutes, *without any hope of appeal*, a *labyrinth*, in other words, the very opposite of the *directives* that current political systems demand from their sources of inspiration.

Alfred Rosenberg

Nevertheless the Hitlerian affirmation is opposed to the prudence of Italian Fascism. It is true that Nietzsche, in the racist pantheon, does not occupy an official place. Chamberlain, Paul de Lagarde, or Wagner are more solidly satisfying to the profound ''admiration of oneself'' practiced by the Germany of the Third Reich. But whatever the dangers of this operation, this new Germany had to recognize Nietzsche and use him. He represented too many mobile instincts, available for virtually any violent action—and the falsification was still too easy. The first fully developed ideology of National Socialism, as it has sprung out of Alfred Rosenberg's brain, accommodates Nietzsche.

Before anything else, the German chauvinists had to get rid of the individualistic Stirnerian interpretation. Alfred Rosenberg, making short work of left-wing Nietzscheanism, seems, with rage, bent on tearing Nietzsche out of the clutches of the young Mussolini and his comrades:

> Friedrich Nietzsche [he says in his *Myth of the Twentieth Century*][16] represents the desperate cry of millions of oppressed people. his savage prediction of the superman was a powerful amplification of individual life, subjugated and annihilated by the material pressure of the epoch. . . . But an epoch gagged for generations grasps, through its impotence, only the subjective side of Nietzsche's great will and vital experience. Nietzsche demanded, with passion, a strong personality; his falsified demand becomes an appeal, a letting loose of all the instincts. Around his banner rally the red battalions and the nomadic prophets of Marxism, the sort of men whose senseless doctrine has never been more ironically denounced than by Nietzsche. In his name, the contamination of the race by blacks and Syrians progressed, whereas he himself strictly submitted to the characteristic discipline of our race. Nietzsche fell into the dreams of colored gigolos, which is worse than falling into the hands of a gang of thieves. From this point on the German people only heard talk of the suppression of constraints, of subjectivism, of "personality," but it was no longer a question of discipline and of inner construction. Nietzsche's most beautiful expression—"From the future come winds with the strange beating of wings, and the good news resounds in his ears"—was nothing more than a nostalgic intuition in the midst of an insane world in which he was, along with Lagarde and Wagner, almost the only seer.

"If you knew how I laughed last spring while reading the works of this vain and sentimental, pigheaded character named Paul de Lagarde"—that is what Nietzsche said about the famous Pan-Germanist.[17] Nietzsche's laugh could obviously be carried over from Lagarde to Rosenberg, the laughter of a man equally nauseated by the Social Democrats and by the racists. The attitude of a Rosenberg must not, moreover, be simply seen as a vulgar Nietzscheanism (as is sometimes supposed, for example, by Edmond Vermeil). The disciple is not only vulgar, but prudent: the very fact that a Rosenberg speaks of Nietzsche suffices to "clip his wings" but it seems to a man of this type that the wings are never clipped back far enough. According to Rosenberg, everything that is not Nordic must be rigorously pruned. But only the gods of the heavens are Nordic!

> Whereas the Greek gods [he writes][18] were the heroes of light and of the heavens, the gods of non-Aryan Asia Minor assumed all the

characteristics of the Earth. . . . Dionysos (at least his non-Aryan side) is the god of ecstasy, of luxury, of the unfettered bacchanal. . . . For two centuries, the interpretation of Greece has continued. From Winckelmann through the German classics to Voss, there was an insistence on light, the gaze turned to the world, the intelligible. . . . The other—romantic—current was fed by the secondary movements indicated at the end of the *Iliad* by the feast of the dead, or in Aeschylus by the actions of the Erinyes. It was fortified by the chthonian gods, established against the Olympian Zeus. Speaking of death and its enigmas, it venerated the mother-goddesses, and first among them Demeter, and it finally blossomed in the god of the dead—Dionysos. It is in this sense that Welcker, Rohde, and Nietzsche made the Earth-mother a creator of life who, herself unformed, perpetually returns through the death in her womb. High German romanticism shuddered with adoration and, as always darker veils were placed before the sky-god's radiant face, it plunged ever more deeply into the instinctive, the unformed, the demonical, the sexual, the ecstatic, the chthonian—into the cult of the Mother.

There is good reason to recall here, first of all, that Rosenberg is not the official philosopher of the Third Reich, and that his anti-Christian stance has not been ratified. But when he expresses repulsion for the gods of the Earth and for the romantic tendencies that do not have as their immediate goal a constitution of force, he expresses beyond the shadow of a doubt the repulsion of National Socialism itself.

National Socialism is less romantic and more Maurrassian than is sometimes imagined, and one must not forget that Rosenberg is its ideological expression closest to Nietzsche; the jurist Carl Schmidt, who incarnates it just as much as does Rosenberg, is very close to Charles Maurras and, with a Catholic background, has always been alien to the influence of Nietzsche.

A "Hygienic and Pedagogical Religion": German Neopaganism

It is German "neopaganism"[19] that has introduced the legend of a poetic National Socialism. It is only insofar as racism leads to this eccentric religious form that it expresses a certain vitalist and anti-Christian current of German thought.

It is a fact that a somewhat chaotic but organized belief freely represents today in Germany the mystical current that first started during the period of high romanticism, and is expressed in writings such as those by Bachofen, Nietzsche, and more recently, Klages.[20] Such a current has never had the slightest unity, but it is characterized by the valuing of life over reason and by the opposition of primitive religious forms to Christianity. Within National Socialism, Rosenberg today represents its most moderate tendency. Much more adventurous theoreticians (Hauer, Bergmann), following Count Reventlow, have set themselves the task of establishing a cultural organization analogous to a Church. This endeavor is not new in Germany, where a "Community of the German Faith" existed in 1908, and where General Ludendorff himself wanted to become, after 1923, the head of a German Church. After Hitler took power the various existing organizations recognized, in a congress, the community of their goals, and were unified in order to form the "Movement of the German Faith."

But if it is true that the proselytes of the new religion do not confine romantic exaltation within Rosenberg's narrow and totally military limits, they are no less in agreement on the point that, once anti-Christianity is proclaimed and life is divinized, the only religion will be race, in other words, Germany. The former Protestant missionary Hauer screams: "There is only one virtue—to be German!" And the extravagant Bergmann, enamored of psychoanalysis and of the "hygienic religion," affirms that "if Jesus of Nazareth, doctor and bene- factor of the people, came back today, he would come down from the cross on which a deceptive knowledge has kept him nailed; he would live again as the doctor of the people, as the authority on racial hygiene."

National Socialism only escapes traditional and pietistic narrowness in order better to assure its mental poverty! The fact that adepts of the new faith have ceremonies in the course of which passages from *Zarathustra* are read defini- tively situates this comedy far from Nietzschean rigor; indeed it is nothing more than the commonest phraseology of buffoons, who assert themselves every- where amid general weariness.

It is finally necessary to add that the leaders of the Reich do not appear in- clined—appear less and less inclined—to support this unusual movement; the account of the role played in Hitler's Germany by a free, anti-Christian enthusi- asm, which gives itself a Nietzschean appearance, thus ends on a note of shame.

More Professorial . . .

There remains—perhaps the most serious—the well-thought-out endeavor of Herr Alfred Bäumler, who uses real knowledge and a certain theoretical rigor to construct a political Nietzscheanism. Bäumler's little book, *Nietzsche, the Philosopher and Politician*,[21] published by Reclam and widely disseminated, draws out of the labyrinth of Nietzschean contradictions the doctrine of a people united by a common will to power. Such a labor is in fact possible, and it was inevitable that someone would do it. It sets forth, on the whole, a precise, new, and remarkably artificial and logical figure. Imagine Nietzsche asking himself just once: "To what can my experiences and my perceptions be *of use*?"

That is in fact what Herr Bäumler has not failed to ask in Nietzsche's place. And as it is impossible to be of use to that which does not exist, Herr Bäumler necessarily invokes the existence that has thrust itself on him, that should have thrust itself on Nietzsche, that of the community to which both of them were destined by birth. Such considerations would be correct on the condition that the hypothesis formulated were capable of having a meaning in the spirit of Nietzsche. Another supposition remains possible: Nietzsche could not see his experiences and perceptions as useful; instead, he saw them as an end. Just as Hegel expected the Prussian state to realize Spirit, Nietzsche could have been able—after vituperating it—to wait obscurely for Germany to give a body and a real voice to Zarathustra . . . But it seems that the intellect of Herr Bäumler, more exacting than that of a Bergmann or an Oehler, eliminates overly comical representations. He has thought it expedient to neglect those things that Nietzsche incontestably experienced as an end and not as a means, and he has neglected them overtly, through positive remarks.

Nietzsche, speaking of the death of God, used a disordered language that manifested the most excessive inner experience. Bäumler writes:

> To understand exactly Nietzsche's attitude in regard to Christianity, one must never forget that the decisive expression "God is dead" has the meaning of a historical fact.

Describing what he experienced the first time the vision of the eternal return came to him, Nietzsche wrote: "The intensity of my feelings makes me both tremble and laugh . . . these were not tears of tenderness, but tears of jubilation. . . . "

> In reality [states Bäumler], the idea of the eternal return is without importance from the point of view of Nietzsche's system. We must consider it the expression of a highly personal experience. It has no connection with the fundamental idea of the will to power and even, taken seriously, this idea would shatter the coherence of the will to power.

Of all the dramatic representations that have given Nietzsche's life the character of a laceration and of the breathless combat of human existence, the idea of the eternal return is certainly the most inaccessible. But to go from the inability to attain it to the resolution not to take it seriously is to follow the traitor's path. Mussolini recognized a long time ago that Nietzsche's doctrine could not be reduced to the idea of the will to power. In his way Herr Bäumler, on the path of the traitor, recognizes this with an incomparable éclat—emasculating in broad daylight . . .

The "Land of My Children"

The pressing into service of Nietzsche requires, first of all, that all of his pathos-laden experience be opposed by the system, and give way to the system. But its requirements go much further than this.

Bäumler opposes the comprehension of Revolution with the comprehension of myth; the first, according to him, would be linked to the awareness of the *future*, the second to an intense feeling for the *past*.[22] It goes without saying that nationalism implies an enslavement to the past. In an article in *Esprit* (November 1, 1934, pp. 199–208), Emmanuel Lévinas[23] has provided, on this point, a philosophical exposition of racism in particular that is more profound than that of its partisans. If we cite the essential part of the article here, the profound difference between the teachings of Nietzsche and their bondage will perhaps appear, this time in a fairly brutal way:

> The importance [writes Lévinas] accorded to this feeling for the body, with which the Western spirit has never been content, is at the basis of a new biological conception of man. The biological, with all the fatality that it implies, becomes more than an object of spiritual life—it becomes its heart. The mysterious urgings of the blood, the call of heredity and of the past for which the body serves as an enigmatic vehicle, lose their status as problems submitted for solution to a Self that is free in a sovereign way. The Self brings to their resolution only the very unknowns of this problem. It is constituted by them. Man's essence is no longer in liberty, but in a kind of bondage. . . .
>
> From that point on, any social structure that announces a liberation in regard to the body and that does not tie it down becomes suspect, as a denial or a betrayal. . . . An inbred society immediately follows from this solidification of the spirit. . . . Any rational assimilation or mystical communion between minds that is not based on a blood-community is suspect. Nevertheless, the new type of truth cannot be capable of renouncing the formal nature of truth and of ceasing to be universal. The truth can very well be *my* truth in the strangest sense of this possessive—it must still tend toward the creation of a new world. Zarathustra is not content with his own transfiguration; he comes down from his mountain and carries a gospel. How can universality be compatible with racism? There will be a fundamental modification of the very idea of universality. *It must give way to the idea of expansion*, for the expansion of a force presents a structure completely different from that of the propagation of an idea. . . . Nietzsche's will to power, which modern Germany has rediscovered and glorified, is not only a new ideal, it is an ideal that brings, at the same time, its own form of universalization: war and conquest.

Lévinas, who introduces (without attempting to justify it) the identification of the Nietzschean attitude with the racist attitude, in fact limits himself to providing (without having attempted it) a striking demonstration of their incompatibility and even of their nature as opposites.

The blood-community[24] and the enslavement to the past are, in their connection, as distant as possible from the outlook of a man who demanded with great pride to be known as the "stateless one." And the understanding of Nietzsche must be seen as closed to those who do not *completely* take into account the profound *paradox* of another name that he claimed with no less pride, that of the CHILD OF THE FUTURE.[25] The understanding of myth linked by Bäumler to an intense feeling for the past is countered by the Nietzschean *myth* of the *future*.[26] The future, the marvelous unknown of the future, is the only object of the Nietzschean celebration.[27] "Humanity [in the thought of Nietzsche] still has much more time before it than behind it—how, in a general way, could the ideal be found in the past?"[28] It is only the aggressive and gratuitous gift of oneself to the future—in opposition to reactionary avarice, bound to the past—that enables the figure of Zarathustra, who demanded to be disowned, to present such a strong image of Nietzsche. The "stateless ones," those who live today, those who have unchained themselves from the past, how can they relax and see chained to this patriotic misery the one who, among them, through his hatred of this misery, devoted himself to the LAND OF HIS CHILDREN? Zarathustra—when the gaze of others was fixed on the land of their fathers, on their fatherland—Zarathustra *saw* the LAND OF HIS CHILDREN.[29] Against this world covered with the past, covered with fatherlands like a man is covered with wounds, there is no greater, more paradoxical, more passionate expression.

"We Who Are Homeless"

There is something tragic in the simple fact that Lévinas's error is possible (for it is no doubt a question in this case of an error, not of a prejudice). The contradictions that are killing men suddenly appear strangely insoluble. For if opposed parties, adopting opposed solutions, have in appearance resolved these contradictions, it is only through gross simplifications—and these apparent solutions only distance the possibility of escaping death. Those freed from the past are chained to reason; those who do not enslave reason are the slaves of the past. In order to constitute itself, the game of politics demands such false positions, and it seems impossible to change them. Transgressing with one's life the laws of reason, answering even against reason the demands of life, is in practice, in politics, to give oneself, bound hand and foot, to the past. Nevertheless, life demands to be freed no less from the past than from a system of rational and administrative measurements.

The passionate and tumultuous movement that forms life, that responds to its demand for the strange, the new, the lost, sometimes appears to be carried along by political action—but that is only a matter of a brief illusion. Life's movement can only be merged with the limited movements of political formations in clearly defined conditions;[30] in other conditions, it goes far beyond them, precisely into the region to which Nietzsche's attention was drawn.

Far beyond, where the simplifications adopted for a little while and for a limited goal lose their meaning, existence and the universe that carries it again appear to be a labyrinth. Toward this labyrinth, which alone encompasses the numerous possibilities of life, and not toward immediate banalities, the contradictory thought of Nietzsche is headed, at the mercy of a skittish liberty.[31] Alone, in the world as it now exists, it even seems to escape the pressing worries that make us refuse to open our eyes wide enough. Those who already see the void in the solutions proposed by parties, who even see nothing more in the hope aroused by these parties than an occasion for wars lacking any fragrance but that of death, seek a faith that corresponds to the convulsions they undergo: the possibility of man's finding not a flag and the senseless butchery before which this flag advances, but everything in the universe that can be an object of laughter, of ecstasy, or of sacrifice . . .

> Our ancestors [wrote Nietzsche] were Christians who in their Christianity were uncompromisingly upright: for their faith they willingly sacrificed possessions and position, blood and fatherland. We—do the same. For what? For our unbelief? For every kind of unbelief? No, you know better than that, friends! The hidden Yes in you is stronger than all the Nos and Maybes that afflict you and your age like a disease; and when you have to embark on the sea, you emigrants, you too are compelled to this by—a *faith*![32]

Nietzsche's teachings elaborate the faith of the sect or the "order" whose dominating will creates a free human destiny, tearing it away from the rational enslavement of production, as well as from the irrational enslavement to the past. The revalued values must not be reduced to use value—this is a principle of such burning, vital importance that it rouses all that life provides of a stormy will to conquer. Outside of this well-defined resolution, these teachings only give rise to inconsequential things or to the betrayals of those who pretend to take them into account. Enslavement tends to spread throughout human existence, and it is the destiny of this free existence that is at stake.

Notes

1. *Oeuvres Posthumes* (trans. Bolle) (Paris: Mercure de France, 1934), section 858, p. 309.

2. On Elisabeth Förster-Nietzsche, see the obituary by W. F. Otto in *Kantstudien*, no. 4, 1935, p. v (two portraits); but better is Erich Podach's *L'Effondrement de Nietzsche* (French translation) (Paris: Gallimard, 1931); Podach confirms the truth of statements by Nietzsche about his sister ("people like my sister are inevitably irreconcilable adversaries of my manner of thinking and of my philosophy"—cited by Podach, p. 68): the disappearance of documents, the shameful omissions of the *Nietzsche-Archiv* can already be attributed to this singular "adversary."

3. Letter of 21 May 1887, published in French in *Lettres choisies* (Paris: Stock, 1931).

4. The second of two letters to Theodor Fritsch, published in French by Marius Paul Nicolas (*De Hitler à Nietzsche* [Paris: Fasquelle, 1936], pp. 131-34). We must note here the value of Nicolas's work, whose purpose is, on the whole, analogous to our own, and which provides important documents. But we must regret that the author is preoccupied above all with showing M. Julien

Benda that he should not be hostile to Nietzsche . . . and hope that M. Benda remains faithful to himself.

5. *Friedrich Nietzsche und die deutsche Zukunft* (Leipzig, 1935). R. Oehler belongs to the family of Nietzsche's mother. [We quote here from the Walter Kaufmann translation of *Beyond Good and Evil* (New York: Random House, 1966), p. 187. Tr.]

6. In the first of two letters to T. Fritsch—see above, note 3.

7. "Is there not a Hegelianism of left and right? There can be a Nietzscheanism of right and left. And it seems to me that already Stalin's Moscow and Rome, the latter consciously and the former unconsciously, pose these two Nietzscheanisms" (Pierre Drieu la Rochelle, *Socialisme fasciste* [Paris: Gallimard, 1934], p. 71). In the article from which these lines are taken (entitled "Nietzsche contre Marx"), Drieu, while recognizing that "there will never be anything but a residue of his thought that can be surrendered to a brutal exploitation by thugs," reduces Nietzsche to the will to initiative and to the negation of optimism concerning progress . . .

In fact, if not in principle, the distinction between the two Nietzscheanisms is no less justified on the whole. Already in 1902, in an article entitled "Nietzsche malgré lui" (*Journal des Débats*, 3 September 1902), Bourdeau ironically spoke of left and right Nietzscheans.

Jean Jaurès (who, in a lecture in Geneva, identified the *superman* with the *proletariat*), Bracke (the translator of *Human, All too Human*), Georges Sorel, Felicien Challaye can be cited in France as men on the left who were interested in Nietzsche.

It is unfortunate that Jaurès's lecture has been lost.

It is important again to note that the principal work on Nietzsche is by Charles Andler, the sympathetic editor of the *Communist Manifesto*. [Bataille refers here to Andler's *Nietzsche, sa vie et sa pensée* (Paris: Bossard, 1920–31). Tr.]

8. *The Will to Power*, section 1026. [Trans. W. Kaufmann (New York: Random House, 1967), p. 531. Tr.]

9. *The Gay Science*. [Trans. W. Kaufmann (New York: Random House, 1974), p. 340. Tr.]

10. Nietzsche speaks of aristocracy, he even speaks of slavery, but, expressing himself on the subject of "new masters," he speaks of "their new holiness," of their "capacity for renunciation." "They give," he writes, "to the lowest the right to happiness, and they renounce it for themselves."

11. *The Will to Power*, section 942. [Kaufmann translation, p. 496—but we retain the French translation's "remarks for asses," whereas Kaufmann has "parenthesis for asses." Tr.].

12. It is well known that Hegelianism, represented by Gentile, is practically the official philosophy of Fascist Italy.

13. Under "Fascismo." The article has been translated as the first article of: Benito Mussolini, *Le Fascisme* (Paris: Denoël et Steele, 1933).   •

14. Mussolini writes with reference to the people: "It is a question neither of race nor of a definite geographical region, but of a group that endures through history, of a multitude unified by an idea that is a will to existence and to power" (Denoël et Steele edition, p. 22).

15. In an article published at the time in a newspaper in Romagna and reprinted by Marguerite G. Sarfatti (*Mussolini*, French translation [Paris: Albin Michel, 1927], pp. 117–21).

16. *Der Mythus des 20. Jahrhunderts* (Munich, 1932), p. 523. [An English translation of this work has very recently been published: *The Myth of the Twentieth Century* (Torrance, Calif.: Noontide Press, 1982). Tr.]

17. First letter to T. Fritsch, cited above, notes 3 and 6.

18. *Der Mythus des 20. Jahrhunderts*, p. 55. This hostility of fascism to the chthonian gods, to the gods of the Earth, is no doubt what locates it most accurately in the psychological or mythological world.

19. On German neopaganism, see the article by Albert Béguin in the *Revue des Deux-Mondes*, 15 May 1935.

20. We should note that, referring to the contemporary writer Ludwig Klages, famous above all

for his work in characterology, Baron Ernest Seillière, (*De la déesse nature à la déesse vie* [Paris: Alcan, 1931], p. 133) uses the expression *acephalic* . . . Klages is, moreover, the author of one of the most important books to have been devoted to Nietzsche, *Die psychologischen Errungenschaften Nietzsches*, second edition (Leipzig, 1930) (first edition: 1923).

21. *Nietzsche, der Philosoph und Politiker* (Leipzig, 1931); the two passages cited are on pp. 98 and 80.

22. See Seillière, op. cit., p. 37.

23. [The title of Lévinas's article is "Quelques réflexions sur la philosophie de l'hitlerisme." Tr.]

24. Nietzsche is generally interested in the beauty of the body and in the race, without this interest determining for him the privileging of a limited blood-community (whether fictive or not). The community ties that he foresees are without any doubt mystical ties; it is a matter of a "faith," not of a fatherland.

25. *The Gay Science*, section 377, entitled "We Who Are Homeless." [Kaufmann translation, pp. 338–40. Tr.]

26. *Den Mythus der Zukunft dichten!* writes Nietzsche in notes for *Zarathustra* (*Werke, Grossoktavausgabe* [Leipzig, 1901], vol. 12, p. 400).

27. *Die Zukunft feiern nicht die Vergangenheit!* (from the same passage as the preceding quote); *Ich liebe die Unwissenheit um die Zukunft* (*The Gay Science*, #287).

28. *Posthumous Works* (*Werke* [Leipzig, 1901], vol. 13, p. 362).

29. *Thus Spoke Zarathustra*, second part, "On the Land of Education": "and I am driven out of fatherlands and motherlands. Thus I now love only my *children's land*. . . . In my children I want to make up for being the child of my fathers. . . . " [Trans. W. Kaufmann, in *The Portable Nietzsche* (New York: Viking, 1954), p. 233. Tr.]

30. The Russian revolution perhaps shows what a revolution is capable of. The questioning of all human reality in a reversal of the material conditions of existence suddenly appears as a response to a pitiless demand, but it is not possible to foresee its consequences: revolutions thwart all intelligent predictions of their results. Life's movement no doubt has little to do with the more or less depressing aftermath of a trauma. It is found in slowly active and creative *obscure determinations*, of which the masses are not at first aware. It is above all wretched to confuse it with the readjustments demanded by the conscious masses, carried out in the political sphere by more or less parliamentary specialists.

31. This interpretation of the "political thought" of Nietzsche, the only one possible, has been remarkably well expressed by Karl Jaspers. The reader is referred to the passage that we cite in our review of Jaspers's book. [Bataille's review of Jaspers's *Nietzsche, Einführung in das Verständnis seines Philosophierens* (Berlin: de Gruyter, 1936), consists chiefly of a French translation (by Pierre Klossowski) of a long quote from Jaspers's book, which may be found on pp. 252–53 of the book's English translation: *Nietzsche: An Introduction to the Understanding of His Philosophical Activity*, trans. C. F. Wallrath and F. J. Schmitz (Tucson: The University of Arizona Press, 1965). The review itself may be found on pp. 474–76 of volume I of Bataille's *Oeuvres Complètes*. Tr.]

32. This is the conclusion of section 377 of *The Gay Science*, "We Who Are Homeless." This paragraph sums up more precisely than any other Nietzsche's attitude toward contemporary political reality.

Propositions

When Nietzsche said he wanted to be understood in fifty years, he could not have meant it in only the intellectual sense. That for which he lived and exalted himself demands that life, joy, and death be brought into play, and not the tired attention of the intellect. This must be stated simply and with an awareness of one's own involvement. What takes place profoundly in the revaluation of values, in a decisive way, is tragedy itself; there is little room left for repose. That the essential for human life is exactly the object of sudden horror, that this life is carried in laughter to the heights of joy by the most degrading events possible, such strange facts place human events, happening on the surface of the Earth, in the conditions of mortal combat, making it necessary to break the bonds of recognized truth in order to "exist." But it is vain and unbearable to try to address those who have at their disposal only a feigned attention; combat has always been a more demanding enterprise than any other. In this sense it becomes impossible to shy away from a meaningful comprehension of the teachings of Nietzsche. All this leads to a slow development where nothing can be left in the shadows.

I. Propositions on Fascism

1. "The most perfect organization of the universe can be called God."[1]

The fascism that recomposes society on the basis of existing elements is the most closed form of *organization*; in other words, the form of human existence closest to the eternal God.

In social revolution (but not in Stalinism as it exists today) decomposition conversely reaches its extreme point.

Existence is constantly situated in opposition to two equally illusory possibilities: an "ewige Vergottung und Entgottung," in other words an "eternal integration that deifies (that produces God), and an eternal disintegration that annihilates God in itself."

The destroyed social system recomposes itself by slowly developing an aversion to the initial decomposition.

The recomposed social structure—whether the result of fascism or of a negating revolution—paralyzes the movement of existence, which demands a constant disintegration. The great unitary constructions are only the warning signs of a religious upheaval that will push life's movement beyond servile necessity.

The charm, in the toxic sense of the word, of Nietzschean exaltation comes from its disintegration of life, while carrying it to the overflow of the will to power and irony.

2. With regard to the community, the character of the individual as substitute is one of the rare certainties that emerges from historical research. It is from the unitary community that the person takes his form and his being. The most opposed crises have led, before our eyes, to the formation of similar unitary communities: thus in these there was neither social sickness nor regression; instead, societies rediscovered their fundamental mode of existence, their timeless structure as it was formed or reformed in the most diverse economic or historical circumstances.

The protest of human beings against a fundamental law of their existence can evidently have only a limited significance. Democracy, which rests on a precarious equilibrium between classes, is perhaps only a transitory form; it brings with it not only the grandeur but the pettiness of decomposition.

The protest against unitarism does not necessarily take place in a democratic sense. It is not necessarily done in the name of a *within*; the possibilities of human existence can from now on be situated *beyond* the formation of *monocephalic* societies.

3. Recognizing the limited scope of democratic rage (in large part deprived of meaning because the Stalinists share it) does not mean in any way the acceptance of a unitary community. Relative stability and conformity to natural law in no way confer on a political form the possibility of stopping the movement of ruin and creation of history, still less of satisfying in a single moment the demands of life. On the contrary, closed and stifling social existence is condemned to the condensation of forces of decisive explosion, which cannot be carried out within a democratic society. But it would be a crude error to imagine that the exclusive, and even simply the necessary, goal of an explosive thrust is to destroy the head and the unitary structure of a society. The formation of a new structure, of an "order" developing and raging across the entire earth, is the

only truly liberating act, and the only one possible, since revolutionary destruction is regularly followed by the reconstitution of the social structure and its head.

4. Democracy rests on a neutralization of relatively free and weak antagonisms; it excludes all explosive condensation. Monocephalic society is the result of the free play of the natural laws of man, but each time it is a secondary formation, it represents a crushing atrophy and sterility of existence.

The only society full of life and force, the only free society, *is the bi- or polycephalic* society that gives the fundamental antagonisms of life a constant explosive outlet, but one limited to the richest forms.

The duality or multiplicity of heads tends to achieve in the same movement the *acephalic* character of existence, because the very principle of the head is the reduction to unity, the *reduction* of the world to God.

5. "Inorganic matter is the maternal breast. To be released from life is once again to become *true*; it is to perfect oneself. Whoever understands this would consider the return to insensate dust as a celebration."[2]

"To grant perception also to the inorganic world; an absolutely precise perception—the reign of 'truth'!—Uncertainty and illusion start with the organic world."[3]

"Loss of all specialization: synthetic nature is superior nature. But all organic life is already a specialization. The inorganic world found behind it represents the greatest synthesis of forces; for this reason, it seems worthy of the greatest respect. In the inorganic, error and the limitations of perspective do not exist."[4]

These three texts, the first summarizing Nietzsche, the other two taken from his posthumous writings, reveal at the same time the conditions of the splendor and poverty of existence. To be free means not to be a function. To allow oneself to be locked in a function is to allow life to emasculate itself. The head, conscious authority or God, represents one of the servile functions that gives itself as, and takes itself to be, an end; consequently, it must be the object of the most inveterate aversion. One limits the extent of this aversion, however, by giving it as the principle of the struggle against unitary political systems: but it is a question of a principle outside of which such a struggle is only a contradiction in terms.

II. Propositions on the Death of God

. . . .

6. The *acephalic man* mythologically expresses sovereignty committed to destruction and the death of God, and in this the identification with the headless man merges and melds with the identification with the superhuman, which IS entirely "the death of God."

. . . .

7. Superman and *acephalic man* are bound with a brilliance equal to the position of time as imperative object and explosive liberty of life. In both cases, time becomes the object of ecstasy, and, secondly, it appears as the "eternal return" in the vision of Surlei or as "catastrophe" ("Sacrifices"), or again as "time-explosion": it is, then, as different from the time of philosophers (or even from Heideggerian time) as the christ of erotic saints is from the God of the Greek philosophers. The movement directed toward time suddenly enters into concrete existence, whereas the movement toward God turned away from it during the earliest period.

8. Ecstatic time can only find itself in the vision of things that puerile chance causes brusquely to appear: cadavers, nudity, explosions, spilled blood, abysses, sunbursts, and thunder.

9. War, to the extent that it is the desire to insure the permanence of a nation, the nation that is sovereignty and the demand for inalterability, the authority of divine right and of God himself, represents the desperate obstinacy of man opposing the exuberant power of time and finding security in an immobile and almost somnolent erection. National and military life are present in the world to try to deny death by reducing it to a component of a glory without dread. Nation and army profoundly separate man from a universe given over to lost expenditure and to the unconditional explosion of its parts: "profoundly," at least to the extent that the precarious victories of human avarice are possible.

10. Revolution must not only be considered in its overtly known and conscious ins and outs, but in its brute appearance, whether it is the work of Puritans, Encyclopedists, Marxists, or Anarchists. Revolution, in its significant historical existence, which still dominates the present civilization, manifests itself to the eyes of a world mute with fear as the sudden explosion of limitless riots. Because of the Revolution, divine authority ceases to found power; authority no longer belongs to God, but to time, whose free exuberance puts kings to death, to time incarnated today in the explosive tumult of peoples. Even in fascism itself authority has been reduced to founding itself on a so-called revolution—a hypocritical and forced homage to the only imposing authority, that of catastrophic change.

11. God, kings, and their sequels have interposed themselves between men and the Earth—in the same way that the father stands before the son as an obstacle to the violation and possession of the Mother. The economic history of modern times is dominated by the epic but disappointing effort of fierce men to plunder the riches of the Earth. The Earth has been disemboweled, but men have reaped from her womb above all metal and fire, with which they ceaselessly disembowel each other. The inner incandescence of the Earth not only explodes in the craters of volcanoes; it also glows red and spits out death with its fumes in the metallurgy of all nations.

12. The incandescent reality of the Earth's womb cannot be touched and possessed by those who misunderstand it. It is the misunderstanding of the Earth, the forgetting of the star on which he lives, the ignorance of the nature of riches, in other words of the incandescence that is enclosed within this star, that has made for man an existence at the mercy of the merchandise he produces, the largest part of which is devoted to death. As long as men forget the true nature of terrestrial life, which demands ecstatic drunkenness and splendor, nature can only come to the attention of the accountants and economists of all parties by abandoning them to the most complete results of their accounting and economics.

13. Men do not know how to enjoy the Earth and her products freely and with prodigality; the Earth and her products only lavish and liberate themselves in order to destroy. Dull war, such as that organized by modern economies, also teaches the meaning of the Earth, but it teaches it to renegades whose heads are full of calculations and plans for the short run; that is why it teaches it with a heartless and depressing rage. In the measureless and rending character of the aimless catastrophe known as modern warfare, it is nevertheless possible for us to recognize the explosive immensity of time. The Earth as mother has remained the old chthonian deity, but with the human multitudes she also tears down the God of the sky in an endless uproar.

15.[5] The search for God, for the absence of movement, for *tranquillity*, is the fear that has scuttled all attempts at a universal community. Man's heart is uneasy not only up to the moment when he finds repose in God: God's universality still remains for him a source of uneasiness, and peace is produced only if God allows himself to be locked up in the isolation and profoundly immobile permanence of a group's military existence. For universal existence is unlimited and thus restless: it does not close life in on itself, but instead opens it and throws it back into the uneasiness of the infinite. Universal existence, eternally unfinished and acephalic, a world like a bleeding wound, endlessly creating and destroying particular finite beings: it is in this sense that true universality is the death of God.

Notes

1. Section 712, *The Will to Power*, trans. W. Kaufmann (New York: Random House, 1967), pp. 379–80.

2. See Charles Andler's *Nietzsche, sa vie et sa pensée*, vol. 6 (Paris: Gallimard, 1931), p. 307, and the *Posthumous Works*, period of *The Gay Science* (1881–82), sections 497 and 498 (*Werke, Grossoktavausgabe* [Leipzig, 1901], vol. 12, p. 228).

3. *Posthumous Works*, 1883–88 (*Grossoktavausgabe*, vol. 13, p. 228).

4. Ibid., same page.

5. [No number 14 was included in the original text. Tr.]

Nietzschean Chronicle[1]

*The current crisis is the same as the one that threatened human
nature at the time of the establishment of Christianity.*

Benjamin Constant[2]

The Apogee of Civilization Is a Crisis

Each time a vast movement of civilization has developed, in Egypt or in the
Greco-Roman world, in China or in the Occident, the values that brought men
together at the dawn of each upheaval, the taboo or sacred acts, places, names,
and laws, have slowly lost, more or less on the whole,[3] a part of their efficacious
force and their ability to inspire awe. The simple fact of the movement itself was
decomposition and, in this sense, civilization can be seen as synonymous with
sickness or crisis. The two meanings, passive and active, of the word *critical—*
questioned and questioning—adequately and clearly account for the identification that must be made between a developing civilization and crisis. On the passive side, there is the crisis of the conventions—the royal or divine sovereignty—that constitute the foundations of the human aggregate; on the active
side, there is the *individual* critical attitude toward these conventions: the individual thus develops in a corrosive way, at the expense of society, and the facilitated individual life sometimes takes on a dramatic meaning. The figure of the
living community little by little loses its tragic appearance—both puerile and
terrible—which reached each being in his most secretly lacerated wound; it loses

the power of provoking the total religious emotion that grows to the point of ecstatic drunkenness, when existence is avidly opened before it.

But because the material organization that has developed demands the conservation of social cohesion, this cohesion is maintained by all the means at the disposal of its principal beneficiaries; when communal passion is not great enough to constitute human strengths, it becomes necessary to use constraint and to develop the alliances, contracts, and falsifications that are called politics. When human beings become autonomous they discover around themselves a false and empty world. The awareness of being a dupe before administrative impudence (and also before terrifying displays of individual satisfaction and stupidity) succeeds the strong and painful feeling of communal unity. The vast results of long centuries of struggle, of prodigious military or material conquest, have always led conquering peoples—whether in the West, or among the Egyptians or the Romans[4]—to a failed and disappointing world, flattened by interminable crises. Through an extreme malaise and through a confusion in which everything appears vain and nearly disastrous, there grows the obsession with

The Recovery of the Lost World

Decomposition can affect, at the same time, economic activity, the institutions of authority, and the principles that establish moral and religious attitudes. Disintegrated societies, obscurely attempting to regain their cohesion, can still be devastated by a multiplicity of useless endeavors: brutal force and intellectual pedantry, both equally blind, find the road wide open before them. The excessive and shattered joy of great disasters can therefore relieve existence, like a hiccup. But behind the facade constituted by affirmations of strength, reason, and cynicism, there is a yawning void, and whatever continues gives way more and more to the feeling that something is missing. Nostalgia for a lost world can be clothed in numerous forms, and generally it is the feat of cowards, who only know how to moan for what they claim to love, who avoid or know how not to find the possibility of FIGHTING. Behind the facade, there is first of all only nervous depression, violent but incoherent noise, aesthetic reverie and chatter. When a man among others, in this world in which a simple representation of the act has become an object of nausea, tries to enter into combat for the ''recovery of the lost world,'' he creates a void around himself, he meets only the infinite evasion of all those who have taken upon themselves the task of knowledge and of thought—for it is almost impossible to imagine a man who thinks without having the constant worry of elminating from the course of his reflections everything that could condense and threaten to explode. Because he could not confuse emasculation with knowledge, and because his thought was open to a lucid explosion that could not stop before exhausting his resources—becoming the *hero* of everything human that is not enslaved—Nietzsche collapsed in humiliating solitude. The destiny of human life, since it is linked to what is most significant for all men, has perhaps never known a moment that justifies a greater uneasiness than the one in which Nietzsche, alone and in a fit of madness, embraced a horse in the streets of Turin.

The Fascist Solution

But the close connection between the will to regain lost life and enervating mental depression is not only the occasion for tragic failures: it constitutes an incentive to grasp at the vulgar and facile solutions whose success at first seems assured, to the exclusion of all others. Since it is a question of regaining what existed in the past, and whose elements are dying or dead, it is simplest to revive, in favorable circumstances, what already exists. It is easier to restore than to create, and since the necessity of a renewed social cohesion can, at certain moments, be felt in the most pressing way, the first movement of recomposition takes place in the form of a return to the past. The crudest and most directly *usable* fundamental values are capable, in bitter and hateful crises, of taking on a dramatic meaning that seems to restore real color to communal existence, whereas on the whole it is a matter of an operation in which the affective values set in motion are in large part *used* for ends other than themselves. The RECOMPOSITION OF SACRED VALUES starts[5] when the boots of human existence are repaired, and it can obediantly march straight ahead once again under the whip of hard necessity. The reestablished Pharaohs and Caesars, the heads of the revolutionary parties that today have betwitched half the inhabitants of Europe, have answered the desire to base life again on an irrational urge. But the amount of constraint necessary for the maintenance of too rapidly imposed edifices indicates their profoundly disappointing character. To the extent that there persists a nostalgia for a community through which each being would find something more tragically taut than anything to be found in himself—to this extent the concern for the recovery of the lost world, which played a role in the genesis of fascism, has as its outcome nothing other than military discipline and a limited calm, produced by a brutality that destroys with rage everything it lacks the power to captivate.

But what is adequate to a possibly dominant faction is nothing more than sundering and deception when one considers the entire living community of beings. The community does not demand a fate similar to that of the different parts it brings together, but it demands as an end that which violently unifies and asserts itself *without alienating life*, without leading it to the repetition of emasculated acts and of external moral formulae. Brief bursts of fascism, set off by fear, cannot deceive such a true, wild, and avid demand.

From the Caesarian Heavens to the Dionysian Earth:
The Religious Solution

If one now imagines the obsession that dominated Nietzsche's life, it seems clear that this common obsession with the lost world, which grows greater in profound depression, can necessarily be followed in opposite directions. The confusion between two responses to the same void, the apparent similarity of fascism and Nietzsche, then becomes easily understandable: any resemblance is reduced to identical traits appearing in two opposites.

Among the various oppositions that maintain the existence of men under the harsh law of Heraclitus, none is truer or more ineluctable than the one that opposes the Earth to the heavens, to the "need to punish" the dark demands of tragedy; on one side are constituted the aversion to sin and the light of day, glory and military repression, the imprescriptible rigidity of the past; on the other, the grandeur of auspicious nights, of avid passion, of the obscure and free dream—power is given to movement and, in that way, whatever its numerous appearances may be, it is torn from the past and projected into the apocalyptic forms of the future. On one side a constitution of communal forces riveted to a narrow tradition—parental or racial—constitutes a monarchical authority and establishes itself as a stagnation and as an insurmountable barrier to life; on the other, a bond of fraternity, which may be foreign to the bond of blood, is established between men, who among themselves decide upon the necessary consecrations: and the goal of their meeting is not a clearly defined action, but life itself—LIFE, IN OTHER WORDS, TRAGEDY.

It is true that, when it comes to man, there are no examples of a real form representing, to the exclusion of the other, one of the possible directions of life: these directions are nevertheless easy to determine and describe. On the whole, they set the chthonian and Uranian world of mythic Greece (and, in the phases of recomposition of each great civilization, in a clearer and clearer way, the properly religious movements—Osirian, Christian, or Buddhist) in opposition to the development of the character of the military sovereign.

The thing that has prevented people from immediately seeing how Nietzsche's representation of values opposes the eternal resumption of military monarchy—a resumption that takes place with an empty regularity, without ever providing anything new—has been Nietzsche's effort to point out the deepest differences less between Dionysianism and Bismarckian National Socialism (a movement which, for good reason, he saw as negligible) than between Dionysianism and Christianity. And the possibility of error is even greater in that the critique of Christian falsehoods led Nietzsche to rail against any renunciation of power, leading in that way to a confusion between the sphere of military solidification and ossification and that of tragic liberty. And even greater in that there can be no question of renouncing a hard-won human virility: the scorn for Caesarian acts, deprived of all human meaning, will no longer lead to the acceptance of boundaries that these acts claim to impose on life; a religious movement that develops in the present world no more has to resemble Christianity or Buddhism than Christianity and Buddhism resembled polytheism. It is because of this necessary dissimilarity that Nietzsche set aside, for good reason, the word *religion*, which alone lends itself to a confusion almost as unfortunate as the confusion between Nietzschean Dionysianism and fascism—and a word that can only be used, in the present world, in defiance.

Nietzsche Dionysos

THE CRITICAL PHASE OF A CIVILIZATION'S DECOMPOSITION IS REGULARLY FOLLOWED BY A RECOMPOSITION, WHICH DEVELOPS IN TWO DIFFERENT DIRECTIONS: THE RECONSTITUTION OF RELIGIOUS ELEMENTS OF CIVIL AND MILITARY SOVEREIGNTY, TYING EXISTENCE TO THE *PAST*, IS FOLLOWED OR ACCOMPANIED BY THE BIRTH OF FREE AND LIBERATING SACRED FIGURES AND MYTHS, *RENEWING* LIFE AND MAKING IT "THAT WHICH FROLICS IN THE *FUTURE*," "THAT WHICH ONLY BELONGS TO A *FUTURE*."

The Nietzschean audacity demanding for the figures it creates a power that bows before nothing—that tends to break down old sovereignty's edifice of moral prohibition—must not be confused with what it fights. The marvelous Nietzschean KINDERLAND is nothing less than the place where the challenging of every man's VATERLAND takes on a meaning that is no longer impotent negation. It is only after Zarathustra that we can "ask our children's forgiveness for our having been the children of our fathers."[6] The very first sentences of Nietzsche's message come from "realms of *dream* and *intoxication*."[7] The entire message is expressed by one name: DIONYSOS. When Nietzsche made DIONYSOS (in other words, the destructive exuberance of life) the symbol of the will to power, he expressed in that way a resolution to deny to a faddish and debilitating romanticism the force that must be held sacred. Nietzsche demanded that the possessors of today's shattering values become dominant—and not that they be dominated by a heaven laden with the need to punish.

The god of the Earth, DIONYSOS, was the son of Semele, the Earth, and Zeus, god of the Heavens. The myth has it that Semele, pregnant with Dionysos, wanted Zeus to appear to her clothed in the attributes of his power; she was reduced to flames and ashes by the heavenly thunder and lightning she had so imprudently provoked. Thus the god was born of a lightning-torn womb.

In the image of the one he wanted to *be* to the point of madness, Nietzsche is born of the Earth torn open by the fire of the Heavens, he is born blasted by lightning and in that way he is imbued with this fire of domination that becomes the FIRE OF THE EARTH.

WHEN THE SACRED—NIETZSCHEAN—FIGURE OF TRAGIC DIONYSOS RELEASES LIFE FROM SERVITUDE, IN OTHER WORDS, FROM THE PUNISHMENT OF THE PAST, HE RELEASES IT AS WELL FROM RELIGIOUS HUMILITY, FROM THE CONFUSIONS AND TORPOR OF ROMANTICISM. HE DEMANDS THAT A *BRILLIANT WILL* RETURN THE EARTH TO THE DIVINE ACCURACY OF THE DREAM.

The Performance of *Numantia*[8]

The opposition of Heaven and Earth has ceased to have a meaningful, communal, and immediately intelligible value. When it appears, it comes up against the desires of the intellect, which no longer knows what such an antiquity is supposed to mean, and which refuses to admit as well that mythological entities can have, at the present time, in a world saturated with science, any meaning at all. But if one considers an everyday reality, only favorable circumstances are needed for men, who are obviously a long way from madness, to enter lucidly into the world of the infernal spirits—and not only men, but the vulgar political passions that animate them.

When Marquino, coming forward in his cowl, calls forth the most somber things of the world, the figures he invokes with terrible names . . . *waters of the black lagoon* . . . cease to be empty and powerless representations. For, in Numantia's agony, within the walls and under the naked rock of the sierra, it is the Earth that is there: the Earth that opens to return the cadaver to the world of the living, the Earth that opens to the living, thrown by delirium into death. And even though this Earth breathes Fury and Rage, even though it appears in the screams of children slaughtered by their fathers, of wives slaughtered by their husbands, even though the bread it brings the starving man is soaked in blood, the feeling its presence inspires is not horror. Because those who belong to it (and thus who belong to frenzy) bring back to life, before our eyes, all of lost humanity, the world of truth and immediate passion for which nostalgia has always been felt. And it is impossible to break apart a profoundly constituted and bound figure. Just as the Romans, commanded by the implacable authority of a leader, are associated with the glory of the sun, in the same way the Numantines, WITHOUT A LEADER, WITHOUT A HEAD, are located in the region of the Night and of the Earth, in the region haunted by the phantoms of the Tragedy-Mother. And insofar as agony and death have entered the city, this city becomes the image of everything in the world that can demand a total love; insofar as this city dies, all the nostalgia for the lost world can now be expressed by the single name, NUMANTIA.

"Numantia! Liberty!"[9]

The tragedy of Numantia is great because in it one is confronted not only with the death of a certain number of men, but with the entry of death into the entire city: it is not individuals who are dying, but an entire people. That must be disconcerting, and in principle it must make *Numantia* inaccessible, because the game destiny plays with men can only appear to most of them clothed in the brilliant colors of individual existence.

Moreover, what is currently in the air—if one is speaking of collective existence—is the poorest thing one can imagine, and no representation can be more disconcerting than one that presents death as the fundamental object of the *communal* activity of men, death and not food or the production of the means of production. No doubt such a representation is based on the totality of religious practices of all ages, but there has been a predominant tendency to see the reality of religion as a surface reality. In the existence of a community, that which is typically religious, in the sure grip of death, has become the thing most foreign to man. No one thinks any longer that the reality of a communal life—which is to say, human existence—depends on the sharing of nocturnal terrors and on the kind of ecstatic spasms that spread death. Thus the truth of *Numantia* is even more difficult to grasp than that of an individual tragedy. It is religious truth—in other words, that which in principle rejects the inertia of men living today.

The idea of a fatherland—which appears as a constituent of dramatic action—has only an external meaning, if one compares it to this religious truth. Whatever their appearance, the symbols that govern the emotions are not among those that serve to represent or maintain the military existence of a people. Military existence even excludes any dramatization of this kind. It is based on a brutal negation of any profound meaning of death and, if it uses cadavers, it is only to make the living march in a straighter line. The most tragic *performance* it knows is the parade and, due to the fact that it excludes all possible depression, it is incapable of basing communal life on the tragedy of dread. In this sense the fatherland, condemned to accept as its own a brutal military poverty, is far from equal to the communal unity of men. In certain cases it can become a force of attraction destroying the other possibilities, but since it is essentially constituted by armed force, it can give to those who submit to its force of attraction nothing that satisfies the great human hungers, because it subordinates *everything* to a *particular* utility. On the contrary, it must force its half-seduced lovers to enter the inhuman and totally alienated world of barracks, military prisons, and military administrations. In the crisis currently depressing existence, the fatherland even represents the greatest obstacle to this unity of life that—it must be forcefully said—can only be based on a communal awareness of profound existence, the emotional and riven play of life with death.

Numantia, which is only the atrocious expression of this play, cannot have any more meaning for the fatherland than it has for the individual who suffers alone. But *Numantia*, in fact, took on for those present at the spectacle a meaning that had to do neither with individual drama nor with national feeling, but with political passion. This was made possible by the war in Spain. That is an obvious paradox, and it is possible that such a confusion is as lacking in importance as the confusion of the inhabitants of Saragossa, who presented the tragedy during a siege. *Numantia*, today, has been performed not only in Paris, but in Spain, in burned-out churches, without any other decor than the traces of the fire, and without any other actors than red militiamen. The fundamental themes of a remote existence, the cruel and unalterable mythological themes developed in the tragedy—are they not, however, as foreign to the political spirit as they are to the military spirit?

If it were necessary to hold to current appearances, the answer would have to be in the affirmative. Not only does a politician, of whatever party, find repugnant the consideration of profound realities, but he has accepted, once and for all, the game of alterations and compromises that makes possible precarious power alliances, and that makes impossible the formation of a true heartfelt community.

In addition, among the various convulsive conflicts in history, the one currently sundering the totality of civilized countries—the conflict between antifascism and fascism—appears the most corrupt. The comedy which—under the pretense of democracy—opposes German Caesarism with Soviet Caesarism, shows what frauds are acceptable to a mob limited by misery, at the mercy of those who basely flatter it.

Nevertheless a reality exists which, behind this facade, is in contact with the most powerful secrets of existence; anyone who wants to enter this reality need only take in the opposite way what is generally accepted. If the image of *Numantia* expresses the grandeur of a people struggling against oppression by the powerful, it reveals at the same time that the struggle currently engaged in most often lacks any grandeur: the antifascist movement, if it is compared to *Numantia*, appears to be an empty mob, a vast decomposition of men linked only by what they refuse.

There is only illusion and comfort in admiring *Numantia* because one sees in it an expression of the current struggle. But tragedy confronts the world of politics with an evident truth: the battle joined will only take on a meaning and will only be effective to the extent that fascist wretchedness comes face to face with something other than troubled negation—namely, the heartfelt community of which *Numantia* is the image.

The principle of this reversal can be expressed in simple terms. CAESARIAN UNITY, ESTABLISHED BY A LEADER—A HEAD—IS OPPOSED BY THE HEADLESS COMMUNITY, BOUND TOGETHER BY THE OBSESSIVE IMAGE OF A TRAGEDY. Life demands that men gather together, and men are only gathered together by a leader or by a tragedy. To look for a HEADLESS human community is to look for tragedy: putting the leader to death is itself tragedy, it remains a requirement of tragedy. A truth that will change the appearance of human things starts here: THE EMOTIONAL ELEMENT THAT GIVES AN OBSESSIVE VALUE TO COMMUNAL LIFE IS DEATH.

The Dionysian Mysteries

This "Dionysian" truth cannot be an object of propaganda. And since, by its own movement, it calls forth power, it gives meaning to the idea of an organization revolving around profound mysteries.

"Mystery" here has nothing in common with a vague esotericism: it is a question of lacerating truths that absorb those to whom they belong, truths that the mob does not seek, and away from which it even tends to move. The disintegration-movement of this mob can only be countered by a crafty deliberation, by what revolves once again around figures of death.

It is only on this open route, where everything is disorienting to the point of drunkenness, that Sade's paradoxical assertions cease to be, for whoever accepts them, a mockery and an implacable judgment.

For men who do not want to follow a consistent and difficult path, what could the following quote mean?

> An already old and corrupt nation, courageously shaking off the yoke of its monarchical government in order to adopt a republican one, can only maintain itself through many crimes, for it is already in crime. . . .

Or this one . . .

> From these first principles, there follows . . . the necessity of softening laws, and above all of annihilating for all time the atrocity of the death penalty, because the law, which in itself is cold, cannot be accessible to the passions that legitimate in man the cruel activity of murder.

Still, those are the least clearly inhuman of Sade's assertions. How could his bloody doctrine have a meaning for anyone who, finding it right, does not live it in trembling? For "killing for pleasure" would only be a literary provocation, and the most inadmissible expression of hypocrisy, if consciousness were not driven by it to a point of extreme lucidity. The awareness of the fact that the pleasure of killing is the truth, charged with horror, for one who does not kill, can remain neither obscure nor tranquil, and it forces life into an unlikely, frozen world, where it tears itself apart.

What else could be the meaning of the fact that, for a number of years, some of the most gifted men did their utmost to shatter their own intellects, hoping in this way to make the intellect itself explode? Dada is generally seen as an unimportant failure, whereas, for others, it becomes liberating laughter, a revelation that transfigures human being.

And as for Nietzsche's glances into the abyss, isn't it time to call to account those for whom they have only been the object of an eclectic curiosity? Many realities are subject to the law of all or *nothing*. This is the case with Nietzsche. The *Spiritual Exercises* of Saint Ignatius of Loyola would be *nothing* if they were not meditated in the greatest silence (and meditated, they are a prison without an exit). What Nietzsche shattered can only be opened to those carried forward by the need to shatter; the others do to Nietzsche what they do to everything else: nothing has meaning for them, and everything they touch decomposes. It is a law of present-day life that an ordinary man must be incapable of thinking about anything at all, and be tied down in every way by completely servile occupations, which drain him of reality. But the existence of this man will end up crumbling into dust, and one day he will no longer be astonished when a living being does not see him as the ultimate limit of things.

Notes

1. Continuation of the article that appeared in the January number, entitled "Nietzsche and the Fascists." This chronicle will be continued. [But the suspension of *Acéphale* prevented this continuation. Tr.]

2. This cyclical representation of history is in reality the current view. Chateaubriand, Vigny, George Sand, Renan all expressed themselves in the same way on the subject of Christianity.

Engels developed at great length the principle of the similarity between the earliest period of Christianity and the nineteenth century (see "On the Early History of Christianity"). [In *Marx and Engels: Basic Writings on Politics and Philosophy*, ed. Lewis Feuer (Garden City, N.Y.: Doubleday Anchor Books, 1959). Tr.]

Nietzsche, seeing himself as the Antichrist and seeing the time in which he lived as a summit of history, also imagined a cyclical movement of things. But for Nietzsche, there was in a certain sense a return to the world that Socrates and Christianity had destroyed (see the review of the book by Löwith, in *Acéphale*, January, p. 31). [Bataille refers here to a review of Karl Löwith's book *Nietzsches Philosophie der ewigen Wiederkunft des Gleichen* (Berlin: Die Runde, 1935), by Pierre Klossowski, in *Acéphale* 2 (1937). Tr.]

It is unfortunate that the cyclical conception of history has been discredited by occultism and by Spengler. It can take shape, however, as soon as it is based on a simple and obvious principle. It will necessarily be linked to a SOCIOLOGICAL INTERPRETATION OF HISTORY—sociological, in other words, separated from both economic materialism and moral idealism.

3. Continuous adjustments have not been able to prevent the continuous downward slide.

4. In the Egyptian civilization, individual values, which were, strictly speaking, nonexistent at

the beginning of the third millennium (in the period of the great pyramids), appear to have been well developed eight or ten centuries later, in a period of social revolutions tending toward nihilism (see Alexandre Moret, *Le Nil et la civilisation égyptienne* [Paris, 1926]. pp. 251ff. and 292ff.); in Western civilization, as in the Chinese civilization, the multiple forms of sovereignty in a feudal society lead to a monarchical individualization that introduces a rational administration. The forms and the sequences of events are different in each cycle, but the coinciding of social troubles, the decline of sacred values, and the enrichment of individual life is constant; the same is true of the recomposition that follows the crisis.

5. It goes without saying that it is impossible to determine an exact date on which a process starts and, on the whole, considerations on the order of those explained here cannot have an extremely precise formal value. The same is true, moreover, of any reflections on a complex subject.

6. *Thus Spoke Zarathustra*, second part, "On the Land of Education." [Trans. W. Kaufmann, in *The Portable Nietzsche* (New York: Viking, 1954), p. 233. The quote here has been modified to conform to the French version that Bataille cites. Tr.] The German term *Kinderland*, land of children, corresponding to *Vaterland*, fatherland, cannot be exactly translated.

7. *The Birth of Tragedy*, section 1. [Trans. F. Golffing (Garden City, N.Y.: Doubleday Anchor Books, 1956), p. 19. Tr.]

8. This tragedy, by Cervantes, was staged in Paris in April and May 1937 by Jean-Louis Barrault. It is important, from the point of view developed here, that Barrault was carried along by the meaning of the tragedy's grandeur. It is even more important that André Masson, through his decors and paintings, created a magic through which the essential themes of mythic existence regained their brilliance. There is no telling here what was Cervantes' and what was Masson's in the representation of the two opposed worlds.

The subject of *Numantia* is the merciless war carried out by the Roman general Scipio against the Numantines in revolt who, besieged and exhausted, kill each other rather than surrender. In the first part, the soothsayer Marquino makes a dead man come out of a tomb, in order to learn from him the terrible fate of the city.

[A translation of this play, entitled *The Siege of Numantia* and translated by R. Campbell, is in the collection *The Classic Theatre*, ed. Eric Bentley, vol. 3 (Garden City, N.Y.: Doubleday Anchor Books, 1959). Tr.]

9. "Numantia! Liberty!" is the war cry of the furious and besieged Numantines.

The Obelisk

The Mystery of the Death of God

A "mystery" cannot be posited in the empty region of spirit, where only words foreign to life subsist. It cannot result from a confusion between obscurity and the abstract void. The obscurity of a "mystery" comes from images that a kind of lucid dream borrows from the realm of the crowd, sometimes bringing to light what the guilty conscience has pushed back into the shadows, sometimes highlighting figures that are routinely *ignored*. From Louis XVI's guillotine to the obelisk, a spatial arrangement is formed on the PUBLIC SQUARE, in other words, on all the public squares of the "civilized world" whose historical charm and monumental appearance prevail over everything else. For it is nowhere but THERE that a man, in some ways bewitched, in some ways overtaken by frenzy, expressly presents himself as "Nietzsche's madman" and illuminates with his dream-lantern the mystery of the DEATH OF GOD.

The Prophecy of Nietzsche

"Have you not heard," cried Nietzsche, "of that madman who lit a lantern in the bright morning hours, ran to the marketplace, and cried incessantly: "I seek God! I seek God!' —As many of those who did not believe in God were standing around just then, he provoked much laughter. Has he got lost? asked one. Did he lose his way like a child? asked another. Or is he hiding? Is he afraid of us? Has he gone on a voyage? emigrated? —Thus they yelled and laughed.

213

The madman jumped into their midst and pierced them with his eyes. 'Whither is God?' he cried; 'I will tell you. *We have killed him*—you and I. All of us are his murderers. But how did we do this? How could we drink up the sea? Who gave us the sponge to wipe away the entire horizon? What were we doing when we unchained this earth from its sun? Whither is it moving now? Whither are we moving? Away from all suns? Are we not plunging continually? Backward, sideward, forward, in all directions? Is there still any up or down? Are we not straying as through an infinite nothing? Do we not feel the breath of empty space? Has it not become colder? Is not night continually closing in on us? Do we not need to light lanterns in the morning? Do we hear nothing as yet of the noise of the gravediggers who are burying God? Do we smell nothing as yet of the divine decomposition? Gods, too, decompose. God is dead. God remains dead. And we have killed him.

'How shall we comfort ourselves, the murderers of all murderers? What was holiest and mightiest of all that the world has yet owned has bled to death under our knives: who will wipe this blood off us? What water is there for us to clean ourselves? What festivals of atonement, what sacred games shall we have to invent? Is not the greatness of this deed too great for us? Must we ourselves not become gods simply to appear worthy of it? THERE HAS NEVER BEEN A GREATER DEED; AND WHOEVER IS BORN AFTER US—FOR THE SAKE OF THIS DEED HE WILL BELONG TO A HIGHER HISTORY THAN ALL HISTORY HITHERTO.' '''[1]

Mystery and the Public Square

While the existence of human beings may have importance within their own lives and within the limits of their personal destinies, it has none in the eyes of others. Beyond these limits—where human meaning begins—existence matters to the extent that they attract and, apart from this attraction, they are less than shadows, less than specks of dust. And the attraction of an isolated human being is itself nothing but a shadow, a pitiful fleeting apparition. It is but the tentative incarnation of WHAT IS ONLY HUMAN LIFE, which has no name and which the agitation of countless multitudes obscurely demands and constructs, in spite of appearances to the contrary. Who knows what bitterness and sanctity are exhaled in this agitation, which is horror, violence, hatred, sobs, crime, disgust, laughter, and human love. Each individual is but one of the specks of dust that gravitate around this bitter existence. The dust so effectively obscures the condensation around which it orbits that many clear minds, whose reality, however, is only a kind of residue formed wherever activity is condensed (and not a stormy light produced in the shelterless solitude of the individual), imagine human existence as inaccurately as someone who would judge the reality of a capital by the appearance of a suburb, who would think that that life must be examined in its empty and peripheral forms, rather than in the monuments and the monumental vistas that are its center.

The Obelisk

Clausewitz writes in *On War*: "Like the obelisks that are raised at the points where the major roads of a country begin, the energetic will of the leader constitutes the center from which everything in military art emanates." The *Place de la Concorde* is the space where the death of God must be announced and shouted precisely because the obelisk is its calmest negation. As far as the eye can see, a moving and empty human dust gravitates around it. But nothing answers so accurately the apparently disordered aspirations of this crowd as the measured and tranquil spaces commanded by its geometric simplicity.

The obelisk is without a doubt the purest image of the head and of the heavens. The Egyptians saw it as a sign of military power and glory, and just as they saw the rays of the setting sun in their funeral pyramids, so too they recognized the brilliance of the morning sun in the angles of their splendid monoliths: the obelisk was to the armed sovereignty of the pharoah what the pyramid was to his dried-out corpse. It was the surest and most durable obstacle to the drifting away of all things. And even today, wherever its rigid image stands out against the sky, it seems that sovereign permanence is maintained across the unfortunate vicissitudes of civilizations.

The old obelisk of Ramses II is thus, at the central point from which the avenues radiate, both a simpler and a more important apparition than any other; is it not worthy of renewed astonishment that, from remote regions of the earth and from the dawn of the ages, this Egyptian image of the IMPERISHABLE, this petrified sunbeam, arrives at the center of urban life?

The Obelisks Respond to the Pyramids

If one considers the mass of the pyramids and the rudimentary means at the disposal of their builders, it seems evident that no enterprise cost a greater amount of labor than this one, which wanted to halt the flow of time.

The Egyptian pharoah was surely the first to give the human individual the structure and the measureless *will to be* that set him upright above the surface of the earth as a kind of luminous and living edifice. When individuals—long after the era of the great pyramids—have wanted to acquire immortality, they have had to appropriate the Osirian myths and the funeral rites that formerly had been the privilege of the sovereign. For it was only to the extent that a considerable mass of power had been concentrated in a single head that the human being raised to the heavens his greed for eternal power, something that had surely never taken place before the *pschent* designated the head of the pharoah to the holy terror of a vast populace. But once it did, each time death struck down the heavy column of strength the world itself was shaken and put in doubt, and nothing less than the giant edifice of the pyramid was necessary to reestablish the order of things: the pyramid let the god-king enter the eternity of the sky next to the solar Râ, and in this way existence regained its unshakable plenitude in the person of the one it had *recognized*. The existing pyramids still bear witness to this calm triumph of an unwavering and hallucinating resolve: they are not only the most ancient and the vastest monuments man has ever constructed, but they are still, even today, the most enduring. The great triangles that make up their sides "seem to fall from the sky like the rays of the sun when the disk, veiled by the storm, suddenly pierces through the clouds and lets fall to earth a ladder of sunlight." Thus they assure the presence of the unlimited sky on earth, a presence that never ceases to contemplate and dominate human agitation, just as the immobile prism reflects every one of the things that surrounds it. In their imperishable unity, the pyramids—endlessly—continue to crystallize the mobile succession of the various ages; alongside the Nile, they rise up like the totality of centuries, taking on the immobility of stone and watching all men die, one after the other: they transcend the intolerable void that time opens under men's feet, for all possible movement is halted in their geometric surfaces: IT SEEMS THAT THEY MAINTAIN WHAT ESCAPES FROM THE DYING MAN.

The "Sensation of Time" Sought by Glory

A moving perspective, represented by the shadows and traces of the successive generations of numberless dead, extends from the banks of the Nile to those of the Seine, from the angles of the pyramids to those of the monolith erected before the Gabriel palace. The long span that stretches from the Ancient Empire of Egypt to the bourgeois monarchy of the Orleans—which raised the obelisk on the Place de la Concorde "to the applause of the immense crowd"—was necessary for man to set the most stable limits on the deleterious movement of time. The mocking universe was slowly given over to the severe *eternity* of its almighty Father, guarantor of profound stability. The slow and obscure movements of history took place here at the heart and not at the periphery of being, and they represent the long and inexpiable struggle of God against time, the combat of "established sovereignty" against the destructive and creative madness of things. Thus history endlessly repeats the immutable stone's response to the Heraclitean world of rivers and flames.

But from the development of this changing perspective over the centuries, a specific result that dominates even the monstrous accumulation of forms has come to light: the boundaries raised in opposition to the atrocious "sensation of time" were tied to this sensation in exactly the same way that all work is tied to a sensation of "need." Whereas "need" and poverty endlessly use up the results of useful labor, the interminable obstinacy of men eventually managed to distance from communal existence the "sensation of time," and the shameful malaise it introduced. Moderation and platitude slowly took over the world; more and more accurate clocks replaced the old hourglasses that retained a funereal meaning. The grim reaper went the way of all other phantoms. The earth has been so perfectly emptied of everything that made night terrifying that the worst misfortunes and war itself can no longer alter its comfortable perception. The result is that human striving is no longer directed at powerful and majestic limits; it now aspires, on the contrary, to anything that can deliver it from established tranquillity. *Everything indicates that it was impossible for man to live without the "sensation of time" that opened his world like a movement of breathtaking speed—but what he lived in the past as fear he can only live now as pride and glory.*

To this vision, whose consequences must be projected before us, is added the fact that life ceaselessly gravitates around limits that up to now held back agitation and dread. It would seem that sovereign protection has sometimes been shaken, sometimes violently toppled, and sometimes ignored—but the horizon none the less remains bound by these great figures. And when someone is carried by glory to meet time and its cutting explosion, he comes upon them again, and it is precisely at that moment that death is revealed. From the very fact that they had become, for the mass of tranquilized lives, increasingly useless, empty, and fragile shadows, the figures stand under the threat of collapse and thus reveal, far more thoroughly than in the fearful obsessions of the past, the despairing fall of lives. They are no longer obstacles to the lost obsessive "sensation of time," but are instead the high places from which the breakneck speed of the fall is possible: and the high places themselves topple, to ensure a total revelation. The lands stray from their sun, the horizon is annihilated. And now, rising before the man who carries within himself the naive uproar of conquest of the "death of God," the very stone that earlier had sought to limit storms is nothing more than a milestone marking the immensity of an unlimitable catastrophe. A feeling of explosion and a vertiginous weightlessness surround an imperious and heavy obelisk.

The "Tragic Time of Greece"

Starting with the immense masonry of the pyramids, this reversal of signs is not, however, the result of a uniform and regular course of things. Time has not been the object of a simple feeling of fear. In the attraction exercised by the majestic figures that impose its limit, a now solid time is no less fascinating than the explosive charge packed in a steel shell. And the affinities between happiness and explosion are so profound that fiery catastrophes have always been at the mercy of transports of joy. Combat has always been preferable to tranquillity, a sudden fall to stability. Thus Greece in its earliest days already revealed the possibilities of affinity between man and violence.

It even seems that ancient Greece was engendered by wounds and crime, just as the strength of Cronus was engendered by the bloody mutilation of his father Uranus, in other words, of precisely the divine sovereignty of the heavens. Cronus, the very "human" god of the golden age, was celebrated in saturnalia; Dionysus, whose coming into the world depended on the murder of his mother by his father—the criminal Zeus striking down Semele in a blast of lightning— this tragic Dionysus, broken in joy, started the sudden flight of the bacchantes. And the least explained of all the "mysteries," TRAGEDY, like a festival given in honor of horror-spreading time, depicted for gathered men the signs of delirium and death whereby they might recognize their true nature.

This happy yet somber receptiveness of life was answered by the aggressive vision of Heraclitus. Nietzsche said that this vision was the equivalent of an earthquake, robbing the earth of its stability. He described it in images that he used ten years later to describe the death of God, images of a total yet brilliantly glorious fall. Thus in the death of God, whose whirlwind tears everything from the past, we find once again this "nostalgia for a lost world" which so painfully riveted the eyes of Nietzsche on Greece in the tragic era.

And which, in the same movement, directed Nietzsche's rage against Socrates: what Socrates introduced to a tumultuous humanity was nothing less than the principle, still weak but bearing with it the quality of *immutability*, whose obligatory value would put an end to the *levity* of combat. What Socrates introduced was the GOOD: it was GOD, and already the gravity of Christianity, which dominated the tragedy of the *passion* of the heavens and reduced "the death of God" to the debasement of men and to sin, and turned TIME into EVIL.

The Obelisk and the Cross

The obelisks of Rome are capped with crosses, which add their metallic fragility to the pyramidal peaks of these great stone figures.

The equivocal image of the "death of God" more than any other shatters the order that had fixed the features of immutable sovereignty. The irritated amusement that derives from this botched copulation captures the essence of the malaise that results from the accumulation of successive forms necessary to the lives of men. Thus are revealed the happy shortcuts of Roman Christianity in which, without logic, life attempts to reconcile its impossible moods. But at the same time it becomes clear that the crafty, baroque edifice that resulted was elevated only to fall. For this occidental world, whose fevers were first exhausted and contained in the terrible expiation of saints, only seems to have torn apart its childhood before God in order to be rid of this father, once it had the strength. Whereas the development of ancient life little by little allowed the divine shadow to grow and rejected tragic time, the movement of occidental life strikes down, one after the other, the risky constructions that the will to endure never maintained in correct propositions. Thus, going in the opposite direction on the road traveled by the ancient world, this world, as its riches accumulate and everything in it decomposes, aspires in its depths to the tragic deliverances of primitive Greek naiveté. It is true that everything takes place in an almost empty expanse, in a world which, in its entirety, is leveled and depressed by rational destruction. But in each place where the massive destiny of men is formed, the rhythm of life and death accelerates and attains a speed so great that it results only in the vertigo of the fall.

Hegel against the Immutable Hegel

What makes this movement difficult to represent is the fact that it is accelerated by increases in the sensation of rest. This is what first became apparent when the vicissitudes of human life were traced back from an obelisk. In particular, the rest attained by means of this shadow was necessary for the intellect to approach time with a light heart.

This movement was not at first clear or assured. Even Hegel describing the movement of Spirit as if it excluded all possible rest made it end, however, at HIMSELF as if he were its necessary conclusion. Thus he gave the movement of time the *centripetal* structure that characterizes sovereignty, Being, or God. Time, on the other hand, dissolving each center that has formed, is fatally known as *centrifugal*—since it is known in a being whose center is already there. The dialectical idea, then, is only a hybrid of time and its opposite, of the death of God and the position of the immutable. But it nevertheless marks the movement of a thought eager to destroy what refuses to die, eager to break the bonds of time as much as to break the law through which God obligates. It is manifestly clear that the liberty of time traverses the heavy Hegelian process, precisely to the feeble extent that Socratic irony introduced into this world an eternal Being imposing man.

The Pyramid of Surlei

Nietzsche is to Hegel what a bird breaking its shell is to a bird contentedly absorbing the substance within. The crucial instant of fracture can only be described in Nietzsche's own words:

"The intensity of my feelings makes me both tremble and laugh . . . I had

cried too much . . . these were not tears of tenderness, but tears of jubilation . . . That day I was walking through the woods, along the lake of Silva-
plana; at a powerful pyramidal rock not far from Surlei I stopped . . . ''²

Nietzsche's thought, which resulted in the sudden ecstatic vision of the eternal return, cannot be compared to the feelings habitually linked to what passes
for profound reflection. For the object of the intellect here exceeds the categories in which it can be represented, to the point where as soon as it is represented it becomes an object of ecstasy—object of tears, object of laughter . . . The *toxic* character of the ''return'' is even of such great importance
that, if for an instant it were set aside, the formal content of the ''return'' might
appear empty.

In order to represent the decisive break that took place—freeing life from the
humilities of fear—it is necessary to tie the sundering vision of the ''return'' to
what Nietzsche experienced when he reflected upon the explosive vision of
Heraclitus, and to what he experienced later in his own vision of the ''death of
God'': this is necessary in order to perceive the full extent of the bolt of lightning
that never stopped shattering his life while at the same time projecting it into
a burst of violent light. TIME is the object of the vision of Heraclitus. TIME
is unleashed in the ''death'' of the One whose eternity gave Being an immutable
foundation. And the audacious act that represents the ''return'' at the summit
of this rending agony only wrests from the dead God his *total* strength, in order
to give it to the deleterious absurdity of time.

A ''state of glory'' is thus deftly linked to the feeling of an endless fall. It
is true that a fall was already a part of human ecstasy, on which it conferred the
intoxication of that which approximates the nature of time—but that fall was the
original fall of man, whereas the fall of the ''return'' is FINAL.

The Guillotine

''The very stone that earlier had sought to limit storms is now nothing more than
a milestone marking the immensity of an unlimitable catastrophe . . . '' Near
Surlei, a rock in the form of a pyramid still bears witness to the fall of the
''return'' . . .

Only protracted futility—attached to servile or useful objects—can today
shelter existence from the feeling of violent absurdity. The great dead shadows
have lost the magical charm that made their protection so effective. And when
an extreme chance wills that they still make up the center of destiny, they protect
only to the extent that there is daily indifference.

The obelisk of Luxor has, after a hundred years, become the measured navel
of the land of moderation: its precise angles now belong to the essential figure
that radiates from its base. But the timelessness given to it is due to the absence
of any intelligible affirmation: it endures by virtue of its discreet value. Where

monuments that had clearly affirmed principles were razed, the obelisk remains only so long as the sovereign authority and command it symbolizes do not become conscious. There was some difficulty in finding an appropriate symbol for the Place de la Concorde, where the images of royalty and the Revolution had proven powerless. But it was contrary to the majesty of the site to leave an empty space, and agreement was reached on a monolith brought back from Egypt. Seldom has a gesture of this type been more successful; the apparently meaningless image imposed its calm grandeur and its pacifying power on a location that always threatened to recall the worst. Shadows that could still trouble or weigh upon the conscience were dissipated, and neither God nor time remained: total sovereignty and the guillotine-blade that put an end to it no longer occupied any place in the minds of men.

This is the deceitful and vague response of exalted places to the fathomless multitude of insignificant lives that, for as far as the eye can see, orbit around them—and the spectacle only changes when the lantern of a madman projects its absurd light on stone.

At that moment, the obelisk ceases to belong to the present and empty world, and it is projected to the ends of time. It rises, immutable—there—dominating time's desperate flight. But even while it is blinded by this domination, madness, which flits about its angles in the manner of an insect fascinated by a lamp, recognizes only endless time escaping in the noise of successive explosions. And there is no longer an image before it, but it *hears* this noise of successive explosions. To the extent that the obelisk is now, with all this dead grandeur, *recognized*, it no longer facilitates the flight of consciousness; it focuses the attention on the guillotine.

The Place de la Concorde is dominated, from the height of the palace balustrades, by eight armored and acephalic figures, and under their stone helmets they are as empty as they were on the day the executioner decapitated the king before them. After the execution, Marly's two horses were brought from the nearby forest and set up at the entrance to the exalted places, before which they rear without end. The central point of the triangle formed by the two horses and the obelisk marks the location of the guillotine—an empty space, open to the rapid flow of traffic.

Nietzsche/Theseus

The pure image of the heavens, the purified image of the king, of the chief, of the *head* and of his firmness, this pure image of the sky crossed by rays, commands the concord and the assurance of those who do not *look at it*, and who are not struck by it; but a mortal torment is the lot of the one before whom its reality becomes naked.

The purified head, whose unshakable commands lead men, takes on in these conditions the value of a derisive and enigmatic figure placed at the entrance to a labyrinth, where those who naively *look* are led astray without guidance, overcome with uneasy torment and glory. It is the "breath of empty space" that one inhales THERE—there where interpretations based on immediate political events no longer have any meaning; where the isolated event is no more than the symbol of a much greater event. For it is the *foundation* of things that has fallen into a bottomless void. And what is fearlessly conquered—no longer in a duel where the death of the hero is risked against that of the monster, in exchange for an indifferent duration—is not an isolated creature; it is the very void and the vertiginous fall, it is TIME. The movement of all life now places the human being before the alternatives of either this conquest or a disastrous retreat. The human being arrives at the threshold: there he must throw himself headlong into that which has no foundation and no head.

Notes

1. [*The Gay Science*, section 125, trans. W. Kaufmann (New York: Random House, 1974), p. 181. Tr.]

2. [*Ecce Homo*, section on *Thus Spake Zarathustra*, trans. W. Kaufmann (New York: Random House, 1967), p. 295. Tr.]

The Sorcerer's Apprentice[1]

I. An Absence of Need More Unfortunate
Than the Absence of Satisfaction

A man carries within himself a large number of needs, which he must satisfy in order to avoid distress. But misfortune can hit him even when he does not suffer. An evil fate can rob him of the means of satisfying his needs, but he is no less affected when he lacks one of his elementary needs. The absence of virility most often involves neither suffering nor distress; satisfaction is not lacking in the one diminished by this absence—but it is nevertheless feared as a misfortune.

Thus there is a first ailment that is not felt by the one it strikes; it is only an ailment for one who must face the menace of an impending mutilation.

Consumption, which destroys the bronchial tubes without causing suffering, is surely one of the most pernicious illnesses. And the same is true for everything that causes silent decomposition, when it is inconceivable that one could be aware of it. The greatest harm that strikes men is perhaps the reduction of their existence to the state of a servile organ. But no one realizes the despair involved in becoming a politician, a writer, or a scientist. There is no cure for the insufficiency that diminishes anyone who refuses to become a whole man, in order to be nothing more than one of the functions of human society.

II. Man Deprived of the Need to Be Man

The harm would not be great if it struck only a certain number of luckless men. The one who mistakes the glory of his literary works for the accomplishment of his destiny could be deluded without human life being led into a general decline. But nothing exists beyond science, politics, and art—which are held to live in isolation, every man for himself, like so many servants of a dead man.

The greatest part of activity is subordinated to the production of useful goods, no decisive change seeming possible, and man is all too inclined to make his enslavement by work an insuperable limit. Nevertheless, the absurdity of such an empty existence still induces the slave to complete his production through a faithful response to what art, politics, or science demand him to be and to believe; he finds therein the fulfillment of his human destiny. The "great men" who practice in these fields thus constitute a limit for all others. And no alarming suffering is tied to this state of half-death—scarcely the awareness of a depression (agreeable if it coexists with the memory of disappointing tensions).

It is permissible for man to love nothing, for the universe without cause and without end that gave him his life did not necessarily grant him an acceptable destiny. But the man who is scared by human destiny, and who cannot endure the linkage of greed, crimes, and misery cannot be virile, either. If he turns away from himself, he doesn't even have a reason to groan to the point of exhaustion. He can tolerate his existence only on the condition that he forget what it really is. Artists, politicians, and scientists have the responsibility of lying to him; those who dominate existence in this way are almost always those who know best how to lie to themselves, hence those who lie best to others. In these conditions virility declines as much as the love of human destiny. All equivocations are welcome when it comes to dismissing the heroic and seductive image of our fate; in a world where the need to be a man is missing, there is room only for the unattractive face of the useful man.

But while this absence of need is the worst thing that can happen, it is experienced as smug bliss. Harm appears only if the persistence of "amor fati" makes a man a stranger to the present world.

III. The Man of Science

The "man deprived by fear of the need to be a man" has placed his greatest hopes in science. He has renounced the character of totality that his acts had as long as he wanted to live his destiny. For the act of science must be autonomous and the scientist excludes all human interests external to the desire for knowledge. A man who bears the burden of science has exchanged human destiny's concern for living with a concern for the discovery of truth. He passes from the totality to a part, and serving this part demands that the other parts no longer count. Science is a function that developed only after occupying the place of the destiny that it was to have *served*. For it could do nothing as long as it served.

It is a paradox that a function could only be fulfilled on condition that it become an end in itself.

The totality of sciences that man has at his disposal is due to this sort of fraud. But if it is true that the human domain has increased because of it, it has been at the cost of a crippled existence.[2]

IV. The Man of Fiction

The function attributed to art is more equivocal. It does not always seem that the writer and artist have been willing to renounce existence, and their abdication is more difficult to detect than that of the man of science. What art and literature express does not have the birdbrained appearance of learned laws; their troubling conceptions, in opposition to methodically represented reality, only seem to be endowed with a shocking seductiveness. But what is the meaning of these painted and written phantoms, invoked to make the world in which we wake a little less unworthy to be haunted by our idle lives? Everything is *false* in images of fantasy. And everything is false with a lie that knows neither hesitation nor shame. The two essential elements of life thus find themselves rigorously dissociated. The truth pursued by science is true only provided that it be without meaning, and nothing has meaning unless it be fiction.

The servants of science have excluded human destiny from the world of truth, and the servants of art have renounced making a true world out of what an anxious destiny has caused them to bring forth. But for all that it is not easy to escape the necessity of attaining a real, and not a fictive, life. The servants of art can accept for their creations the fugitive existence of shadows; nevertheless they themselves must enter living into the kingdom of truth, money, glory, and social rank. It is thus impossible for them to have anything other than a lame life. They often think that they are possessed by what they represent, but that which has no true existence possesses nothing; they are only truly possessed by their careers. Romanticism replaces the gods who possess from the outside with the unfortunate destiny of the poet, but through this he is far from escaping lameness; romanticism has only made misfortune into a new form of career and has made the lies of those it has not killed even more tiresome.

V. Fiction Placed in the Service of Action

Hypocrisy linked to the career and, in a more general way, to the *ego* of the artist or writer, commits him to place fictions in the service of some more solid reality. If it is true that art and literature do not form a self-sufficient world, they can subordinate themselves to the real world, contribute to the glory of the Church or the State or, if this world is divided, to the action of religious or political propaganda. But, in this case, there is nothing more than ornament or service to others. If the institutions one serves were themselves agitated by the contradictory movement of destiny, art would encounter the possibility of serving and expressing profound life; if it is a question of organizations whose interests are tied to circumstances, to particular communities, art introduces between profound life and partisan action a confusion that sometimes shocks even the partisans.

Most often, human destiny can be lived only in fiction. But the man of fiction suffers from not accomplishing on his own the destiny he describes; he suffers from escaping fiction only through his career. He then tries to make the phantoms that haunt him enter into the real world. As soon, however, as they belong to the world that action makes true, as soon as the author ties them to some particular truth, they lose their privilege of realizing human life to the fullest; they are nothing more than the boring reflections of a fragmentary world.

VI. The Man of Action

If the truth that science reveals is stripped of human sense, if the *fictions* of the spirit alone respond to the strange will of man, then the accomplishment of this will demands that these fictions be *made true*. The one who is possessed by a need to create only experiences the need to be a man. But he renounces this need if he renounces creating anything more than fantasies and lies. He only remains virile by trying to make reality conform to what he thinks: each force in him demands that the failed world in which he has appeared be submitted to the caprice of dreams.

However, this necessity most often appears only in an obscure form. It appears vain to limit oneself to reflecting reality as in science, and vain to escape it as in fiction. Action alone proposes to transform the world, in other words, to make it similar to dreams. "To act" resonates in the ear with the blast of the trumpets of Jericho. No imperative possesses a more basic efficacy and, for whoever hears it, the necessity to take action is imposed without possible delay and without condition. But he who demands that action realize the will that animates him quickly receives strange responses. The neophyte learns that the will to efficacious action is the one that limits itself to dismal dreams. He accepts; then he slowly understands that action will leave him only the benefit of having acted. He believed in transforming the world according to his dream, but he only transformed his dream on the level of the poorest reality: he can only stifle in himself the will he carried—*in order to be able to ACT.*

VII. Action Changed by the World, Action
Incapable of Changing the World

The first renunciation that action demands of the one who wants to act is that he reduce his dream to the proportions described by science. The concern for giving human destiny a field other than fiction is scorned by doctrinaire politicians. It cannot be set aside in the practice of the extremist parties that demand from militants that they wager their lives. But the destiny of a man does not become real on the sole condition that he enter into combat. This destiny must still mingle with that of the forces in whose ranks he confronts death. And the doctrinaire politicians, with this destiny at their disposal, reduce it to equal well-being for all. The language of action accepts only a formula conforming to the rational principles that govern science and keep it foreign to human life. No one thinks that political action can be defined and take shape in the personal form of legendary heroes. The just distribution of material and cultural goods alone allays their all-consuming concern with avoiding everything that resembles the human face and its expressions of avid desire or happy defiance before death. They have been persuaded that it is hateful to address the struggling multitudes as one would address a crowd of already dying heroes. Thus they speak the language of self-interest to those who are, in some ways, already dripping blood from their own wounds.

Men of action follow or serve *that which exists*. If their action is a revolt, they still follow *that which exists* when they get themselves killed in order to destroy it. Human destiny possesses them, in fact, when they destroy; it escapes them as soon as they have nothing more than the will to order their faceless world. Destruction has hardly been achieved, and they find themselves, along with others who follow, at the mercy of what they have destroyed, which then starts to reconstruct itself. The dreams that science and reason have reduced to empty formulae—these amorphous dreams themselves cease to be anything more than the dust raised by the passage of ACTION. Enslaved, and breaking everything that is not bent by necessity—which they undergo before others— men of action blindly abandon themselves to the current that sweeps them away and that is accelerated by their impotent agitation.

VIII. Dissociated Life

The life thus broken into three pieces has ceased to be *life*; it is nothing more than art, science, or politics. In the region where savage simplicity had made men dominant, there are now nothing but scientists, politicians, and artists. The renunciation of life in exchange for a function is the condition consented to by each of them. A few scientists have artistic or political concerns, and politicians and artists can also look outside of their fields; they only add up three infirmities, which together do not make a valid man. A totality of life has little to do with a collection of abilities and areas of expertise. One can no more cut it into pieces than one can cut up a living body. Life is the virile unity of the pieces that go to make it up. In it there is the simplicity of an ax blow.

IX. Full Life and the Image of the Loved One

Simple and strong life, which has not yet been destroyed by functional servility, is possible only to the extent that it has ceased to subordinate itself to some particular project, such as acting, depicting, or measuring; it depends on the *image of destiny*, on the seductive and dangerous myth with which it feels itself to be in silent solidarity. A human being is dissociated when he *devotes himself* to a useful labor, which has no sense by itself; he can only find the plenitude of total life when seduced. Virility is nothing less than the expression of this principle: when a man no longer has the force to respond to the image of desirable nudity, he recognizes the loss of his virile integrity. And just as virility is tied to the allure of a nude body, full existence is tied to any image that arouses hope and terror. THE LOVED ONE in this broken-up world has become the only power that has retained the virtue of returning to the heat of life. If this world were not ceaselessly traversed by the convulsive movements of beings who seek each other, if it were not transfigured by the face "whose absence is painful," it would still appear as a mockery to those it causes to be born: human existence would be present there, but only in the form of a memory or of a film of "primitive" countries. It is necessary to exclude fiction, with a feeling of irritation. The lost, the tragic, the "blinding marvel," possessed in one's innermost being, can no longer be met anywhere but on a bed. It is true that satisfied dust and the dissociated concerns of the present world also invade bedrooms; locked bedrooms nevertheless remain, in the almost unlimited mental void, so many islands where the images of life reconstitute themselves.

X. The Illusory Character of the Loved One

The image of the loved one appears, first of all, with a precarious brilliance. It illuminates and at the same time frightens the one who follows it with his eyes. He sets it aside and smiles at his puerile agitation if he holds above all else his concern for his duties. A man who has become "serious" believes it easy to find existence anywhere else than in the necessary response to this attraction. However, even if someone else, less weighty, lets himself be burned by the seduction that frightens him, he must still recognize the illusory character of such an image.

Living, in itself, contradicts this image. Eating, sleeping, and speaking empty it of meaning. If a man meets a woman and if it becomes evident to him that she is his destiny, then everything that invades him like a silent tragedy is incompatible with her necessary comings and goings. The image through which, in an instant, destiny has become alive thus finds itself projected into a world foreign to everyday agitation. The woman toward whom a man is drawn, as to his human destiny, no longer belongs to the space that money controls. Her sweetness escapes the real world, through which she moves without allowing herself to be any more imprisoned than a dream. Misfortune would ravage the spirit of anyone who lets himself be possessed by the need to reduce her. Her reality is as doubtful as a gleam that vacillates, but which the night makes violent.

XI. The True World of Lovers

The first doubtful appearance of the lovers who meet again in their night of destiny is not, however, of the same order as the illusions of the theater or books. For theater and literature cannot by themselves create *a world where beings relocate each other*. The most rending visions represented by art have never created anything more than a fugitive link between the people they have touched. If they meet, they must be content to express what they have experienced in phrases that substitute comparison and analysis for communicable reactions, whereas lovers commune even in the most profound silence, where each movement, charged with burning passion, has the power to convey ecstasy. It would be vain to deny that this flaming hearth constitutes a real world, the world where lovers find themselves, as they once appeared to one another, each of them having taken on the moving form of the other's destiny. Thus the stormy movement of love makes true what was only an illusion on the first day.

The obstacle met by the fragmentary activities oblivious to others—by action oblivious to the dream—is thus surmounted when two beings in love physically unite. Shadows pursued to the point of an embrace are no less amazing than the remote creatures of legends. The sudden apparition of a woman seems to belong to the unsettled world of dreams—but possession throws the nude and pleasure-drowned dream figure into the narrowly real world of a bedroom.

Happy action is the "sister of dreams," on the very bed where the secret of life is revealed to knowledge. And knowledge is the ecstatic discovery of human destiny, in this guarded space where science—as much as art or practical action—has lost the possibility of giving a fragmentary meaning to existence.[3]

XII. Series of Chances

The renunciation of dreams and the practical will of the man of action thus do not represent the only ways to touch the real world. The world of lovers is no less *true* than that of politics. It even absorbs the totality of life, which politics cannot do. And its characteristics are not those of the fragmentary and empty world of practical action, but those that belong to *human life* before it is reduced to servility: the world of lovers is constructed, like life, out of a *series of chances that give the awaited answer to an avid and powerful will to be.*

What determines the election of the loved one—so that the possibility of another choice, represented logically, inspires horror—is in fact reducible to a *series of chances*. Simple coincidences arrange the meeting and constitute the feminine figure of destiny to which a man feels bound, sometimes to the point of death. The value of this figure is dependent on long-term obsessive exigencies, which are so difficult to satisfy that they lend the loved one the colors of extreme luck. When a certain configuration of cards is introduced into a game, it determines the fate of the stakes; the unexpected meeting of a woman, as in the case of a lucky hand of cards, determines existence. But the best hand of cards only has meaning if the conditions under which it is dealt allow one to win the pot. The winning hand is only an arbitrary combination; the desire to win, and the winnings themselves, make it real. *Consequences* alone give a true character to random series that would have no meaning if human caprice had not chosen them. Meeting a woman would only be an aesthetic emotion without the will to possess her and make true what her apparition had seemed to mean. Only once conquered, or lost, the fugitive image of destiny ceases to be an aleatory figure and becomes reality determining fate.

An "avid and powerful will to be" is thus the condition of truth, but the *isolated individual* never possesses the power to create a world (he only tries it if he himself is in the power of forces that *alienate* his senses and thus make him mad); the coincidence of wills is no less necessary to the birth of human worlds than is the coincidence of chance figures. Only the accord of lovers, like that of gamblers at a table, creates the living reality of still shapeless correspondences (if the accord is lacking, sorrow, in which love remains real, is always the consequence of a first complicity). Moreover, the accord of two, or of several, must be added to the general belief that assigns a value to the previously described figures of destiny. The meaning of love is determined in legends that illustrate the destiny of lovers in everyone's mind.

But this "avid will to be," even in relation to the fact that it is held *in common*, is in no way similar to the will that deliberates and intervenes. It is will as blind fearlessness before death and must, following the example of one who confronts murderous gunfire, trust itself in large part to *chance*. Only a *random* movement can give the response that obscure passion demands, upon the fortuitous appearance of "series." A good game only has value if the cards are properly shuffled and cut, and not set up in a prior arrangement, which would constitute *cheating*. The player's decisions must themselves be *chancy*, due to his ignorance of the other players' hands. The secret force of *loved ones* and the value of their conjunction cannot result from decisions or intentions determined in advance. It is true that, even beyond prostitution or marriage, the world of lovers is still more the realm of trickery than is the world of gambling. There are no precise limits, but instead there are numerous nuances between the ingenuous meeting of persons incapable of hidden motives, and the impudent flirtation that ceaselessly arranges frauds and maneuvers. But naive uncon-sciousness alone has the power to conquer the world of miracles where lovers meet.

Luck, which struggles with the teleological disposition and with the coordi-nation of means and ends, thus triumphs, suddenly appearing with divine ardor. For a long time now the intellect has ceased to imagine the universe in the grasp of a prescient reason. Existence recognizes that it is at the disposal of chance, provided that it can see itself on the same scale as the starry sky, or death. It recognizes itself in its magnificence, made in the image of a universe untouched by the stain of merit or intention.

XIII. Destiny and Myth

It is impossible to imagine, without soon succumbing to extreme dread, the crowd that turns away from this "horrible" influence of chance. This crowd in fact demands that assured life no longer depend on anything but calculations and appropriate decisions. But the "life that only measures itself against death" escapes those who lose the taste for burning "in the flames of hope and dread," a taste shared by lovers and gamblers. Human destiny wants capricious chance to command; what reason substitutes for the rich vegetation of chance is no longer an adventure to be lived, but is instead the empty and correct solution to the difficulties of existence. Acts undertaken with some rational end are only servile responses to a necessity. Acts undertaken in pursuit of seductive images of chance are the only ones that respond to the need to live like a flame. For it is human to burn and consume oneself to the point of suicide at the baccarat table; even if the cards reflect a degraded form of good or bad fortune, their meaning, which wins or loses money, also possesses the virtue of signifying des-tiny (the queen of spades sometimes signifies death). It is, on the contrary, in-human to abandon life to a chain of useful acts. One aspect of human options is inevitably devoted to a concern with freeing oneself from problems such as hunger, cold, and social constraints. What escapes servitude—life—risks itself; in other words, it places itself on the level of the chances it meets.

Life risks itself, the project of destiny is realized. What was only a dream figure becomes myth. And *living* myth, which intellectual dust only knows as *dead* and sees as the touching error of ignorance, the myth-lie represents destiny and becomes *being*. Not the being that rational philosophy betrays by giving it the attributes of the immutable, but the being expressed by the given name and the surname, and then the double being that loses itself in an endless embrace, and finally the being of the city "that tortures, decapitates, and makes war . . ."

Myth remains at the disposal of one who cannot be satisfied by art, science, or politics. Even though love by itself constitutes a world, it leaves intact everything that surrounds it. The experience of love even augments lucidity and suffering; it develops the malaise and the exhausting impression of emptiness that results from contact with decomposed society. Myth alone returns, to the one who is broken by every ordeal, the image of a plenitude extended to the community where men gather. Myth alone enters the bodies of those it binds and it expects from them the same receptiveness. It is the frenzy of every dance; it takes existence "to its boiling point": it communicates to it the tragic emotion that makes its sacred intimacy accessible. For myth is not only the divine figure of destiny and the world where this figure moves; it cannot be separated from the community to which it belongs and which ritually assumes its dominion. It would be fiction if the *accord* that a *people* manifests in the agitation of festivals did not make it a vital human reality. Myth is perhaps fable, but this fable is placed in opposition to fiction if one looks at the people who dance it, who act it, and for whom it is living *truth*. A community that does not carry out the ritual possession of its myths possesses only a truth in decline; it is living to the extent that its will to be animates the sum of mythical chances that represent its intimate existence. A myth thus cannot be assimilated to the scattered fragments of a dissociated group. It is in solidarity with *total* existence, of which it is the tangible expression.

Ritually lived myth reveals nothing less than true being; in it life appears no less terrible or beautiful than the *loved woman*, nude on a bed. The darkness of the sacred place, which contains the real presence, is no more oppressive than that of the bedroom where lovers have locked themselves; the knowledge to be gleaned is no less foreign to the science of laboratories in the sacred place than it is in the lovers' hideaway. In the sacred place, human existence meets the figure of destiny fixed by the caprice of *chance*: the *determining laws* that science defines are the opposite of this play of fantasy constituting life. This play separates itself from science and coincides with the delirium that engenders the images of art. But while art recognizes the ultimate reality and the superior character of the true world that constrains men, myth enters into human existence like a force demanding that *inferior* reality submit to its dominion.

XIV. The Sorcerer's Apprentice

It is true that this return to the old human house is perhaps the most upsetting moment of a life devoted to the succession of disappointing illusions. As a strange step draws nearer to it, the old house of myth appears no less deserted than the "picturesque" rubble of temples. For the representation of the myth that expresses the totality of existence is not the result of any current experience. The past alone, or the civilizations of "backward" peoples, have made possible the knowledge but not the possession of a world that seems henceforth inaccessible. It is possible that total existence is nothing more for us than a simple dream, nourished by historical descriptions and by the secret gleams of our passions. Contemporary men can master only a heap that represents the debris of existence. This recognized truth, however, quickly appears at the mercy of the lucidity controlled by the need to live. At the very least a first experience should be followed by failure before the denier acquires the right to *sleep* guaranteed by his denial. The methodical description of the experience to be attempted indicates, moreover, that it only demands attainable conditions. The "sorcerer's apprentice," first of all, does not encounter demands that are any different from those he would encounter on the difficult road of art. Inconsequential fictional figures are no less exclusive of determined intention than are arid mythical figures. The requirements of mythological invention are only more rigorous. They do not refer—as a rudimentary conception would have it—to obscure faculties of collective invention. But they would refuse to see any value in figures whose share of willed arrangement has not been set apart with the rigor proper to *sacred* feeling. From beginning to end, moreover, the "sorcerer's apprentice" must accustom himself to this rigor (supposing that it does not respond to his most intimate command). Secrecy, in the domain where he advances, is no less necessary to his strange procedures than it is to the transports of eroticism (the total world of myth, the world of *being*, is separated from the dissociated world by the very limits that separate the *sacred* from the *profane*). The "secret society" is precisely the name of the social reality constituted by these procedures. But this novelistic expression must not be understood, as it usually is, in the vulgar sense of a "spy ring." For secrecy has to do with the constitutive reality of seductive existence, and not with some action contrary to the security of the State. Myth is born in ritual acts hidden from the static vulgarity of disintegrated society, but the violent dynamism that belongs to it has no other object than the return to lost totality; even if it is true that the repercussions are decisive and transform the world (whereas the action of parties is lost in the quicksand of contradictory words), its political repercussion can only be the result of existence. The obscurity of such projects only expresses the disconcerting reorientation necessary at the paradoxical moment of despair.

Notes

1. This text does not exactly constitute a sociological study, but the definition of a point of view through which the results of sociology can appear as responses to the most virile concerns, and not to a specialized scientific preoccupation. Sociology itself, in fact, has difficulty avoiding a critique of pure science to the extent that it is a phenomenon of dissociation. If the social fact represents by itself the totality of existence, and if science is only a fragmentary activity, then the science that envisages the social fact cannot attain its object if that object, to the extent that it is attained, becomes the negation of science's principles. Sociological science thus no doubt demands other conditions than the disciplines that are concerned with the dissociated aspects of nature. It seems to have devel-

oped—in particular in France—insofar as those who have taken it on have been aware of the coinciding of the social fact and the religious fact. The results of French sociology run the risk, however, of remaining nonexistent if the question of *totality* is not first posed in all its magnitude.

2. It does not follow that science must be rejected . . . Its *moral* ravages are alone criticized, but it is not impossible to contravene them, as far as sociology is concerned, in the name of the principle of knowledge (see above, note 1).

3. The description of the "world of lovers" in this text has, however, only a *demonstrative* value. This world constitutes one of the rare possibilities for present life, and its realization presents a character that is much less distanced from the totality of existence than are the worlds of art, politics, or science. It however does not fulfill human life. It would in any case be an error to consider it the elementary form of society. The conception that holds that the couple is at the basis of human society had to be abandoned for reasons that seem decisive.

The Practice of Joy before Death

*All this I am, and I want to be: at the same time dove, serpent,
and pig.*

Nietzsche

When a man finds himself situated in such a way that the world is happily reflected in him, without entailing any destruction or suffering—as on a beautiful
spring morning—he can let himself be carried away by the resulting enchant-
ment or simple joy. But he can also perceive, at the same time, the weight and
the vain yearning for empty rest implied by this beatitude. At that moment,
something cruelly rises up in him that is comparable to a bird of prey that tears
open the throat of a smaller bird in an apparently peaceful and clear blue sky.
He recognizes that he cannot fulfill his life without surrendering to an inexorable
movement, whose violence he can feel acting on the most remote areas of his
being with a rigor that frightens him. If he turns to other beings who do not go
beyond beatitude, he experiences no hate, but, on the contrary, he sympathizes
with necessary pleasures; he clashes only with those who pretend to attain fulfillment in their lives, who act out a risk-free charade in order to be recognized
as having attained fulfillment, while in fact they only speak of fulfillment. But
he should not succumb to vertigo. For vertigo swiftly exhausts and threatens to
revive a concern for happy leisure or, if that cannot be attained, for a painless
emptiness. Or if he does not give in, and if he tears himself completely apart

in terrified haste, he enters death in such a way that nothing is more horrible. He alone is happy who, having experienced vertigo to the point of trembling in his bones, to the point of being incapable of measuring the extent of his fall, suddenly finds the unhoped-for strength to turn his agony into a joy capable of freezing and transfiguring those who meet it. But the only ambition that can take hold of a man who, in cold blood, sees his life fulfilled in rending agony, cannot aspire to a grandeur that only extreme chance has at its disposal. This kind of violent decision, which disrupts his repose, does not necessarily entail either his vertigo or his fall in sudden death. In him, this decision may become an act and a power by which he devotes himself to the rigor whose movement ceaselessly closes in on him, as cutting as the beak of a bird of prey. Contemplation is only the context, sometimes calm and sometimes stormy, in which the rapid force of his action must one day be put to the test. The mystical existence of the one whose "joy before death" has become inner violence can never attain the satisfying beatitude of the Christian who gives himself a foretaste of eternity. The mystic of "joy before death" can never be seen as cornered, for he is able to laugh complacently at every human endeavor and to know every accessible enthusiasm: but the totality of life—ecstatic contemplation and lucid knowledge *accomplished in a single action* that cannot fail to become risk—is, however, just as inexorably his lot as death is that of the condemned man.

The texts that follow cannot alone constitute an initiation into the *exercise* of a mysticism of "joy before death." While admitting that a method of initiation might exist, they do not represent even a part of it. Since oral initiation is itself difficult, it is impossible to give in a few pages more than the vaguest representation of that which by nature cannot be grasped. On the whole, these writings represent, moreover, less exercises strictly speaking than simple descriptions of a contemplative state or of an ecstatic contemplation. These descriptions would not even be acceptable if they were not given for what they are, in other words, as free. Only the very first text could be proposed as an exercise.

While it is appropriate to use the word *mysticism* when speaking of "joy before death" and its practice, this implies no more than an affective resemblance between this practice and those of the religions of Asia or Europe. There is no reason to link any presuppositions concerning an alleged deeper reality with a joy that has no object other than immediate life. "Joy before death" belongs only to the person for whom there is no *beyond*; it is the only intellectually honest route in the search for ecstasy.

Besides, how could a *beyond*, a God or what resembles God, still be acceptable? No words are clear enough to express the happy disdain of the one who "dances with the time that kills him" for those who take refuge in the expectation of eternal beatitude. This kind of fretful saintliness—which first had to be sheltered from erotic excess—has now lost all its power: one can only laugh at a sacred drunkenness allied with a horror of debauchery. Prudery may be healthy for backward souls, but those who would be afraid of nude girls or whisky would have little to do with "joy before death."

Only a shameless, indecent saintliness can lead to a sufficiently happy *loss of self*. "Joy before death" means that life can be glorified from root to summit. It robs of meaning everything that is an intellectual or moral *beyond*, substance, God, immutable order, or salvation. It is an apotheosis of that which is perishable, apotheosis of flesh and alcohol as well as of the trances of mysticism. The religious forms it rediscovers are the naive forms that antedate the intrusion of a servile morality: it renews the kind of tragic jubilation that man "is" as soon as he stops behaving like a cripple, glorifying necessary work and letting himself be emasculated by the fear of tomorrow.

I

"I abandon myself to peace, to the point of annihilation."

"The noises of struggle are lost in death, as rivers are lost in the sea, as stars burst in the night.
The strength of combat is fulfilled in the silence of all action.
I enter into peace as I enter into a dark unknown.
I fall in this dark unknown.
I myself become this dark unknown."

II

"I AM joy before death.
Joy before death carries me.
Joy before death hurls me down.
Joy before death annihilates me."

"I remain in this annihilation and, from there, I picture nature as a play of forces expressed in multiplied and incessant agony."

"I slowly lose myself in unintelligible and bottomless space.
I reach the depths of worlds.
I am devoured by death.
I am devoured by fever.
I am absorbed in somber space.
I am annihilated in joy before death."

III

"I AM joy before death."

"The depth of the sky, lost space is joy before death: everything is profoundly cracked."

"I imagine the earth turning vertiginously in the sky.
I imagine the sky itself slipping, turning, and lost.
The sun, comparable to alcohol, turning and bursting breathlessly.
The depth of the sky like an orgy of frozen light, lost.
Everything that exists destroying itself, consuming itself and dying, each instant producing itself only in the annihilation of the preceding one, and itself existing only as mortally wounded.
Ceaselessly destroying and consuming myself in myself in a great festival of blood.
I imagine the frozen instant of my own death."[1]

IV

"I focus on a point before me and I imagine this point as the geometric locus of all existence and all unity, of all separation and all dread, of all unsatisfied desire and all possible death."

"I adhere to this point and a profound love of what I find there burns me, until I refuse to be alive for any reason other than for what is there, for this point which, being both the life and death of the loved one, has the blast of a cataract."

"And at the same time it is necessary to strip away all external representations from what is there, until it is nothing but a pure violence, an interiority, a pure inner fall into a limitless abyss; this point endlessly absorbing from the cataract all its inner nothingness, in other words, all that has disappeared, is 'past,' and in the same movement endlessly prostituting a sudden apparition to the love that vainly wants to grasp that which will cease to be."

"The impossibility of satisfaction in love is a *guide* toward the *fulfilling leap* at the same time that it is the nullification of all possible illusion."

V

"If I imagine myself in a vision and in a halo that transfigures the ecstatic and exhausted face of a dying being, what radiates from that face illuminates with its necessity the clouds in the sky, whose grey glow then becomes more penetrating than the light of the sun itself. In this vision, death appears to be of the same nature as the illuminating light, to the extent that light is lost once it leaves its source: it appears that no less a loss than death is needed for the brilliance of life to traverse and transfigure dull existence, for it is only its free uprooting that *becomes in me* the strength of life and time. In this way I cease to be anything other than the mirror of death, just as the universe is only the mirror of light."

VI. Heraclitean Meditation

"I MYSELF AM WAR."

"I imagine human movement and excitation, whose possibilities are limitless: this movement and excitation can only be appeased by war.

I imagine the gift of an infinite suffering, of blood and open bodies, in the image of an ejaculation cutting down the one it jolts and abandoning him to an exhaustion charged with nausea.

I imagine the earth projected in space, like a woman screaming, her head in flames.

Before the terrestrial world whose summer and winter order the agony of all living things, before the universe composed of innumerable turning stars, limitlessly losing and consuming themselves, I can only perceive a succession of cruel splendors whose very movement requires that I die: this death is only the *exploding* consumption of all that was, the joy of existence of all that comes into the world; even my own life demands that everything that exists, everywhere, ceaselessly give itself and be annihilated.

I imagine myself covered with blood, broken but transfigured and in agreement with the world, both as prey and as a jaw of TIME, which ceaselessly kills and is ceaselessly killed.

There are explosives everywhere that perhaps will soon blind me. I laugh when I think that my eyes persist in demanding objects that do not destroy them."

Note

1. One night, dreaming, X. is struck by lightning; he understands that he is dying and he is suddenly, miraculously, dazzled and transformed; at this point in his dream, he attains the *unexpected*, but he wakes up.

The Sacred

The moment has probably come to designate the crucial element toward which an obscure and uncertain search was directed, through the detours of the creation of forms or verbal invention. The great "quest" of what has been given the poor name "modern spirit" was certainly not obsessed with a "grail" as easily accessible as the "beautiful"; it distanced itself with distrust, sometimes even with an ostentatious distrust, from all the paths leading to the "true," and seemed to have only equivocal feelings about "the good," going from profound modesty to insulting rage, from affirmation to an equally trenchant negation. The conditions for the search were, moreover, obscurity and the limitless character of the goal that it had resolved to attain. Long torment and abrupt violence alone bore witness to the fundamental importance for all life of this "quest" and its indeterminable object.

First of all, it is necessary to show that there are no examples of such a movement of passion raging within the narrow domain of artistic invention. Even romanticism seems to have been traversed by a strictly intellectual uneasiness, if it is compared with the agitation of the "modern spirit." In the order of formal invention, the romantics did not *create*. They permitted themselves some license, and did nothing but extend the domain of myths and, in general, *given* poetic themes, which for them, just as before them, served as motifs for verbal creation. Today's restlessness has not had an intellectual development comparable to that of romanticism and the German philosophy dependent on it, but this restlessness has been applied, with a sort of vertigo, to the discovery of verbal or figurative formulae that are the key to this ponderous existence, which so often defies investment with a *raison d'être*. Surrealism today has made itself the *supporter* of this enterprise, but it recognizes itself as the heir to an earlier obsession: the history of poetry since Rimbaud, that of painting since Van Gogh, testify to the extent and the meaning of the new upheaval.

If one now wants to represent, with an initial clarity, the "grail" obstinately pursued through successive, deceptive, and cloudy depths, it is necessary to insist upon the fact that it could never have been a *substantial* reality; on the contrary, it was an element characterized by the impossibility of its enduring. The term *privileged instant*[1] is the only one that, with a certain amount of accuracy, accounts for what can be encountered *at random* in the search; the opposite of a *substance* that withstands the test of time, it is something that flees as soon as it is seen and cannot be grasped. The will to fix such instants, which belong, it is true, to painting or writing is only the way to make them *reappear*, because the painting or the poetic text *evokes* but does not *make substantial* what once appeared. This gives rise to a mixture of unhappiness and exultation, of disgust and insolence; nothing seems more miserable and more dead than the stabilized thing, nothing is more desirable than what will soon disappear. But, as he feels what he loves escaping, the painter or writer trembles from the cold of extreme want; vain efforts are expended to create pathways permitting the endless reattainment of that which flees.

It is decisively important in this movement that the search, intellectually undertaken at the promptings of unsatisfied desire, has always preceded theory's delineation of the object sought. The belated intervention of discriminating intelligence certainly opened up a field of possibilities for empty error, whose extent became discouraging, but it is no less certain that an experience of this nature would not have been possible if some clairvoyant theory had tried to fix in advance its direction and its limits. It is only when things are already settled and night has fallen that the "Owl of Minerva" can give the goddess an account of the events that have taken place and can decide upon their hidden meaning.

It appears after the fact that art, no longer capable of expressing whatever it is that, coming to it from outside, is incontestably *sacred*—romanticism having used up the possibilities of renewal—it appears after the fact that art could no longer live if it did not have the force to attain the *sacred instant* by its own resources. The techniques put into play up to that point only had to express a *given* that had its own value and meaning. They added to this given only the achieved perfection of expression, to which the "beautiful" could be restored; in relation to them the "true" was only the crudest way of deciding whether the perfection of means sought had been attained, and the "good" remained foreign to them, since its judgments can have no bearing on whatever is expressed. The results were relative facility, absence of worry, and innocence; profound bitterness was excluded from this execution of plans, for which society, its traditions, and its powers took both the initiative and the responsibility. This bitterness was experienced only when doubt was cast on the value of these plans; the authority denied to present reality was then transferred onto the deceptive specters of the past and the elusive phantoms of dreams. Up to the moment, that is, when art, which was still fundamentally only a means of expression, became aware of the *created* share that it had always added to the world it expressed; at that moment it could turn away from all past or present reality and create from itself its own reality, which can no longer be simply beautiful or true, and which must dominate the struggle of good against evil—because of the supreme value this reality represents—in the same way that a violent earth tremor dominates and paralyzes the most catastrophic of battles.

Certainly the possibility of now assigning a definable object to such a strange endeavor is more the result of the endeavor's failure than it is of any moments of fugitive success. A foolish bitterness and an arrogant aversion to oneself have been its most accomplished results. Such results—Rimbaud's name alone sums up their capacity to make nearly everything despicable—underscore the extent to which the cycle of possible exchanges between connoisseurs, painters, and poets moves away from the "grail" without which—and this has become all the more clearly and distinctly apparent, by the very fact of this failure—human existence cannot be justified.

As long as the identification introduced by Christianity between God and the object of religion was imposed upon the spirit, all that could be recognized on the subject of this "grail" was that it could not be confused with God. This distinction had the drawback of setting aside the still profound identity between this "grail" and the very object of religion. But the development of knowledge touching on the history of religions has shown that the essential religious activity was not directed toward a personal and transcendent being (or beings), but toward an impersonal reality. Christianity has made the sacred *substantial*, but the nature of the sacred, in which today we recognize the burning existence of religion, is perhaps the most ungraspable thing that has been produced between men: the sacred is only a privileged moment of communal unity, a moment of the convulsive communication of what is ordinarily stifled.

Such a disjunction between the sacred and transcendental substance (consequently impossible to create) suddenly opens a new field—a field perhaps of violence, perhaps of death, but a field which may be entered—to the agitation that has taken hold of the living human spirit. For if the field of the sacred is accessible, there can be no question of this spirit not breaking through the barrier; this spirit must simply recognize, since it sought and seeks without

Figure 13. Sacred site in Lithuania. The crosses planted by the peasants only perpetuate the meaning of a pagan tumulus where sacrifices were carried out.

Figure 14. The Torero Villalta before the bull he has just killed. Modern bullfights, owing to their ritual enactment and their tragic character, represent a form close to ancient sacred games.

*Figure 15. The Phallus of Delos. Choregic monu-
ment of Karystios, ca. 300 B.C.* The words in
various languages that designate the sacred signify
both ''pure'' and ''filthy.'' The meaning of the
sacred can be seen as lost to the extent that the
awareness of the secret horrors at the basis of religions is lost.

*Figure 16. Sacrifice through the
tearing out of the heart, in Aztec
Mexico. Post-Hispanic Mexican
manuscript, Codex Vaticanus
3738.* Human sacrifice is loftier
than any other—not in the sense
that it is crueler than any other,
but because it is close to the only
sacrifice without trickery, which
can only be the ecstatic loss of
oneself.

respite, that it never sought, and does not seek, to reach less far. The fact that "God is recognized to be dead" cannot lead to a less decisive consequence; God represented the only obstacle to the human will, and freed from God this will surrenders, nude, to the passion of giving the world an intoxicating meaning. Whoever creates, whoever paints or writes, can no longer concede any limitations on painting or writing; *alone*, he suddenly has at his disposal all possible human convulsions, and he cannot flee from this heritage of divine power—which belongs to him. Nor can he try to know if this heritage will *consume* and *destroy* the one it *consecrates*. But he refuses now to surrender "what possesses him" to the standards of salesmen, to which art has conformed.

Note

1. Emile Dermenghem has used the expression "privileged instants"—which for him are at the basis of poetry and mysticism—in an article in *Mesures* (July 1938): "The Instant in the Works of the Mystics and Some Poets." This article refers in particular to the conceptions of the Sufis, who attribute to the "instant" a decisive value, and who compare it to a slicing sword. "The instant," a Sufi says, "cuts the roots of the future and the past. The sword is a dangerous companion; it can make its master a king but it can also destroy him. It does not distinguish between the neck of its master and the neck of another." The profoundly ambiguous, dangerous, and mortal character of the sacred is reflected in this violent representation.—Jean-Paul Sartre in *Nausea* has already spoken of "perfect moments" and "privileged situations" in a significant way.

The College of Sociology

[July 4, 1939] This meeting was to have been devoted to the College of Sociology itself. Because the College of Sociology is, up to a certain point, a singular enterprise, difficult to reduce to the usual forms of activity, there was cause to clarify its meanings and intentions, especially since this singular character may have disconcerted those who have watched us debate, and given rise to doubts in their minds. To tell the truth, the circumstances are such that there exists, between those who up to this point had tried to see things through to a successful conclusion, such strained relations that I should speak of a crisis rather than of the common development of an organization. The talk I am starting now will thus only be the expression of a profound disagreement that has already opened a crack in the wall. It had been understood that three of us would speak tonight, Caillois, Leiris, and I—but I am alone. I do not recognize this without sadness. Caillois left for Argentina a few days ago, and his absence was evidently inevitable; it was no less meaningful. The few texts that I have received from him since his departure are in any case of a nature that would suspend the accord that existed between us. I will not put these things forward today, for it seems possible to me that an oral explanation—Caillois will return in September—will resolve the differences that they establish between us. For the moment I would rather speak of the substance of a disagreement than of terms that may only give rise to misinterpretations. It is possible that by elevating the debate, moreover, and displacing it to the point where love and death alone are still in question, I do nothing more than set aside any chance of ultimate reconciliation. Even though that appears to be the case, I retain the conviction that at this moment

I am acting in the opposite way, but if I was aware that in doing it I was smashing the possibilities that remain, I would still do it, and in the same way, because other things count more than the College of Sociology. If I have come here this evening, if I have come here for two years, it is in fact less with the concern for founding an influential organization than with the will to create a force, starting from an awareness of the misery and the grandeur of this perishable existence that has befallen us; STANDING AND FACING DESTINY remains in my eyes the essential aspect of knowledge. Having perceived that the results put forward by the science of the sacred take away from man his ability to hide from what he is, it seemed to me opportune to found an association that would have this science in particular as its object. No one is more avid than I to find the virtues of association, no one is more frightened than I of the deception that founds individual isolation, but the *love of human destiny* exists in me with enough force to relegate to the background the concern for the forms through which it can enter.

It seems to me that the interest aroused by the College of Sociology—both within and without—depended on its effectiveness in putting everything in question. The intentions of various people were perhaps different, and I have not wanted, in speaking of my reasons, to make it appear that they were not exclusively mine. It goes without saying, however, that only long-range intentions and the capacity that we had for defining crucial new problems justified our existence. To the extent that the College of Sociology is not an open door on the chaos in which every form moves, arises, and perishes, on the convulsion of festivals, of human powers and deaths, it in truth represents only the void. This is why I suffer when I see Leiris, who refrains from speaking today due to doubts on the soundness of our activity—I suffer to see Leiris reproach us for not further resembling the scientists we claim as our authorities. Leiris thinks that we do not follow the rules of Durkheim's sociological method, and that the role we assign the sacred does not conform to the doctrine of the total phenomenon of Mauss. He adds to these considerations the fear of seeing our efforts lead to the formation of the worst of literary cliques. I said I would raise the level of the discussion resulting from the crisis I have spoken of. I will raise it as high as I can. I think that Caillois's work, or my work, will be criticized, but that it will command respect. That, however, is not the question. Above all, the question is whether it is still possible to discuss fundamental problems, if one agrees to go as far as one can in the possible questioning of matters of life, to demand *everything* of which our remaining strength is capable. Methodological and doctrinal points, the inevitable obstacles, the inevitable chances of failure, all this is certainly important, but one can also look beyond these necessary difficulties.

That a beyond—by this I mean a terrestrial beyond—belongs to present-day man is a truth that is difficult to contest. It is no less contestable that access to this beyond must appear, first of all, in the form of combat and danger. And no one doubts that the *internal* dangers, that the inner dangers of all movements must be formidable, and even more, demoralizing.

The disagreement emphasized by Leiris does not exclude, moreover, the possibility of a subsequent collaboration, once limits and ends have been well defined, and above all once the modes of freedom necessary for the development of an effort—which is still somewhat unsure of itself—have been made clear. The questions posed by the differences arising between Caillois and myself are more serious, at least to the extent that they have more to do with the foundations than with the forms of an activity. But since, as I say, they have to do with the very foundations of the enterprise, you will permit me to speak about them through a digression, and, straying from this specific discussion, to limit myself to speaking about the profound reality that this discussion calls into question. The very absence of Caillois moreover seems to make any other procedure impossible. At the outset it suffices to indicate that my emphasis on mysticism, drama, madness, and death seems to Caillois difficult to reconcile with the principles from which we start. I must add that Caillois is not the only one to feel uneasy about this incompatibility. Paulhan and Wahl have conveyed to me the same impression. Thus I have every reason to introduce today, as one of the expressions of a state of crisis, an effort at elucidation. I will there-fore try to show how the development of the College of Sociology caried within itself the necessity of the present crisis, only too happy to have gone to the bases of my thought, not in the calm of solitary reflection, but in the disorder of dispute.

I thus find myself led to develop a general representation of the things that will fall within the order of philosophical representations. And only when I have completed this representation will it be possible for me to show how communal unity, namely power, is formed, as well as this kind of mental turmoil that goes from mysticism to madness. I would not, however, want people to become uneasy, seeing me enter into the dense underbrush of philosophical reflection. Although I must tackle the central problem of metaphysics, it seems to me that I can still be clear; in any case I am sure that I will speak of what touches all human beings, to the extent that they are enemies of torpor.

One of the most widely accepted results of man's efforts to discover what he really is is without a doubt that he lacks unity of being. Men in the past repre-sented themselves as an indivisible reality. Some animals can be cut into two sections; after a certain length of time these two sections form two complete animals, distinct from each other. But nothing could be more shocking to those who limit themselves to a classical conception of the human soul than conducting such an experiment on man. Habits of thought are so well established that it remains difficult for each of us to see himself doubled, one side seeing, loving, or fleeing the other. It is true that surgery, operating on man or very similar animals, remains far from such brutal possibilities. It can only carry out mixtures that leave the essential intact. At most in the distant future we might see really troubling possibilities, such as the exchange of the cerebral hemispheres of two big apes . . . I speak of this less out of interest in a possible experiment than to introduce, into the usual perspectives, a maximum of disorder. I imagine that the idea of a composite being, resulting from the coupling of two of our brains, will provoke a kind of vertiginous malaise. This idea can, however, become familiar. It is nothing more than a banality to consider a human being as a whole "ajar," consisting of distant, badly connected, and even unknown parts. It has generally been recognized that the individual is only an unfinished aggregate; an animal and a human being are seen simply as narrow and stable compositions, whereas a society is only united by connections that are very loose and easily done away with. One has to admit at the same time that an individual or a society are not exceptions, and that each element in nature is an aggregate of parts, at least as long as we do not reach the simplest stage, that of the electron. Science enumerates atoms—in spite of their name—as groupings of elementary particles, molecules as groupings of atoms, and going from stage to stage it arrives at the individual—a grouping of cells—and finally at society (where, it is true, it hesitates to recognize—but it is unclear for what reason—a simple case of unified composition on the basis of multiple elements).

I do not want to insist upon what is only a scientific introduction to what I will present today. I am in a hurry, and my haste in arriving at images that are less external to the reality that we are is perhaps understandable. I will now speak directly of what each of us can experience, and I will speak first of all about an aspect of our lives that apparently is as separate as possible from our union with the social group—I will speak about the erotic activity that the majority of us enter into with one or with, successively, a number of our fellow beings. This digression has the advantage of putting us in the presence of realities that are not only the most obscure, but also the most familiar. In fact nothing is more vivid in our minds than the image of the union of two beings of the opposite sex. But as common and as convincing as it is, its meaning nevertheless remains hidden; all that one can say is that each being blindly obeys its instinct. Giving a name to this instinct, or seeing it as an expression of the will to reproduce that belongs to nature, is not a way of escaping this darkness. In fact other needs than the need to reproduce are satisfied in the act of coupling.

The introduction of a sociological point of view throws an unforeseen light on this natural darkness.

If I consider the reproduction of a simple asexual cell, the birth of a new cell seems to result from an inability, on the part of the whole, to maintain its integrity: a split, a wound is produced. The growth of the minuscule being has as its effect an excess, a laceration, a loss of substance. The reproduction of sexual animals and men can be divided into two phases, each one presenting these same aspects: excess, laceration, and loss of substance. In the first phase two beings communicate with each other through their hidden rents. There is no communication more profound: two beings are lost in a convulsion that binds them together. But they only communicate when losing a part of themselves. Communication ties them together with wounds, where their unity and integrity dissipates in fever.

Two beings of the opposite sex lose themselves in each other, and together form a new being, different from each of them. The precariousness of this new being is manifest: the two parts always remain distinct; there is nothing more than, in short moments of obscurity, a tendency to lose consciousness. But if it is true that the unity of the individual reemerges with greater clarity, this unity is no less precarious as well. Between these two cases there is, no doubt, only a difference of degree.

Love expresses a need for sacrifice: each unity must lose itself in some other, which exceeds it. But the happy movements of the flesh have a double orientation. Because going through flesh—going through the point where the unity of a person is torn apart—is necessary if, in losing oneself, one wants to rediscover oneself in the unity of love, it does not follow that the moment of tearing apart is itself devoid of meaning for torn-apart existence. It is difficult to know, in a coupling of beings, how much is passion for another being, how much is erotic frenzy, up to what point the being looks for life and power, and up to what point it is led to tear itself apart and lose itself, at the same time tearing apart and losing another (and of course the more a woman is beautiful the more her tearing apart, her loss, or simply her sudden nudity are desirable). Beyond the will to leave one's narrow being for one that is more vast, there is—very often mixed with this first will to loss—a will to loss that now only finds limits to its immoderate movements in fear, and even more that takes advantage of the fear it provokes in order to become all the more inflamed and delirious.

To this description of the first forms of being revealed by love, it is necessary to add the union that results from marriage. Many possibilities exist, going for the movement of passion to the sort of oppressive conjugal life where the heart is no longer at stake. At the most extreme point, self-interest and law found the joyless unity of beings for whom physical love is only a concession to nature. If one now thinks of the various social groups that correspond to the various forms of sexual union, all in opposition to each other, juridical and administrative society have close ties with the conjugal union founded on self-interest, the community formed through heartfelt ties recalls the passionate unity of lovers, and forms are not lacking that have in common with erotic perversions the fact that the loss of self in a vaster being is the occasion for a loss of self in a formless universe and in death.

There is, I know, a paradoxical element here; these parallels will necessarily appear to be very arbitrary. However I do not introduce them with the intention of making their meaning precise. I propose to admit, as a law, that human beings are only united with each other through rents or wounds; this notion has, in itself, a certain logical force. If elements are put together to form a whole, this can easily happen when each one loses, through a rip in its integrity, a part of its own being, which goes to benefit the communal being. Initiations, sacrifices, and festivals represent so many moments of loss and communication between individuals. Circumcisions and orgies show adequately that there is more than one link between sexual laceration and ritual laceration; the erotic world itself has been careful to designate the act in which it is fulfilled as a "little death" [*petite mort*]. But one of the two domains exceeds the other; the domain of social laceration that coincides with sexual laceration has a changed and richer meaning, and the multiplicity of its forms extends from war to the bloody cross of Christ; the execution of a king and the sexual act only have in common the fact that they unify through the loss of substance. And it is in the creation or the maintenance of a new unity of being that they resemble each other; it would be vain to claim that the one, like the other, is the effect of an obscure instinct of generation whose action accounts for all human forms.

Thus I can say that the "sacred" is communication between beings, and thereby the formation of new beings. The notion elaborated by sociologists, according to which it is possible to describe the play of the sacred by comparing it to electrical currents and charges, permits me to introduce an image that will explain my position. The wounds or rents of which I have spoken take place, opening the way for any number of eruptions of accumulated force. But this eruption of force out of oneself, produced for the benefit of social power, in religious sacrifice as well as in war, is not in any way produced like the easily understood expenditures necessary to acquire a necessary or desirable object. Although sacrifices and festivals are generally useful, they possess in themselves a value of attraction independent of the conscious or unconscious results they favor. Men, assembling for a sacrifice and for a festival, satisfy their need to expend a vital excess. The sacrificial laceration that opens the festival is a liberating laceration. The individual who participates in loss is obscurely aware that this loss engenders the community that supports him. But a desirable woman is necessary to he who makes love, and it is not always easy to know if he makes love in order to be united with her, or if he uses her because of his need to make love. In the same way, it is difficult to know to what extent the community is but the favorable occasion for a festival and a sacrifice, or to what extent the festival and the sacrifice bear witness to the love individuals give to the community.

In fact, it appears that this question, which might seem simply quaint, appears as the final question of man, and further on as the final question of being. Being is indeed constantly enticed in two directions, one leading to the formation of durable organizations and conquering forces, the other leading, through the intermediary of expenditures of force and of increasing excess, to destruction and death. We confront these options even in life's most commonplace circumstances: the debate over the opportuneness of a useful or seductive expenditure has behind it the weighing of acquisition against loss. But in everyday practice the extreme points have disappeared so thoroughly that everything is almost unrecognizable. The movement only regains its full meaning when it is a question of sexual commerce. The union of lovers finds itself facing this infinite interrogation: supposing that the unified being that they form counts more for them than love, lovers find themselves condemned to a slow stabilization in their relations. The empty horror of regular conjugality already encloses them. But if the need to love and to lose oneself is stronger in them than the concern for finding oneself, then there is no other outcome than laceration, the perversions of tumultuous passion, drama, and if it is a question of a total need, death. I must add that eroticism constitutes a kind of flight before the rigor of this dilemma. But I only speak of it now in order to pass on to a more general consideration.

When a man and a woman are united by love, they together form an association, a being entirely closed in on itself, but when the first equilibrium is compromised, a naked erotic search may be added to or substituted for the search of the lovers, who at first had as their object only themselves. The need to lose oneself, in them, goes beyond the need to find oneself. At this moment the presence of a third is no longer, as it was at the start of their love, the final obstacle. Beyond the common being that they meet in their embrace, they search for a measureless annihilation in a violent expenditure whereby the possession of a new object, of a new woman or a new man, is only a pretext for an even more annihilating expenditure. In the same way, men more religious than others cease to have a narrow concern for the community for which sacrifices are performed. They no longer live for the community; they only live for sacrifice. Thus little by little they are possessed by the desire to extend, through contagion, their sacrificial frenzy. Just as eroticism slides without difficulty toward the orgy, sacrifice, becoming an end in itself, lays claim to universal value, beyond the narrowness of the community.

In the case of social life, however, the first movements can only be extended to the extent that the aspiration to sacrifice finds a god who supports it. As were closed forms, in other words the simplest forms, the community was for certain people the occasion for sacrifice; it is necessary to find again the equivalent of the community in the form of a universal god, in order to extend endlessly the sacrificial orgy. Dionysus and the Crucified thus lead a tragic procession of bacchantes and martyrs. But the rent opened by the irruption of the universal god out of the old local community eventually recloses. The god of the Christians is in turn reduced to the status of guarantor of the social order. But he becomes, again, the wall against which the rage of love for love throws itself. And it is without a doubt at this point that the final question of being takes shape. The eternal extension of God serves, first of all, the objective of enabling each person who loses himself to refind himself in him. But what is then missing is the satisfaction of those who aspire only to be lost, without remission. When Theresa of Avila screamed that she was dying of not dying, her passion, moving beyond any possible barrier, broke an opening that leads into a universe where perhaps there is no composition either of form or of being, where it seems that death rolls from world to world. For the organized composition of beings is apparently deprived of the slightest meaning when it is a matter of the totality of all things; this totality cannot be the analog of composite beings, animated by the same movement that we know.

At this point, then, I suppose that my plan seems strange. But I have only wanted to describe, to the fullest extent, the problem that imposes its dangers from the moment man agrees to question the sociological sphinx. It seems to me that meeting this sphinx has singularly increased the precision and the brutality of metaphysical interrogation. Essentially, what I wanted to say is that a College of Sociology as we have conceived it necessarily opens this bottomless interrogation. It is possible that I sometimes give the impression of lingering over morose preconceptions in my consideration of the impossible. I could answer with a single sentence. I will not do so today. Today I will be satisfied with introducing a few practical statements concerning the means proper to the College of Sociology.

Text of Caillois's letter.

Is it possible to find a reason to fight and die different from those that have to do with fatherland and class, a reason to fight that would not be founded on material interests? Can the concern for human grandeur, taken on by a small number, constitute by itself a sufficient reason to exist? But what exactly does one [mean] when one speaks of grandeur?

Since it has been a question of [classes], could there be classes without a Church, without the sacred, without sacrifice?

Could there be a society without spiritual power, radically distinct from temporal power?

A Commentary on the Texts

A Commentary on the Texts

None of Bataille's writings from the prewar period were included in a larger volume in his lifetime (with three exceptions: *Histoire de l'oeil*, privately published [134 copies were printed] in a collection of pornographic novels in 1928; the novel *Le Bleu du ciel* [1935], first published in 1957; and "Le Bleu du ciel" [a short article, not the novel], which first appeared in *Minotaure* in 1936 and which reappeared as part of *L'Expérience intérieure* [1943]). Bataille's prewar writings were only collected in book form when the first two volumes of the *Oeuvres Complètes*, edited by Denis Hollier, were published in 1970.

In choosing from the nearly 1,000 pages of material in volumes I and II, I have attempted to include Bataille's most significant writings. In virtually all cases, however, I think the problems covered in pieces not included in this collection are also treated in those presented here.

The latter part of volume II of the *Oeuvres Complètes* (pp. 291–374) contains eight lectures given by Bataille before the Collège de Sociologie, which date from 1937–39. These have since been reedited (by Denis Hollier) in a volume entitled *Le Collège de sociologie* (Paris: Gallimard, Collection "Idées," 1979); also in this volume are the lectures given by all the other participants in the Collège (Leiris, Caillois, Klossowski, Lewitzky, etc.). A translation of this collection is to be published in 1985 by the University of Minnesota Press.

The writings are presented in roughly chronological order—roughly, because many of the posthumous writings cannot be precisely dated. The publication of some texts took place several years after composition; in these cases, I have held to the date of composition for determining the order. All texts are presented in their entirety. Ellipsis dots are those of Bataille.

I (1927-1930)

[Dream]. First published in the *Oeuvres Complètes* (henceforth *OC*) II, 9–10. The manuscript is marked "Recorded in 1927, around June." This dream was recorded as part of Bataille's psychoanalysis, done under Dr. Adrien Borel. Dr. Borel reappears in "Sacrificial Mutilation and the Severed Ear of Vincent Van Gogh" as one of the authors of the case report on the automutilator, Gaston F.

The Solar Anus. Written in 1927; first published in 1931 by Editions de la Galérie Simon, Paris, and illustrated with drypoint etchings by André Masson. Reprinted in *OC* I, 81–86.

The Language of Flowers. First published in *Documents* 3 (June 1929):160–68. Reprinted in *OC* I, 173–78. After Breton attacked the veracity of the story of Sade and the rose petals (see the "Introduction," above), Bataille had his friend, the Sade expert Maurice Heine, research it. Unfortunately, the story turned out to be apocryphal (see *OC* II, 422).

Materialism. *Documents* 3 (June 1929):170. Reprinted in *OC* I, 179–80. This was a contribution to a "Critical Dictionary," a regular feature of *Documents* that presented definitions written by the various contributors—Desnos, Leiris, Limbour, as well as Bataille.

Eye. *Documents* 4 (September 1929):216. Reprinted in *OC* I, 187–89.

The Big Toe. *Documents* 6 (November 1929):297–302. Reprinted in *OC* I, 200–204.

The "Lugubrious Game," *Documents* 7 (December 1929):297–302. Reprinted in *OC* I, 211–16. This article is the most direct response to Breton that Bataille published in *Documents*. Bataille could only include a sketch of Dali's *Lugubrious Game* because Dali, at this time still under the influence of Breton, refused permission to reproduce a photograph of the painting (several of Dali's paintings had earlier been reproduced in *Documents* 4, including *Blood Is Sweeter than Honey*).

Formless. *Documents* 7 (December 1929):382. Reprinted in *OC* I, 217. An entry in the "Critical Dictionary."

The "Old Mole" and the Prefix *Sur* in the Words *Surhomme* [Superman] and *Surrealist*. First published in *Tel Quel* 34 (Summer 1968), and reprinted in *OC* II, 93–109. Although the date of this essay is uncertain, it clearly dates from the height of the Bataille/Breton controversy and therefore probably from

1929–30. It was accepted for publication by the short-lived avant-garde review *Bifur* (which published, in this period, articles by Heidegger and Sartre, among others), the last issue of which appeared in June, 1931. *Bifur* ceased publication, however, before "The "Old Mole"" could see the light of day. This translation is by Donald M. Leslie, Jr.

Base Materialism and Gnosticism. *Documents*, second year, 1 (1930):1–8. Reprinted in *OC* I, 220–26. Many of the illustrations accompanying this article are of stones from the collection of the Cabinet des Médailles of the Bibliothèque Nationale in Paris; Bataille worked in the Cabinet des Médailles at the time this article was written.

The Deviations of Nature. *Documents*, second year, 2 (1930):79–83. Reprinted in *OC* I, 228–30. Eisenstein was attempting to develop a kind of dialectical materialist ideational montage in films such as *October*. Eisenstein's theories of dialectical *shock* in fact bear a certain resemblance to Bataille's early theory of heterogeneity, (and the attempt to situate it in a materialist dialectic), though they are less scabrous (see in this context especially Bataille's "Psychological Structure of Fascism"). (Important essays by Eisenstein are collected in *The Film Sense*, trans. and ed. Jay Leda [New York: Harcourt, Brace and World, 1947].) Materialist theories of montage and shock were very much the order of the day, as in Walter Benjamin's "constellation" theory of materialism (see note 18 of our Introduction, above).

Rotten Sun. *Documents*, second year, 3 (1930):173–74. Reprinted in *OC* I, 231–32. This article was part of an "Hommage à Picasso."

Mouth. *Documents*, second year, 5 (1930):299. Reprinted in *OC* I, 237–38. Another entry in the "Critical Dictionary."

Sacrificial Mutilation and the Severed Ear of Vincent Van Gogh. *Documents*, second year, 8 (1930):10–20. Reprinted in *OC* I, 258–70.

The Jesuve. First published in *OC* II, 13–20. This piece was evidently written in 1930, for a crossed-out note in the manuscript indicates that the "pineal eye" obsession first came to Bataille "three years ago," in 1927. The word "Jesuve," which also appears in "The Solar Anus" and "The Pineal Eye," is apparently a word devised by Bataille himself; its meaning is open to conjecture. In it, we can perceive a number of words: "je" ("I"), "Jésus" (which in French is also a kind of sausage), "sève" ("sap"), etc.

The Pineal Eye. First published in *L'Ephémère* 3 (1967); reprinted in *OC* II, 21–35. Although the date is uncertain, it is clearly from roughly the same period as "The Jesuve." Among other fragmentary notes connected with "The Pineal Eye" found among Bataille's papers, there is this one (II, 418):

> All the plants of the earth are raised to the sky, and they continuously throw myriads of brilliant multicolored jets of spittle at the sun, in the form of flowers, and there is only an obscene Van Gogh, surrounded by madmen, to throw at this same sun the phallic spit of his eyes. The other human creatures miserably drag themselves around like giant impotent and correct phalluses, their eyes riveted on soporific surroundings.
>
> It is necessary to break oneself in pieces and feel in one's body the madness of a contortionist; at the same time one must become a fetishist to the point of slavering, a fetishist of the eye, of the buttocks and of the feet, all at once, in order to find again in oneself what miserably miscarried at the beginning of the constitution of the human body.

This piece is followed in *OC* II by three short variants.

The Use Value of D. A. F. de Sade (An Open Letter to My Current Comrades). First published in *OC* II, 54–69. This position paper is from 1929 or 1930. While it clearly is connected with Bataille's polemic against André Breton (and Breton's view of Sade), it also looks forward to a number of positions that Bataille developed in the *Critique sociale* essays. It is followed in *OC* II by a short variant.

II (1932-1935)

The Critique of the Foundations of the Hegelian Dialectic. First published in *La Critique sociale* 5 (March 1932):209–14. Reprinted in *Deucalion* 5 (1955) and in *OC* I, 277–90. This article was written jointly with Raymond Queneau (1903–76); Queneau's contribution (including note 13) is in brackets. Queneau, after breaking with Bataille in the late 1930s (he disapproved of the Acéphale project and its rituals) went on to become well known as an experimental novelist (*Exercises de style*, 1947; *Zazie dans le métro*, 1959) and as an editor (he assembled the various notes and articles to make Alexandre Kojève's *Introduction à la lecture de Hegel* [1947]).

The Notion of Expenditure. *La Critique sociale* 7 (January 1933):7–15. Reprinted in *OC* I, 302–20. This translation was first published in *Raritan Review*, Winter 1984.

Sacrifices. The manuscript is dated "Summer 1933"; first published by Editions G. L. M. in October 1936 (G. L. M. was also the publisher of the review

Acéphale) as the text accompanying an album of etchings by André Masson. Reprinted in *OC* I, 89–96.

The Psychological Structure of Fascism. *La Critique sociale* 10 (November 1933):159–65, and 11 (March 1934):205–11. Reprinted in *OC* I, 339–71. This translation, by Carl R. Lovitt, was first published in *New German Critique* 16 (Winter 1979).

Popular Front in the Street. First published in the *Cahiers de Contre-Attaque* 1 (May 1936)—the only issue of the *Cahiers* to be published. Reprinted in *OC* I, 402–12. This speech was given by Bataille at a Contre-Attaque meeting of November 24, 1935.

It must be recalled when reading Bataille's writings from 1935 to 1940 that there is an assumption that democracy in the West is doomed; the choice is between some form of communism and fascism. In this light, Bataille's espousal of a revolution through sexuality and myth takes on added force: faced with a choice between the clear tyranny of fascism and the tendency of bureaucratic Communists to dessicate life—and with democracy not a viable alternative—the only option was to affirm Revolution, while attempting to situate it in relation to values that all "official" parties refused to consider seriously. Bataille then had two alternatives: either to work somehow in conjunction with the Communists, as a Marxist, a course of action he advocates in "Popular Front in the Street," or to refuse the mode of struggle of the Stalinist Communist party entirely (thereby refusing to be a Communist), while not refusing the inevitability of a Marxist "end of history"—the position Bataille takes in the Acéphale period. In either case, his relations with Communist party orthodoxy were bound to be strained.

A bit of history may be in order here: the Croix de Feu ("Cross of Fire") was a paramilitary organization headed by Colonel François de la Rocque; like the early Nazis, it was half party, half right-wing war veterans' organization. Disbanded in the later 1930s, it regrouped under another name. In 1934 its strength was about 20,000 or 30,000 men.

The "events of February" 1934 started with the revelation of the Stavisky affair. The disclosure of high-level corruption gave right-wing paramilitary organizations the opportunity they had been waiting for; their rioting in Paris on February 6–7, while not resulting in the desired coup d'état, nevertheless caused the Radical party's government to fall. The Republic held firm, if not the government; the "forces of order" were responsible for the death of at least twelve right-wing agitators, members of a group that unsuccessfully attempted to reach the Palais-Bourbon.

The response on the left was immediate: first the non-Communist groups organized, marching on February 7 and calling for a peaceful general stri' against fascism—but not against the government—for February 12. The Communists first called for immediate action against the government for February 9; this resulted in fighting with the police in the eastern (working class) sections of Paris, with a number of Communists killed. At that point the Communists agreed to join forces with the non-Communist left and participate in the strike on February 12.

This strike, a success, opened the way for an antifascist alliance of the Communist and non-Communist left, the Popular Front, which finally came to power in June 1936.

Of course this alliance was not without tension—Bataille's speech indicates the frustration of many intellectuals of the left both with the Communists' reluctance to maintain an alliance with other parties of the left and with the Communist tendency to support implicitly the French Army (Pierre Laval, head of the government, visited Moscow in May 1935, where Stalin indicated his approval of the anti-German—and thus necessarily the militaristic, "patriotic"—orientation of Laval's government).

III (1936-1939)

The Labyrinth. First published in *Recherches philosophiques* 5 (1935-36): 364-72. Reprinted in *OC* I, 433-41. A different version of this article appeared in *L'Expérience intérieure* under the title "Le Labyrinthe (ou la composition des êtres)."

The Sacred Conspiracy. First published in *Acéphale* 1 (June 1936):2-4. Reprinted in *OC* I, 442-46. The first three issues of *Acéphale* were illustrated by André Masson.

One way of looking at the changeover from Contre-Attaque to Acéphale might be this. As Bataille makes clear in section 18 of "The Use Value of D. A. F. de Sade" (written around 1930), there are two distinct phases: the "revolutionary phase" and the "postrevolutionary phase." In the first phase, orgiastic and destructive drives are coordinated with the (political and social) revolution. In the second phase, with the revolution carried out, there is a *separation* between political and social organizations on the one hand, and an "antireligious and asocial organization" (an anticipation of Acéphale?) on the other. And in fact, strangely enough given the murky political situation of the later 1930s, Bataille in 1937 considers the end of history to be at hand, the totalizing revolution just around the corner, after the collapse of democracy (see the "Letter to X [Kojeve]" of 1937 [V, 369-71]). Thus, with the coming to power of the Popular Front, Bataille gives up his open advocacy of Communist revolution. But then a much larger problem emerges: to what extent does the *separation* of the political and economic organization from the antireligious and asocial one lead to a *conflict* between the two? This problem, never posed explicitly in Bataille's theoretical writings, nevertheless emerges in his fiction—especially in the novels *Le Bleu du ciel* (1935) and *L'Abbé C.* (1950).

Nietzsche and the Fascists. *Acéphale* 2 (January 1937):3–13. Reprinted in *OC* I, 447–65.

Propositions. *Acéphale* 2 (January 1937):17–21. Reprinted in *OC* I, 467–73.

Nietzschean Chronicle. *Acéphale* 3–4 (July 1937):15–23. Reprinted in *OC* I, 477–90. It should be recalled that Bataille's attempt at founding a Nietzschean "faith," or even "church," was a short-lived one; by September 1939 (the outbreak of the war) he had given it up, dismissing it as a "fad." For more on the permutations of Nietzsche in Bataille, see my article "From *Acéphale* to the Will to Chance: Nietzsche in the Text of Bataille," in *Glyph 6* (Baltimore: Johns Hopkins University Press, 1979).

The Obelisk. First published in *Mesures*, fourth year, 2 (April 15, 1938):35–50. Reprinted in *OC* I, 501–13. Bataille's fascination with the execution of the king (specifically, Louis XVI, on January 21, 1793) took many forms: a Contre-Attaque meeting of January 21, 1936 commemorated the king's death; the topic of the talk was the question of the "200 Families" who ruled France (a common theme in the days of the Popular Front) and who, by implication at least, faced the same fate as the king (I, 394) (the flyer announcing the meeting bears a sketch of a calf's head on a plate). One of the Acéphale rituals—which was never carried out—was to soak a human skull in brine until it became soft and malleable, then place it at the base of the obelisk in the Place de la Concorde on January 21 (1938?); the Press was then to be notified of the very mysterious reappearance of the king's skull.

The Sorcerer's Apprentice. First published in the *Nouvelle Revue Francaise* 298 (July 1938):5–54. Reprinted in *OC* I, 523–37. This was Bataille's only article to appear in the prewar *NRF*, which at the time was the hegemonic intellectual review *par excellence*. Bataille's article appeared along with one by Michel Leiris ("Le Sacré dans la vie quotidienne") and one by Roger Caillois ("Le Vent d'hiver"); the appearance of these articles signaled to the public the activities of the Collège de Sociologie. (The Caillois and Leiris articles will appear in the forthcoming translation of Hollier's *Le Collège de sociologie* anthology.)

The Practice of Joy before Death. *Acéphale* 5 (June 1939):1–8. Reprinted in *OC* I, 552–58. Bataille wrote all the pieces in this last issue of *Acéphale*; as is clear in the "meditation" presented here, by this time Bataille recognized the likelihood of the violent death he had contemplated for so long—but now death starts to appear in the guise of the imminent world war. The fragmentary writing on an individual "practice of meditation" looks forward to the method and subject matter of Bataille's *Somme Athéologique* (*L'Expérience intérieure, Le Coupable, Sur Nietzsche*).

The Sacred, First published in *Cahiers d'art*, fourteenth yeaar, 1–4 (1939): 47–50. Reprinted in *OC* I, 559–63.

The College of Sociology. Presented on July 4, 1939, before the Collège; first published in *OC* II, 364–74. This was the last meeting of the Collège. Leiris's letter, dated July 3 (II, 454–55) raises three objections to the Collège as Bataille conceived it: 1) the Collège, having set itself the task of studying "social structures," has not properly defined the term, has compared societies that are profoundly different, and thus has violated the rules of Durkheimian methodology; 2) the "moral community" desired by Bataille threatens to turn itself into an Order or a Church, if not simply literary clique (this in fact is the criticism Bataille himself later directed against the Acéphale group), and a doctrine for this community has not even been elaborated (a doctrine is never established by a community—instead, communities are founded to follow an already-constituted doctrine); 3) by stressing "sacred" sociology, Bataille ignores all the other aspects of society, as sketched out by Marcel Mauss in his notion of the "total phenomenon."

A.S.

Index

Index

267

Georges Bataille (1897-1962), by profession a librarian, was a member of the Collège de Sociologie and founder of the French review *Critique*. Virtually an underground figure in his lifetime, he left a vast and heterogeneous collection of writings—pornographic novels, poetry, essays on literary, economic, and historical topics; the importance of this work has come to be recognized only in the last twenty years. Among his books are *Story of the Eye, Blue of Noon, L'Abbé C., Literature and Evil, Death and Sensuality* (all available in English), *La Part maudite*, and *L'Expérience intérieure*.

Allan Stoekl is assistant professor of comparative literature and French at Yale University. He is the author of *Politics, Writing, Mutilation: The Cases of Bataille, Blanchot, Roussel, Leiris, and Ponge*, forthcoming from the University of Minnesota Press.

Carl R. Lovitt is assistant director of English programs at the Modern Language Association in New York and a lecturer at New York University. He is also translation editor of *Sub-Stance*. **Donald M. Leslie** is a technical writer at Lotus Development Corporation in Cambridge, Massachusetts.